Believers Church
Bible Commentary

Douglas B. Miller and Loren L. Johns, Editors

BELIEVERS CHURCH BIBLE COMMENTARY

Old Testament
Genesis, by Eugene F. Roop, 1987
Exodus, by Waldemar Janzen, 2000
Joshua, by Gordon H. Matties, 2012
Judges, by Terry L. Brensinger, 1999
Ruth, Jonah, Esther, by Eugene F. Roop, 2002
Psalms, by James H. Waltner, 2006
Proverbs, by John W. Miller, 2004
Ecclesiastes, by Douglas B. Miller, 2010
Isaiah, by Ivan D. Friesen, 2009
Jeremiah, by Elmer A. Martens, 1986
Lamentations, Song of Songs, by Wilma Ann Bailey, Christina Bucher, 2015
Ezekiel, by Millard C. Lind, 1996
Daniel, by Paul M. Lederach, 1994
Hosea, Amos, by Allen R. Guenther, 1998

New Testament
Matthew, by Richard B. Gardner, 1991
Mark, by Timothy J. Geddert, 2001
John, by Willard M. Swartley, 2013
Acts, by Chalmer E. Faw, 1993
Romans, by John E. Toews, 2004
2 Corinthians, by V. George Shillington, 1998
Galatians, by George R. Brunk III, 2015
Ephesians, by Thomas R. Yoder Neufeld, 2002
Colossians, Philemon, by Ernest D. Martin, 1993
1-2 Thessalonians, by Jacob W. Elias, 1995
1-2 Timothy, Titus, by Paul M. Zehr, 2010
1-2 Peter, Jude, by Erland Waltner, J. Daryl Charles, 1999
1, 2, 3 John, by J. E. McDermond, 2011
Revelation, by John R. Yeatts, 2003

Old Testament Editors
Elmer A. Martens, Mennonite Brethren Biblical Seminary, Fresno, California
Douglas B. Miller, Tabor College, Hillsboro, Kansas

New Testament Editors
Willard M. Swartley, Anabaptist Mennonite Biblical Seminary, Elkhart, Indiana
Loren L. Johns, Anabaptist Mennonite Biblical Seminary, Elkhart, Indiana

Editorial Council
David W. Baker, Brethren Church
W. Derek Suderman, Mennonite Church Canada
Christina Bucher, Church of the Brethren
John R. Yeatts, Brethren in Christ Church
Gordon H. Matties (chair), Mennonite Brethren Church
Jo-Ann A. Brant, Mennonite Church USA

Believers Church Bible Commentary

Lamentations
Wilma Ann Bailey

Song of Songs
Christina Bucher

HERALD PRESS
Harrisonburg, Virginia
Kitchener, Ontario

Library of Congress Cataloging-in-Publication Data
Bailey, Wilma A.
　　Lamentations / Wilma Ann Bailey. Song of Songs / Christina A. Bucher.
　　　　pages cm. -- (Believers church Bible commentary ; 27)
　　　ISBN 978-0-8361-9932-1 (pbk. : alk. paper) 1. Bible. Lamentations--Commentaries. 2. Bible. Song of Solomon--Commentaries.   I. Bucher, Christina, joint author. II. Bucher, Christina. Song of Songs. III. Title.
　　BS1535.53.B35 2015
　　223'.907--dc23

　　　　　　　　　　　　　　　　　2014037104

Lamentations: Except as otherwise indicated, Bible text is from *New Revised Standard Version Bible*, copyright 1989 by the Division of Christian Education of the National Council of the Churches of Christ in the USA, and used by permission. Other versions briefly compared are listed with Abbreviations.

Selvan, S. D. P. "Lamentation: A Rereading of Vanni in the Perspective of Underside History," in *Sri Lanka Journal of Theological Reflection*, vol. 7, no. 1 (July 2013): 1–9. Used with permission of the Theological College of Lanka, publishers of the *Sri Lanka Journal of Theological Reflection*, and of the author, Fr. S. D. P. Selvan.

Song of Songs: Scripture quotations, unless otherwise indicated, are from the Holy Bible, New International Version®, NIV®. Copyright © 1973, 1978, 1984, 2011 by Biblica, Inc.™ Used by permission of Zondervan. All rights reserved worldwide. www.zondervan.com. The "NIV" and "New International Version" are trademarks registered in the United States Patent and Trademark Office by Biblica, Inc.™ Other versions briefly compared are identified with Abbreviations.

Copyright © 2015 by Herald Press, Harrisonburg, Virginia 22802
　　Released simultaneously in Canada by Herald Press,
　　Kitchener, Ontario N2G 3R1. All rights reserved.
Library of Congress Control Number: 2014037104
International Standard Book Number: 978-0-8361-9932-1
Printed in the United States of America
Cover and interior design by Merrill Miller

All rights reserved. This publication may not be reproduced, stored in a retrieval system, or transmitted in whole or in part, in any form, by any means, electronic, mechanical, photocopying, recording, or otherwise without prior permission of the copyright owners.

To order or request information, please call 1-800-245-7894 or visit www.heraldpress.com.

19 18 17 16 15　　10 9 8 7 6 5 4 3 2 1

With deep appreciation, to my mother and father

—*Wilma Ann Bailey*

To Ted

—*Christina Bucher*

Abbreviations

*	The Text in Biblical Context
+	The Text in the Life of the Church
AEL	*Ancient Egyptian Literature.* Edited by M. Lichtheim. 2 vols. Berkeley: University of California Press, 1976.
ANET	*Ancient Near Eastern Texts Relating to the Old Testament.* Edited by James B. Pritchard. 3rd ed. with supplement. Princeton, NJ: Princeton University Press, 1969.
ASV	American Standard Version
AT	author's translation
b.	born
BCBC	Believers Church Bible Commentary
BCE	before the Common Era (= BC before Christ)
ca.	*circa,* approximately
CE	Common Era (= AD *anno Domini*)
CEB	Common English Bible
cf.	*confer,* compare
ch./chs.	chapter/chapters
CWMS	*The Complete Writings of Menno Simons, c. 1496–1561.* Translated by J. C. Wenger. Scottdale, PA: Herald Press, 1956.
d.	died
ed.	edition, editor
e.g.	*exempli gratia,* for example
emph.	emphasis
ESV	English Standard Version (ESV Bible)
et al.	*et alia,* and others
etc.	et cetera, and the rest
GASB	Thomas von Imbroich, Konrad Koch, and Matthias Servaes. *Golden Apples in Silver Bowls: The Rediscovery of Redeeming Love.* Translated by L. Gross and E. H. Bender. Lancaster, PA: Lancaster Mennonite Historical Society, 1999.
Gk.	Greek
GNT	Good News Translation
HALOT	Koehler, L., W. Baumgartner, and J. J. Stamm. *The Hebrew and Aramaic Lexicon of the Old Testament.* Translated and edited under the supervision of M. E. J. Richardson. 5 vols. Leiden: E. J. Brill, 1994–2000.
Heb.	Hebrew
HMEC	*Hymnal of the Methodist Episcopal Church: With Tunes.* New York: Phillips & Hunt, 1882.
HWB	*Hymnal: A Worship Book.* Edited by Rebecca Slough et al. Elgin, IL: Brethren Press; Newton, KS: Faith & Life Press; Scottdale, PA: Herald Press, 1992.

i.e.	*id est*, that is
KDP	*Das kleine Davidische Psalterspiel der Kinder Zions.* Germany, 1829.
KJV	King James Version of the Bible
Lectionary	"Masses for the Dead," *Lectionary for Mass*, U.S.A. edition, 2002.
lit.	literally
MT	versification/readings in the Masoretic Text, the standard Hebrew version of the OT, preserved by Masoretes, a group of early medieval Jewish scribes
NASB	New American Standard Bible
NET	New English Translation (NET Bible)
no.	number
NIDB	*New Interpreters Dictionary of the Bible.* 5 vols. Nashville: Abingdon. 2006–9.
NIV	New International Version of the Bible, 2011
NIV 1984	New International Version of the Bible, 1984
NJPS	New Jewish Publication Society version of the Bible, 1999
NKJV	New King James Version
NRSV	New Revised Standard Version of the Bible, 1989
NT	New Testament
OT	Old Testament
pseud.	pseudonym
rev.	revised
Rev. Lect.	*Revised Common Lectionary Daily Readings.* Minneapolis: Fortress, 2005.
RSV	Revised Standard Version of the Bible
s.v.	*sub verbo*, under the word
TBC	Text in Biblical Context, in the commentary
TDOT	*Theological Dictionary of the Old Testament.* Edited by G. J. Botterweck and H. Ringgren. Translated by J. T. Willis, G. W. Bromiley, and D. E. Green. 15 vols. Grand Rapids: Eerdmans, 1974–2006.
TLC	Text in the Life of the Church, in the commentary
T/NIV	agreement between the NIV and Today's New International Version of the Bible, 2006
v./vv.	verse/verses
WDP	*The Writings of Dirk Philips*, 1504–1568. Translated and edited by C. J. Dyck, W. E. Keeney, and A. J. Beachy. Classics of the Radical Reformation. Scottdale, PA: Herald Press, 1992.
WPM	*The Writings of Pilgram Marpeck.* Translated and edited by W. Klassen and W. Klaassen. Classics of the Radical Reformation. Kitchener, ON: Herald Press, 1978.

Pronunciation Guide for Certain Transliterated Hebrew Consonants

ʾ	(not pronounced)
ʿ	(not pronounced)
ḥ	ch (Scottish *loch*)
ṣ	ts
ś	s
š	sh
ṭ	t

Contents

Abbreviations 6
Pronunciation Guide 8
Series Forward 15

Lamentations, by Wilma Ann Bailey
Preface to Lamentations 19

Introduction to Lamentations 22
  Sorrow Songs 22
  Title 23
  Historical and Theological Background 23
  The God of Lamentations 26
  Date and Purpose 27
  Authorship 28
  Structure 29
  Content 30
  The Grief Process 30

There Is No Comforter for Zion, 1:1-22 34
  *The Source of Evil 47
  *How to Prevent Evil from Happening 48
  +Lamentations and Anabaptists 48
  +Opportunities to Grieve in the Church Year 49
  +Shame 50

The Lord Has Become Like an Enemy, 2:1-22...............51
    *God's Anger..60
    *Prophetic Blame...60
    *Concern about the Perception of Others 61
    *Suffering of the Innocent..................................61
    +Waves of Grief 62
    +Wrestling with the Origins of Evil 62
    +Limits to God's Responsibility 64

The Lord Will Not Reject Forever, 3:1-66..................65
    *Acrostics and Repetition 77
    *Lament Metaphors 77
    +Liturgical Use of Lamentations 78
    +Searching Oneself 79

War Changes Behavior and Social Structures, 4:1-22.......80
    *Children and the Poor.....................................87
    +Serving Those Affected by War............................87
    +How Communities Bring Healing to Those Affected
        by Mass Traumas 89

Restore Us to Yourself, 5:1-22...........................90
    *Inequities and the Poor 97
    +Women in War 98
    +Reading on Two Levels 99
    +Remembering and Forgetting 99
    +Healing and Hope..100
    Lamentations: A Rereading 101

Outline of Lamentations 109
Essays for Lamentations 111
    Acrostic 111
    Capture and Destruction of Jerusalem......................112
    City 113
    Communal Lament..114
    Covenant 114
    Credo...115
    Dirge 115
    Elephantine Papyri 115
    The Elite..115
    Evil Spirits 116
    Hebrew Poetry 116

Historiography 117
Morpheme 117
Orality 118
Targum 118
Yahweh 118
Zion Theology 119

Map of Palestine for Lamentations 120
Map of the Ancient Near East for Lamentations 121
Bibliography for Lamentations 122
Selected Resources for Lamentations 126
Index of Ancient Sources for Lamentations 128
The Author of the Commentary on Lamentations 131

Song of Songs, by Christina Bucher
Preface to Song of Songs 135

Introduction to Song of Songs 139
Major Themes of the Song of Songs 140
Lyric Love Poetry or Drama? 142
Who Are the Characters in the Poems? 144
One Poem, or Many? 146
Did Solomon Write the Song of Songs? 147
Setting of the Poems 149
Imagery of the Poems 150
Song of Songs in the Context of the Christian Canon 151
The Song of Songs in the Life of the Church 152

In Celebration of Love, 1:1-8 155
*Kisses and Kissing 164
*Wine and Anointing Oils 165
*Vines and Vineyards 166
+ Embodiment 168
+God's Kiss 169
+Following Jesus 171

Poems of Admiration and Desire, 1:9–2:7 174
*Salvation Imagery: The Land Bursts into Bloom 181
+Flowers and Spirituality 182
+Jesus Christ, the Apple Tree 182

An Invitation to Love, 2:8-17 ....**184**
    *Fig Trees and Vines.......................................190
    *Doves and Turtledoves..................................190
    *The Voice of the Beloved...............................192
    +Incarnation 192
    +New Beginnings 193
    +Taking Refuge in Jesus 196

Seeking and Finding the Beloved, 3:1-11 ....**199**
    *Quests..203
    *Where is God?..205
    +The Absence of God 206

A First Description of Her Beauty, 4:1–5:1 ....**208**
    *Gardens 217
    +The Garden of God's Love.............................218

Seeking the Beloved (Again), 5:2–6:3 ....**222**
    *Imagery of Well-Being 229
    *The Beauty of God and of Creation 230
    +Seeking God..231
    +Divine Beauty 232

Overwhelmed by Love, 6:4–7:13........................**234**
    *Tirzah and Jerusalem 238
    *Return..239
    +Sexual Desire and Sexual Ethics 240
    +The Lure of God's Love 241

Love Is Strong as Death, 8:1-14 ....**242**
    *Divine Passion..251
    +The Overwhelming Power of God's Love............253

Outline of Song of Songs 256
Essays for Song of Songs 258
    Allegorical and Figural Interpretation 258
        Allegorical Interpretation 258
        Figural Interpretation..................................259
    Aromatics..260
    Authorship and Date 261
    Daughters of Jerusalem..................................262
    Descriptive Inventories..................................263

Dramatic Interpretations 263
Embodiment 264
Erotic Imperative 266
Figures of Speech 267
    Metaphor 267
    Simile 267
    Allegory 267
Flowers 268
    Lotus 268
    Rose of Sharon 269
Geography 269
History of Interpretation 270
    Early and Medieval Period 270
    Reformation Period 272
    Seventeenth and Eighteenth Centuries 275
King Fiction 278
Love and Desire 279
    Love 279
    Desire 280
Nuptial Imagery in the New Testament 282
Sexuality 283

Map of Palestine for Song of Songs 287
Map of the Ancient Near East for Song of Songs 288
Bibliography for Song of Songs 289
Selected Resources for Song of Songs 297
Index of Ancient Sources for Song of Songs 299
The Author of the Commentary on Song of Songs 303

Series Foreword

The Believers Church Bible Commentary Series makes available a new tool for basic Bible study. It is published for all who seek more fully to understand the original message of Scripture and its meaning for today—Sunday school teachers, members of Bible study groups, students, pastors, and others. The series is based on the conviction that God is still speaking to all who will listen, and that the Holy Spirit makes the Word a living and authoritative guide for all who want to know and do God's will.

The desire to help as wide a range of readers as possible has determined the approach of the writers. Since no blocks of biblical text are provided, readers may continue to use the translation with which they are most familiar. The writers of the series use the New Revised Standard Version and the New International Version on a comparative basis. They indicate which text they follow most closely and where they make their own translations. The writers have not worked alone, but in consultation with select counselors, the series' editors, and the Editorial Council.

Every volume illuminates the Scriptures; provides necessary theological, sociological, and ethical meanings; and in general makes "the rough places plain." Critical issues are not avoided, but neither are they moved into the foreground as debates among scholars. Each section offers Explanatory Notes, followed by focused articles, "The Text in Biblical Context" and "The Text in the Life of the Church." This commentary aids the interpretive process but does not try to supersede the authority of the Word and Spirit as discerned in the gathered church.

The term *believers church* has often been used in the history of the church. Since the sixteenth century, it has frequently been applied to the Anabaptists and later the Mennonites, as well as to the Church of the Brethren and similar groups. As a descriptive term, it includes more than Mennonites and Brethren. *Believers church* now represents specific theological understandings, such as believers baptism, commitment to the Rule of Christ in Matthew 18:15-20 as crucial for church membership, belief in the power of love in all relationships, and willingness to follow Christ in the way of the cross. The writers chosen for the series stand in this tradition.

Believers church people have always been known for their emphasis on obedience to the simple meaning of Scripture. Because of this, they do not have a long history of deep historical-critical biblical scholarship. This series attempts to be faithful to the Scriptures while also taking archaeology and current biblical studies seriously. Doing this means that at many points the writers will not differ greatly from interpretations that can be found in many other good commentaries. Yet these writers share basic convictions about Christ, the church and its mission, God and history, human nature, the Christian life, and other doctrines. These presuppositions do shape a writer's interpretation of Scripture. Thus this series, like all other commentaries, stands within a specific historical church tradition.

Many in this stream of the church have expressed a need for help in Bible study. This is justification enough to produce the Believers Church Bible Commentary. Nevertheless, the Holy Spirit is not bound to any tradition. May this series be an instrument in breaking down walls between Christians in North America and around the world, bringing new joy in obedience through a fuller understanding of the Word.

—*The Editorial Council*

Lamentations

Wilma Ann Bailey

Preface to Lamentations

When the editorial council of the Believers Church Bible Commentary series asked me to write the commentary on Lamentations, I accepted only because I thought that being a short book, the task would be quickly accomplished. However, other projects got in the way, and it ended up taking a long time to finish. That was fortuitous because there are more resources available now than there were at the start of the project, resources in the form of new commentaries on Lamentations as well as a few books and articles that examine the phenomenon of whole communities that experience grief at the same time due to a trauma such as war, tsunamis, and economic downturn. Earlier, most studies on trauma and the response to trauma focused solely on the experience of the individual.

In order to understand community grief better, I twice traveled to the site of the Alfred P. Murrah Federal Building, where the Oklahoma City bombing took place in 1995. I spoke to a number of people, including a couple of pastors and a counselor, to gain a perspective on the impact of that event on the community. During a trip to Halifax, Nova Scotia, I reflected on how the Halifax Explosion catastrophe of 1917 reshaped the geography and residents of that town. I pored over church bulletins and documents in the Goshen College archives for information about the 1965 Palm Sunday tornadoes and how they affected the Mennonite community in the area. Visiting villages in Ukraine that were formerly settled by Mennonites who were forced out due to war, and becoming acquainted with their first-person accounts as well as secondary material—all this educated me in the meaning of the loss of community that accompanied individual loss. The more I read and the more I experienced, the more engaged I became with the topic of how communities deal with community-wide trauma.

After the first draft of this manuscript was completed, I had the privilege of spending nine weeks in Sri Lanka, a country emerging from nearly thirty years of civil war (and a devastating tsunami that killed and displaced many people). That experience helped me to gain a clearer perspective of what it is like to live in the aftermath of war, the same existential context surrounding the writers of the poems in Lamentations. I thank the people of Sri Lanka for sharing their reflections with me. These include students and faculty at Christian Theological Seminary in Chunnakam, Jaffna District, Sri Lanka; the Uduvil Girls' College; and the war widows of Vanni. A written source titled *Write to Reconcile*, edited by Shyam Selvadurai, provides a collection of short stories, essays, and reflections that were also helpful in shaping my understanding of the thoughts and feelings of Sri Lankans, both Tamil and Sinhala, in relation to the war and its aftermath. My deep appreciation goes to Fr. S. D. P. Selvan, my translator/interpreter, for granting me permission to reprint his poem "Lamentation: A Rereading of Vanni in the Perspective of Underside History."

Work on this project also spun into shorter articles, such as "The Lament Traditions of Enslaved African American Women and the Lament Traditions of the Hebrew Bible," which I wrote for *Lamentations in Ancient and Contemporary Cultural Contexts*, edited by Nancy C. Lee and Carleen Mandolfo (Society of Biblical Literature, 2008).

My reading of Lamentations highlights class, gender, and age differences in the voices that emerge in the poems. It notes that different segments of society, as groups and not only individuals—the rich, the poor, men, women, adults, and children—experience war and the aftermath of war in different ways. It is easy to declare "War is hell," leveling the trauma for all involved. But it is not that simple. The truth is that war is much worse for some people than for others. A child sitting by the body of his dead mother experiences war differently from the general sitting in a command center who orders others to fight. Some people profit from war and continue to reap the benefits in the postwar period. Some cry out for justice. Others just want a return to normalcy. Some are hopeful. Others give in to despair. Some are too young to know what they lost; others, too old to start over again. Most of the voices in the poems in Lamentations are profoundly sad, hurt, confused, and angry. It is a scary book of raw emotions that will not be quieted. But we all need the poems in

Preface to Lamentations

Lamentations because they express what people really feel at some point in their lives. They foster the catharsis and hope for which some people are desperately searching. Congregations do a disservice to their worshiping community when they become absorbed in praise and thanksgiving without noticing that pain is also a normal part of life, and it ought to be acknowledged. Congregations become irrelevant when they cannot meet people at their points of need.

I thank those who read the book in manuscript form and offered suggestions to improve it. They include Dagne Assefa, John Stanley, and Patricia Shelly. Thank you to David Garber for his careful work as copy editor of this book.

I also thank the board, administration, and faculty of Christian Theological Seminary for granting me a sabbatical, during which time I was able to do further research and writing for the commentary.

A special thanks goes to my editor, Douglas Miller, who went over every word with a critical eye to improve it and patiently nudged and advised me over many years to keep this project going.

Wilma Ann Bailey
Indianapolis, Indiana

Introduction to Lamentations

Sorrow Songs

There is an old Negro spiritual titled "I Didn't Hear Nobody Pray." The words are simple:

> I didn't hear nobody pray
> Oh, I didn't hear nobody pray,
> way down yonder by myself,
> and I didn't hear nobody pray.

This "sorrow song" could serve well as a thematic refrain for the biblical book of Lamentations, a book of anguish and inescapable grief, a book dissonant with feel-good religion that admits to no doubt, confusion, insecurity, or pain. Lamentations is a collection of five sorrow songs from ancient Israel. The songs were originally sung, and they were passed from generation to generation as oral compositions before they were written down in the form in which we see them today *[Orality, p. 118]*. Focusing on a community experiencing the aftermath of war, a variety of voices within ancient Israel mourn what has been and is now while holding on to the hope that there will be a future for them. It grants permission to grieve, to be angry at God, to purge the soul, and to dare to hope when there are no visible signs of hope.

Lamentations is regularly read every summer in Jewish synagogues during the ninth day of the month of Ab on the Jewish

Introduction to Lamentations

calendar, the day set aside for the commemoration of the fall of Jerusalem. Ab usually falls during July or August on Western calendars. In the Roman Catholic Church, Lamentations 3:17-26 is a lectionary reading during the Mass for the Dead (*Lectionary*). The reading is modified by five verses when the deceased is a child; in that case, only verses 22-26 are read. Lamentations 3:1-9, 19-24 is an alternate reading for the Saturday before Easter in most Christian liturgical traditions (except in the Episcopal tradition, where it is never read). Anabaptists do not have a tradition of following lectionary readings. Therefore, the frequency of reading selections from Lamentations cannot be known. However, the middle verses of chapter 3 are familiar to persons in those communions. They are read and quoted frequently:

> *The steadfast love of the Lord never ceases,*
> *his mercies never come to an end;*
> *they are new every morning;*
> *great is your faithfulness....*
> *The Lord is good to those who wait for him,*
> *to the soul that seeks him.*
> *It is good that one should wait quietly*
> *for the salvation of the Lord.* (3:22, 25-26)

Title

The title of the book in Jewish Bibles—*'ekah*, or *How!*—is taken from the first word of the first verse, which in the New Revised Standard Version reads, *How lonely sits the city that once was full of people!* The English title Lamentations derives from the content that consists of a series of five laments (*qinot* in Heb). Laments are poems that express sorrow or grief. The poems lament the fall of Jerusalem to the Babylonians in the year 587/586 BCE *[Capture and Destruction of Jerusalem, p. 112]*. This event was particularly catastrophic because it represented the end of an independent Israelite kingdom. (The northern Israelite kingdom had been conquered by Assyria about 130 years earlier.) In graphic detail the poems recount the suffering and confusion of the Jerusalemite community as it attempted to grapple with that experience and understand what had happened to it from a theological and ethical standpoint *[Communal Lament, p. 114]*.

Historical and Theological Background

In what we call the Old Testament, Israel told a powerful story of its emergence as a people that stretched back to a period of servitude in Egypt. God had freed their ancestors from Egyptian rule and placed them under divine protection. God prepared them for their special role in history through an extended wilderness experience, during which they received instruction (Torah) in how they were to live and respond to God's gracious acts toward them (Deut 6:21-24; 26:5-9; Josh 24:2-13). They were a mixed people, a motley collection of diverse tribes and clans, some of whom claimed Mesopotamian origin through their eponymous ancestor (the ancestor whose name becomes the name of a tribe) Jacob (also known as "Israel"), and his wives: Leah, Rachel, Bilhah, and Zilpah (Gen 29–30, 49). Others who were not biological descendents of these ancestors chose to cast their lot with them (Exod 12:37-38; Josh 6:25; Josh 9) and were absorbed into the community. During the period described in the books of Joshua and Judges, the Israelite tribes functioned independently. It was only during the monarchy that their collective identity as Israel jelled.

Another development at a later point in history was the creation of a covenant with King David assuring that a Davidic descendent would sit upon the throne of Israel forever (2 Sam 7:12-16) *[Covenant, p. 114]*. Simultaneously, a new "Zion" theology emerged that gave special status to the city of Jerusalem as the place where God's divine presence would be manifested to the people (Pss 78:68-71; 132:13-18). According to Israel's account of its history as found in the books of 1 and 2 Samuel and 1 Kings, David brought the principal cultic object of north Israel, the ark of the covenant, to Jerusalem, and Solomon built a temple to house it. This created a centralization of worship in ancient Israel that had not existed before these actions. By the eighth century BCE, the Jerusalemites had come to believe in the inviolability of Zion as expressed in the prophecies of the Jerusalemite prophet Isaiah (17:12-14; 37:33-35) *[Zion Theology, p. 119]*.

Not all Israelite theologies granted primacy to Jerusalem. The David/Zion traditions did, but those traditions represent the southern tribe of Judah, in whose territory the city was located. The northern Israelite tribes found spiritual centers at Bethel and Dan. Both were old sites of Israelite worship that existed long before David conquered Jerusalem and made it his political and religious capital. It was precisely the political connections that made Jerusalem controversial for many of the Israelite tribes. David's successor and son, Solomon—the same person who introduced taxation and forced labor into Israelite life—promoted a major shift in the worship life of Israel by building a temple in the city and setting a

Introduction to Lamentations

direction for prayer toward it in his dedicatory prayer (1 Kings 6–8). Persons who did not live in or close to the city had less access to certain aspects of the worship life (such as sacrifice) than those living nearby. Therefore they continued their localized worship at high places and later at synagogues. They did not embrace the notion of the supremacy of Jerusalem until it was uncoupled from its royal and political associations.

Because of the Davidic and Zion traditions, it was very difficult for the people of Jerusalem and Judah to understand what had happened to them when they witnessed the destruction of their cities and towns by the Babylonian army. Up to the end they had been confident in the inviolability of Jerusalem, that God would never let Jerusalem fall, because Jerusalem was God's own city. After all, God had permitted the divine name to be placed there (1 Kings 9:3-5) and had said to Solomon several centuries earlier, "My eyes and my heart will be there for all time" (9:3). Moreover, in the common theological understanding of the ancient Near East, the conquest of a kingdom by a foreign entity illustrated either the weakness of the god of that people or that their own god was punishing them. The God of the people of Jerusalem, Yahweh, had not protected them from Babylonian aggression. Theologically, they could only conclude either that the Babylonian god was stronger or that their own god was punishing them *[Yahweh, p. 118]*.

Rejecting the idea that the Assyrian or Babylonian gods were stronger, one school of thought, as articulated in 2 Kings 17:7-20, blamed the fall of the northern kingdom on the sins of all the people. As named, those sins include various forms of idolatry and neglect of the commandments. Although the prophet Amos is less concerned about idolatry and more with the lack of justice and compassion in the land, he also charges Judah with having rejected God's divine instruction (Amos 2:4).

The prophet Ezekiel, on the other hand, blames not all of the people but specifically the leaders and the elite who have abused and neglected the common folk. According to Ezekiel 34, the leaders have used their positions to enrich themselves. They have neglected their leadership responsibilities. The prophet castigates them: "You have not strengthened the weak, you have not healed the sick, you have not bound up the injured, you have not brought back the strayed, you have not sought the lost, but with force and harshness you have ruled them" (Ezek 34:4) *[Elite, p. 115]*.

The God of Lamentations

God is mentioned multiple times in each chapter of the book of Lamentations. God is called *Yahweh*, usually translated as *the* LORD in every chapter. Yahweh is the personal name for God. It was the common designation for God in the southern tribe of Judah. God is also referred to as *Adonai*, translated as *Lord*, in several places (2:1, 2, 7) and *Elyon, Most High,* in one place (3:38). *El*, translated as *God,* appears only once (in 3:41). *El* was more commonly used by the northern Israelite tribes. Some English translations of the Bible insert the word "God" into 3:1, but it does not appear there in Hebrew. The Hebrew has only "he" in that place, leaving the identity of the "he" unanswered *[Yahweh, p. 118]*.

Appeals are made to the LORD (Lam 1:9, 11, 20; 2:20; 5:21), but Yahweh responds only once, in 2:13-16 (though this may also simply be the voice of a narrator speaking for God), leaving the people of Judah to wonder whether God cares or does not care about the suffering of his people.

Many of the divine images in the book are disturbing. Several of the poems accuse God of playing an active role in the events that led to the suffering and exile of the people of Judah. Strident voices accuse the Lord of having become *like an enemy* who destroys and kills (2:4-5). The Lord is charged with having abandoned the people to starvation and humiliation, rape and murder. But the book is not simply a series of complaints. The poets also express a hope that God can and will relieve their suffering and avenge it. They are convinced that if God is able to see how bad things really are, God will relent. At the very center of the book, in poem 3, there is a statement about positive attributes of God, including love, mercy, and goodness. It is confidence in these positive attributes that leads the poets of Lamentations to believe that God will not react negatively to their complaints and may act to ameliorate their situation.

As the poets of Lamentations reflect on God's role in the suffering of the people of Jerusalem, difficult theological questions emerge. Even if they are guilty of the charges that God has brought against them, they refuse to believe that their sins and failures are so grievous as to merit the suffering that has ensued. The book does not rush to comfort the aggrieved people of Judah. Rather, it allows the pain to linger and the questions to be asked and accusations to be made. It ends with a plea for restoration, a healing of their relationship with God that had been broken.

Introduction to Lamentations

Date and Purpose

Most of the poems may have been written shortly after the events themselves. This determination is based on the sharpness of the pain that permeates the book and the absence of expressions of consolation, amelioration, restoration, or reconciliation. However, it is important to keep in mind that in the immediate aftermath of war, many survivors are still traumatized, and everyone has been changed. Community networks of family, neighbors, and friends have been shattered. Institutions that provided structure and support before the war—such as the temple, courts, the weekly market, the gathering of elders—no longer function. Trade has been disrupted. Survivors are in the process of reestablishing enterprises that will provide a living for them. They are building new houses or repairing old ones that were damaged during the war. They are searching for family members who disappeared. Some were killed. Some were taken into exile. Some fled to safer places. Food and other commodities are scarce in the urban areas. Those who prior to the war were educated, who thus had the leisure to reflect and write, have been exiled, killed, or preoccupied with earning a living. The end of the fighting is not the end of the war for survivors. Many years after the catastrophic events have taken place, some triggering event can psychologically take a person back to the pain. The poems in Lamentations may have been written close to the events described but not in the immediate years following them.

In addition, there are expressions of hope that the fortunes of Jerusalem will be reversed, but they are not yet realized. Most likely, the purpose of the book is to provide a vehicle for expressing grief. It affirms grieving as a legitimate and needed human expression that serves as a catharsis, a purging. Other scholars have offered suggestions as to what they think the purpose of the book is. Kathleen O'Connor (2002: 3) calls Lamentations "a book of comfort" because readers can see "they are no longer alone in their pain." F. W. Dobbs-Allsopp (2002: 37) thinks that the book's "implicit message is that grief, no matter how debilitating, is finally survivable." Claus Westermann (81) writes that laments function in such a way as to "allow the suffering of the afflicted to find expression." Delbert Hillers (4) views Lamentations as "a confession, and testimony to a search for absolution." I believe, however, that although there are statements of confession, the lack of content within them and the adjacent statements of the suffering of the people suggest a certain insincerity. It is as if they are saying, "We are supposed to say this but we really do not believe it. We do not believe that our sins, whatever they were, merited such a response to us and to our community." Following this line of reasoning, Lamentations is also protest literature because it rejects the notion that suffering is always a result of sin and that justice is always realized.

Authorship

The author of the book is unknown. Some Christian and Jewish sources assign it to Jeremiah because, according to tradition, he lived during the period of Jerusalem's fall and was present in the city and witnessed the devastation (Jer 39–42; *Targum Lamentations* 1:1, in Levine). Moreover, Jeremiah is known to have composed at least one lament, as indicated in 2 Chronicles 35:25. But some scholars object, questioning whether Jeremiah would have written a line such as "her prophets obtain no vision from the Lord" (Lam 2:9). Jeremiah, being a prophet himself, certainly thought that he had experienced divine revelation. In response, Nancy Lee (2002: 152) points out that prophets (other prophets) are frequently criticized in the book of Jeremiah itself. Moreover, there are many similarities in the use of idioms, themes, and grammatical structures in the two books. Although in Christian Bibles, Lamentations follows the book of Jeremiah, in Jewish Bibles the book is in a separate section (sometimes sandwiched between Ecclesiastes and Esther), hence physically dissociated from Jeremiah. While it is possible that Jeremiah contributed to what became the book of Lamentations, it is also possible that a variety of poets composed the poems.

In ancient Israel both men and women composed and sang songs of lament. In the book of Jeremiah, the prophet says of himself, "Over the mountains, I lift up weeping and wailing and over a meadow I speak a lament . . ." (Jer 9:10 [9] AT). And it is taken for granted that women composed and sang laments under the inspiration of God. "Listen, women! A word of the Lord! Your ear will take in the word of his [God's] mouth. And you will teach your daughters wailing and each woman [will teach] her neighbor a lament" (Jer 9:20 [19] AT). In the previous text and the one following, the words go directly from God's mouth into the ears of women. Ezekiel 32:16 reads, "It is a lamentation. The daughters of the nations will lament it and they [men and women] will lament it" (AT). The women in the Jeremiah text are referred to as *haḥakamot*, "the wise women" (9:17 [16]). Ancient Israel was not the only country that listened to the words of wise women. Even today such women play a role in the social, religious, and political life of people. For example, in traditional societies of the southern Sudan, the "wise women" compose and sing songs of lament, valor in war, peace, love, and so forth. The songs of these women influence the behavior of men in war and peace, helping the community to mourn its losses and celebrate its joys (Lacey: 1-2). It is certainly within the realm of possibility that a woman or women composed some of the laments in the book of Lamentations. And it is very likely that the poets were witnesses to the events reported and that they lived in the city shortly afterward and felt the lingering effects of the carnage.

Structure

The book of Lamentations consists of five poems, four of which are alphabetic acrostics: the first word of each line begins with a successive letter of the alphabet in order *[Acrostic, p. 111]*. It has been suggested that the acrostic form is used in these laments to express the fullness and completion of grief. The use of the alphabetic form indicates that the poems were either composed in a literate society or restructured into alphabetic acrostics during a period of literacy. Karl Budde proposes that there is a quasi-metrical structure in the book of Lamentations (71). Frequently, though not always, he writes, the first line of a pair of lines is longer than the second. This is referred to as a "limping meter" or a "qinah" meter. It brings to mind an image of a person moving forward and then falling back as the cause of the grief is remembered. According to Levine, that musical scale is also found among Syrian and Egyptian Christians in their worship services (13). Delbert Hillers points out that ancient Sumer in Mesopotamia provides many examples of laments over cities and temples. Those laments are similar in content and style to the laments in the book under study (32-35). Dobbs-Allsopp found nine commonalities in city laments that originated in Mesopotamia, commonalities that are also found in the poems in Lamentations (2002: 7-9). They include a common subject matter (the destruction of a city) and a somber mood, a similar structure and use of poetic devices, a theme of divine abandonment, the assignment of responsibility to gods, the god as the agent of destruction, the use of stock images, statements about the disruption in the life of the community, the lament itself, and a statement of restoration.

Toni Craven (27), building on the work of the form critics Hermann Gunkel and Claus Westermann, identifies a sixfold structure that is characteristic of a lament. It begins with an address to God, followed by a complaint, confession of trust, petition, words of assurance, and a vow of praise. Some or all of the six are present in each of the poems in Lamentations.

Content

The content and style of each of the five poems is unique. The first poem centers on the figure that Zion personified as a female in several roles: the widow, the princess, the violated woman. Israel's God is seen as the perpetrator of the violence against Jerusalem and, paradoxically, the one to whom appeals are made for sympathy and revenge. In the second poem, the Lord is described as having become *like an enemy*, and the language of war is employed with descriptions of battle tactics and weaponry. The third poem opens with the image of a man under attack. It moves to words of hope and grace before reverting to a cry for vengeance. Chapter 4 notices the plight of children in the devastated city. Prophets and priests are blamed for the fall of the city. Chapter 5 complains about the social reversals that have taken place. The affluent are now working like slaves, and slaves are ruling them.

These poems are not to be understood narrowly as historical accounts. They are poems, and as poems they are meant to stir the emotions—to cause the reader or hearer to connect with the pain so keenly felt by those left in the devastated city of Jerusalem *[Communal Lament, p. 114]*. With the possible exception of chapter 3, the book of Lamentations does not reflect personal grief. No individuals are named, and no individual experiences are recounted. The book expresses collective grief for a community now gone, a way of life that perished, a loss of innocence, a crisis of faith.

The Grief Process

In ancient Israel, grief following a catastrophic event that affected an entire community was expressed in a variety of ways. Some of those ways were communally sanctioned and expected. The grieving people were accustomed to tearing their clothing, placing ashes on their heads, sitting on the ground, and refraining from eating as they were weeping and uttering expressions of lament (2 Sam 12:15-22; Gen 37:34-35). The tearing of clothing and placing of ashes on the head indicated a lack of concern for one's appearance. These actions alerted others to their mourning state so that they could respond to mourners appropriately.

Many modern Protestant congregations have no set rituals for loss except in the case of death. And in some congregations, the funeral service itself has undergone a metamorphosis. A memorial service of celebrating the life of the deceased individual has taken its place. Many people welcome this change. But some mourners feel that the memorial celebration has taken away an opportunity for them to mourn their loss. Sometime in the last third of the twentieth century and into the twenty-first century, it became unacceptable in the West to mourn, to show or express grief in public. When the widows of Dr. Martin Luther King Jr. and President John F. Kennedy lost their husbands, the media and ordinary folk noticed how "well" they had handled their loss. They did not weep or collapse or scream or faint. They held up well. They modeled a respectable way of mourning. Many took notice and began to imitate them.

Concomitantly, death became invisible. People near death were sent to a hospital. When they died, they were taken directly from the hospital to the funeral home by funeral directors. From the funeral home or church, the body was taken to the grave site or cremated. Earlier in history, people died at home, and the family or neighbors prepared the body, the casket, and the grave site. The reality of death was visibly present. These actions enabled the grieving process. Thomas Long (38–46) points out that there was more to the funeral than comforting the mourners. In the past, the funeral service was a ritual that reenacted the story of the Christian life from baptism to death, death with a small d because it served only as a passageway to the resurrected life with Christ. Mourners walked the body to the graveyard just as they had walked beside the deceased in life (87–92, 97).

Psychiatrist Elizabeth Kübler-Ross was a pioneer in the study of the psychological process through which many persons go as they face the end of their mortal life. She noticed that often the following five steps are present in the grieving process: denial, anger, bargaining, depression, and acceptance (38–137). Although it is probably not helpful to think of the list as steps, as if everyone experiencing grief passes through the steps in order, the list does represent some of the ways that some individuals express grief. During periods when an entire community is affected by loss at the same time—as occurs during wars, tsunamis, and plagues—so many deaths occur at once or in tandem that one cycle of grief is not completed before the next one starts. This is the type of catastrophe experienced by the Jews who wrote these poems. There was no one to comfort them because they were all bereaved at the same time through the same event.

Communal trauma and communal grieving take on a different character than that which primarily affects an individual. Arthur Neal (4) points out that whereas individual traumas may separate that person from the community, "a national trauma . . . is shared with others." It can function in such a way as to bring people together. It causes people to realize that what appears to be order in society is in fact a human creation that can be disrupted. In response, the community embeds the trauma into social life, and it becomes a "reference point" in the telling of the history of the people. Young adults, at the age when they are making many major decisions in life as a cohort, are shaped by the trauma (Neal: 6, 9, 12, 13, 204). The American Civil War is an example of a trauma of this sort.

Colin Turnbull, on the other hand, noticed that massive trauma to a community may lead to "the total disintegration of family and community" (Robben and Suárez-Orozco: 22). This is illustrated by the prolonged conflict in the Congo that spanned the last years of the twentieth century and the first ones of the twenty-first century. Rapes of women in front of family and community members, for example, cause such deep distress and shame that community members are not able to face each other. The community falls apart.

Ancient Israel's trauma at the fall of Jerusalem during the Babylonian invasion affected the urban elite, the urban middle class, and the royal family to a greater extent than other Judahites. The Babylonians destroyed the city and exiled the royals and those who had the resources to foment a rebellion. The rural folk, the urban poor, and others who probably were simply overlooked were left in place. The various communities within Israel were affected in different ways. The elite experienced the battle for Jerusalem and exile immediately afterward. Some of those elite were settled together in Babylon; once they got over the shock of their loss and adjusted to a new reality in a foreign land, they built thriving communities there. The rural folk may have been disoriented by a sudden loss of their urban center, with its markets and courts, but they were left intact on the land, and much of their life went on as normal. What changed for them was that they were now paying taxes to a new and foreign administration *[Elite, p. 115]*. The book of Lamentations reflects the lot of urban dwellers who survived but now live among the ruins of the city and their shattered community. The survivors of each of these groups and their descendents developed their collective sense of self based on what they had been through. The books of Ezra and Nehemiah illustrate the tensions between the ones who returned from exile and those who never left the city and the surrounding countryside: both see themselves as legitimate descendents of the former people who lived there. The aftermath of the fall of Jerusalem mirrors both ways in which communities respond to catastrophic events. The community that experienced exile developed an identity based on that communal experience.

Introduction to Lamentations

The community that remained in the land developed an identity distinct from that of those who left.

This commentary pays most attention to the NRSV and NIV (2011). All translations of Lamentations are given in italics, including those of the author (AT). Unless otherwise noted, translations of the Bible will appear as NRSV (not flagged). English versification is indicated, and differing Hebrew (MT) versification sometimes is added within parentheses or brackets. The NRSV rendering of "the LORD" is often changed here to "Yahweh," to reflect the MT.

Lamentations 1:1-22

There Is No Comforter for Zion

PREVIEW

This poem articulates the grief experienced by the Jewish community as a result of the devastation of their beloved city, Jerusalem, by a Babylonian military force in 587/586 BCE. It is primarily an expression of loss, pain, and suffering. Words of hope and encouragement are absent except indirectly in appeals to God. Their appeals to God are an expression of hope, hope that God will hear them and respond [*Capture and Destruction of Jerusalem, p. 112*].

In the poem, Zion (the city of Jerusalem) makes a confession, blaming itself for its present state. But there is no specific statement as to what Zion thinks it did wrong. There are only vague references to transgressions and rebellion. The absence of a specific listing of sins casts doubt on the sincerity of Zion's confession (1:5, 18, 20). The truth is that Zion is baffled. The implication is that Zion does not know what it could have done to merit such treatment. Everyone falls short of what God desires, but total destruction is too severe a punishment for being human. God is clearly the one who is held responsible for the suffering in the poem (1:5, 12, 13, 15, 21, 22), not Zion (Jerusalem) itself. The theological crisis that Zion is experiencing is more significant than the political one [*Zion Theology, p. 119*]. Why would God permit the destruction of God's own people and the city that was a symbol of the divine presence within it? The Babylonians who captured and pillaged the city are never mentioned by name because they were thought to be nothing more than an instrument of God. The poem has no happy ending. There are no words of comfort. It is meant to function as a catharsis and a form of protest, protest against unmerited suffering.

This first chapter of the book, like three of the other four, is structured as an alphabetic acrostic formed by the twenty-two consonantal letters of the Hebrew alphabet. The first word of each line begins with a successive letter of the alphabet in order. The twenty-two letters yield the twenty-two verses that appear in English Bibles. In Hebrew, each verse contains three lines except for the seventh verse, which has four lines *[Acrostic, p. 111]*.

Persons who read Lamentations in English translations easily miss the effect that the sounds, wordplays, and rhythms of the ancient Hebrew language had on the ancient listeners. Ancient poetry was usually sung or recited to musical notations. The emotion of the poem was conveyed not just in the meanings of the words but also in their sounds, accompanying music, and syntactical structures. Even today, in synagogues, the entire book of Lamentations is sung, not read *[Hebrew Poetry, p. 116]*.

Laments in the Old Testament often have several but not all of the characteristics that help to define the lament genre: address to God, complaint, confession of trust, petition, words of assurance, and vow of praise (Craven: 27; see the Introduction on "Structure"). That is true in this poem, where only four characteristics appear. There is an address to God in verses 9c, 11c, and 20a. Virtually the whole chapter is a statement of the complaint. Verse 18 contains the statement *Yahweh is right*, which perhaps indicates a glimmer of trust that God has not been out of character in God's treatment of Israel *[Yahweh, p. 118]*. A petition appears in the form of a request for revenge on the enemy in verses 21 and 22. Significantly, there are no words of assurance and no vow of praise. Hence, this poem lacks two characteristic features of the lament form. This may be an indication that a call to end the grieving period must not come too quickly. Grief must first be fully engaged and fully expressed *[Communal Lament, p. 114]*.

Key ideas in the poem revolve around the word "comfort" (Heb. *menaḥem*), particularly the lack of a comforter (vv. 2, 16, 17, 21); the LORD (Yahweh) as the source of Zion's troubles (5, 12, 14, 15, 17); and Jerusalem (7, 8, 17), also named *Zion* (4, 6, 17), as the literal and spiritual center of Israel.

OUTLINE

A Lonely City, 1:1-2
Exile, 1:3
Zion Mourns, 1:4-6
Jerusalem Remembers, 1:7
The Charge against Jerusalem, 1:8-9
Violation, 1:10-11
The Charge against God, 1:12-17
Confession, 1:18-21b
Call for Vengeance, 1:21c-22

EXPLANATORY NOTES

A Lonely City 1:1-2

The very first word of the poem, ʾekah (How!), is sometimes translated as a cry of distress, Alas! This is one of the dirgelike elements of the poem. A dirge is technically not a lament but rather a funeral song *[Dirge, p. 115]*. The dirge offers no hope because in dirge theology the dead one will not live again. The anguished cry—How!—is followed by a description of the city of Jerusalem in metaphorical language as it appeared after its conquest by the army of Babylon in 587/586 BCE:

> How lonely sits the city
>   that once was full of people!
> How like a widow she has become,
>   she that was great among the nations!
> She that was a princess among the provinces
>   has become a vassal.

This is a representation of the second dirgelike element. The structural element of contrast, comparing the way things are now to the way they used to be, is frequently found in both dirges and lament literature. The city was once full of people; now it is almost empty. The elite have been killed or taken into exile *[Elite, p. 115]*. The lower classes have fled to the countryside to eke a living out of the soil. Frequently in dirges and laments, memories of the past are rosier than the reality of the past—to create a sharp contrast with a painful present *[Capture and Destruction of Jerusalem, p. 112]*.

Female imagery appearing in the form of metaphors and similes abound in this first poem. Part of the reason for this is that Hebrew is a gendered language. Nouns are either masculine or feminine grammatically. In the Hebrew language, places are usually feminine.

Jerusalem and Zion are both referred to as "she" and "her." Often when feminine-gendered language is used to refer to Jerusalem or Zion, it means all the people of Jerusalem, not just the women. Its function, in part, is to engender sympathy. In the first verse Jerusalem is likened to a widow. Being a "widow" means that a woman has lost her husband, her status, and her source of livelihood. Widows were probably not as common a sight in ancient Israelite villages as we might think. In contrast to the situation today, women usually died at a young age, before their husbands (Meyers: 99). Those who survived their husbands could be left in dire straits. There were no pensions and few social safety nets beyond the family. The social structure of ancient Israel was primarily patrilocal. That means that upon marriage a woman left her birth family and went to live with her husband's family. The reason for this practice was that in an economy based on subsistence agriculture, most of the resources were held in land. Land was usually (but not always) owned by the husband or the husband's family or clan. If the husband's family no longer wanted the widow because she could no longer produce sons to work the fields for them or she became a liability for them, she might be expelled from the household. There were few options for a widow. She could return to her birth family if it was able and willing to take her back. She could glean, become a prostitute, or beg. If she had a particular skill, such as midwifery, she might be able to eke out a living on her own. If she were still young and strong, she might become someone's concubine or second wife. Widowhood was not just a descriptor for persons whose husbands had passed away; it had social, economic, and political implications that would have been recognized by readers of this text in ancient times (1 Tim 5). Jewish exegesis emphasizes that Jerusalem is *not* a widow but rather, as the text says, "like" a widow—like one whose husband is temporarily absent. It is like a widow in its destitution and spouseless state, with all that implied. The distinction, not "a widow" but "like a widow," is made to convey the understanding that God has not abandoned the Jewish people (Levine: 19). This is a temporary situation.

Jerusalem is compared to a princess, the pampered daughter of a king. Princesses did not work; their function was to be the collateral in treaty relations between kingdoms. Her presence, her marriage, and the production of children were the guarantee that two kingdoms would live together in peace. Jerusalem is likened to a princess who has lost her status, privilege, and security. She has become like a forced laborer. Now she not only works; she also works for the benefit of someone else. She will not accrue personal wealth or benefit from her labor, nor will her own kingdom benefit. She is like a slave. In ancient times, kingdoms conquered other kingdoms partly to enrich their own kingdom. Conquered kingdoms were forced to pay tribute to their overlords and supply laborers to build roads and fortifications. Jerusalem was conquered by the Babylonian army. No longer free, Jerusalem is a vassal people subject to the whims of Babylon.

These two initial verses emphasize that Jerusalem sits alone, abandoned by both friends and allies who have turned against it and become like enemies. An appeal was made to Egypt for help (2 Kings 18:21), but the help never came. Judah and Jerusalem had earlier been vassals to the great Babylonian Empire long before their fall in 587/586 BCE. Their days as an independent city-state were long over but not forgotten [City, p. 113].

The first verse of Lamentations contains hyperbole in stressing the greatness of Jerusalem. *She that was great among the nations! She that was a princess among the provinces. . .* Jerusalem probably was never very significant among the nations as a political or economic power before the conquest. It was a hinterland, tucked away in the Judean hill country, far from the major trade routes. Even the united kingdom of Israel under King David was never the equal of Egypt, Babylon, or Assyria. Its leading city would not have stood out. Jerusalem was made the political and religious capital by David. He built a palace there and brought the ark of the covenant from its temporary home in Baale-judah to the city in order to ensure its religious status (2 Sam 6:2). Later Solomon constructed a temple to house the ark (1 Kings 6; 8). The problem was that Solomon's temple was closely associated with the royal family and therefore the political realities of the day. It was not until the exile, when there was a separation between the political and religious structures of Israelite society, that Jerusalem took on the significance for which it is later revered. Then the city became more and more a symbol and a hope for Jewish people there and around the world. It gained in significance and, particularly, spiritual value.

Not all Israelite traditions granted primacy to Jerusalem. The David/Zion traditions did, but those traditions represent the southern tribe of Judah, in whose territory the city was located. The northern Israelite tribes found spiritual centers at Bethel, located in the central hill country, and Dan, which was north of the Sea of Galilee. Both were old centers of Israelite worship that existed long before David conquered Jerusalem and made it his political and religious capital. It was precisely the political connections that made Jerusalem controversial for many of the northern Israelite tribes. David's successor and son, Solomon, the same person who introduced taxation and forced labor into Israelite life, promoted a major shift in the worship life of Israel not just by building the temple but also by setting a direction for prayer, according to 1 Kings 6–8. In his dedicatory prayer Solomon requested that all prayer be directed toward the city of Jerusalem, thereby elevating it above other Israelite shrine cities (1 Kings 8). The temple in Jerusalem was long considered to be the king's shrine, a place for the elite but not for ordinary folk [Elite, p. 115]. Elaborate rituals controlled by a priestly aristocracy, and demands for pilgrimages and sacrifices that ordinary people could ill afford, created alienation between them and the official cult. Most of the people of Israel worshiped at local shrines and later synagogues that they controlled. It was not until the end of the kingship that ordinary Israelites could accept Jerusalem as their city and the symbol of Israel [Zion Theology, p. 119].

Exile 1:3

Biblical poetry is often difficult to translate, and the first bicolon (one line) of verse 3 is an example [Hebrew Poetry, p. 116]. The NRSV reads, *Judah has gone into exile with suffering and hard servitude*. In this translation, the suffering and hard servitude accompanies Judah into exile. The NIV reads, *After affliction and harsh labor, Judah has gone into exile*. This translation suggests that the affliction and harsh labor are things of the past, left behind by those who went into exile. The *Tanakh*, a modern Jewish translation of the Hebrew Bible/Old Testament (NJPS), translates *Judah has gone into exile because of misery and harsh oppression*. The question that the translations are dealing with is whether the suffering and hard work accompany Judah into exile, or whether Judah leaves suffering and hard work behind as it goes into exile. The uncertainty hinges on a preposition that can be translated in several ways. Likely the NIV and Tanakh have it right. This poetic account of the exile suggests that survivors of the conflict who were not forced into exile left of their own accord as a result of harsh conditions in the homeland. The infrastructure had been destroyed. Some of its inhabitants settled among the nations (Jer 43:1-7), but for some there was no rest because pursuers overtook them. The book of Lamentations, however, is not primarily concerned about the exiles. It focuses on those who have remained in the city of Jerusalem and its environs amid the destruction.

Noticing that the book of Lamentations lacks a listing of specific sins that led to the devastation of Jerusalem and the exile of its prominent citizens, a later Targum (a translation of the Old Testament into the Aramaic language with commentary) supplies them [*Targum, p. 118*]. Targum Codex Urbinates 1, which dates to at least the first century CE, accuses the Israelites of having oppressed widows and orphans, of having levied excessive forced labor, of not freeing their Israelite slaves, and of not making the three yearly pilgrimages to Jerusalem (Levine: 63). The last of these appears in the Targum as a comment on verse 4. This addendum must be read as a theodicy, an attempt to justify God's actions in the poem. The theological assumption is that God would not have permitted the destruction of Jerusalem unless it was deserved. But keep in mind that the writers of the Targum were not witnesses to the destruction and had not lived there at that time. They were proposing a justification for the fall of Jerusalem.

Zion Mourns 1:4-6

In verse 4 there is a reversal of direction from going out to coming in. Judah has *gone* into exile. No one is *coming in* to Zion for the *festivals* because they have been suspended. The temple was looted and destroyed. There were no accommodations for pilgrims. The one-way traffic is causing the city to empty, an issue that is also mentioned in the book of Nehemiah (7:3-5; 11:1-4).

As Xuan Huong Thi Pham (48-50) points out, the image is not just of people in mourning. With anthropomorphizing (speaking of the nonhuman in human terms), the text declares that even the infrastructure of the city (the roads, the gates; 1:4) participate in the mourning. Similar imagery is found in the book of Jeremiah, where there are references to the land as mourning (4:28; 12:4). In Jeremiah 4:28, the land mourns in anticipation of the destruction of Jerusalem and its people; in 12:4, the land mourns before the destruction because of the wickedness of those who live on it. Zechariah 12:12 similarly images the land as lamenting (the NRSV translates as "mourn"), using a different Hebrew word. However, the context in Zechariah seems to refer not to the physical space but to society.

In the second and third bicola (two half-line pairs) of verse 4, Zion's priests groan (or sigh), and the *young women* (*betulot*, sometimes translated *virgins*) *grieve* (NRSV, NIV) or are *unhappy* (NJPS). This pairing of priests and young women is unexpected. More common is the pairing of young women and young men, as in Lamentations 1:18, or pairings of young and old, as in 2:21 and elsewhere in the Old Testament. Priests and young women represent life and continuity. Their uncharacteristic behavior in these verses signals the bleakness of the situation that they are in. Other places where priests and young women are mentioned together in a similar setting are Psalm 78:63-64 and Joel 1:8-9. In all cases the pairing occurs to express a situation of extreme abnormality brought about by calamity. According to Levine (64), one of the Targums claims that the young women are mourning because they no longer dance on the fifteenth of Ab and the Day of Atonement *[Targum, p. 118]*. Priests ought to be reassuring the people that God is still with them through the rituals. Young women ought to be happily looking forward to becoming full participants as adults in the community and mothers who continue life cycle. Instead the young women and the priests have nothing to offer but their grief and despair.

These verses (1:4-6) offer an explanation as to why Jerusalem is in the situation that it is in. The Lord has made the city suffer because of its many transgressions or rebellions. The nature of the transgressions is not mentioned. The reference to the children, *her children have gone away* (1:5), immediately after the statement about transgressions, calls it into question. The word used for children here refers to young children, not adult children or the people as a whole. The poet insists that the little children could not have been guilty of multiple rebellions and transgressions even if the adults were. The statement is meant to elicit sympathy from the audience.

The phrase *daughter Zion* (*bat ṣion*) is often used as an expression of tenderness. In verse 6, it is a poetic synonym for Zion that may also have been chosen for metrical purposes. Lamentations 1 is a poem. The poem may have been set to a particular meter that required a particular length or number of syllables for this verse.

The statement in verse 6, *All her honor* (or *splendor*) *has gone out from Daughter Zion* (AT), coupled with the rest of the verse and its reference to *leaders* (*princes* in the NIV and NRSV), appears to be a reflection on the leaders who were exiled when Jerusalem fell to the Babylonians. The ordinary people who did not present a threat to Babylon were left behind. Several of the poems, including this one, indicate that the poets are more focused on the elite of society than on the plight of the common people *[Elite, p. 115]*.

Jerusalem Remembers 1:7

"Remembering" is an important concept in ancient Israel's theology and ethics. In the Bible, God's claim on Israel is frequently expressed in terms of what God has done for Israel in the past. A series of statements that scholars call *credos* are found in Deuteronomy 6:20-23;

26:5-11; and Joshua 24:2-15 [*Credo, p. 115*]. Each statement recalls that Israel was formed in the trauma of slavery in Egypt. God freed Israel and brought it into the Promised Land. Therefore God has a claim on Israel. When Israel strays, what calls it back is remembering what God has done for it. In the book of Jonah, the prophet turns his life around when he remembers the Lord (see 2:7). In Lamentations 1:7, Jerusalem first remembers better days and then the fall of the city. The literary device used in this verse, contrasting the present circumstances with more favorable ones of the past, is common in lament poetry.

Verse 7 exhibits a structural aberration in the poem in that it has four lines in the Hebrew, while all the others have three lines. It is possible that the verse originally had three lines just as the others do. Some scholars think that line 7b (7a in English), *in the days of her affliction and wandering* (NIV), was probably not original to the text. They think that it was added later because it can be eliminated without violating the thought sequence. Others argue that verse 7c, *all the treasures that were hers in days of old* (NIV), can be omitted without harm to the thought. Another suggestion is that there may have been two versions of the poem and the two were combined here (Hillers: 69).

The final phrase of verse 7, the *foe looked on mocking over her downfall*, expresses a theme found elsewhere in Lamentations and the book of Psalms. Israel was concerned about what others, even enemies, thought about it. The book of Obadiah contains a prophecy of the fall of Edom, a neighboring kingdom that had kinship ties to Israel. According to the tradition, Esau the brother of Jacob, was the eponymous ancestor of the Edomite people (Gen 36), that is, the ancestor after which the nation was named. The complaint against Edom is that it stood by and did not help when Jerusalem was attacked (cf. Ps 137:7). It even participated by preventing people from escaping from the city (Obad 10-15). This statement in Lamentations may be a reference to Edom's actions or lack of action when Judah was conquered by Babylon.

The Charge against Jerusalem 1:8-9

Female imagery, this time negative and explicitly sexual in content, continues. Jerusalem is compared to a wanton woman in verses 8-9, and in the very next verse (10) to a violated one. The poet confesses that Jerusalem did sin and therefore bears some responsibility for its downfall. But the enemy has triumphed, and surely Israel's enemy is God's own enemy; therefore God should respond positively and ease Zion's suffering.

The victim, Jerusalem, is blamed for the current situation by the narrator (v. 9). It is not the fault of outsiders but Jerusalem's own *uncleanness* and disregard of the future that has led to the current state of affairs. In this context, to be unclean refers to a ritual state of impurity that prevents a person from participating in certain religious rituals for a period of time. That state may be brought about by sin but also by bodily discharges or by certain diseases (see Lev 11–12, 14–15). Jerusalem does not let that charge go by without response. She disagrees, and her voice is heard for the first time in the poem in a direct appeal to God to *see my affliction*. The reader's (or in the ancient context, audience's) attention is redirected to the affliction itself and what the enemy has done. Jerusalem is the victim, not the perpetrator.

There is a shift in the voice from the third person (she, her) to the first person (I, my) here in verse 9 as well as in verses 11-16 and 18-22. As R. B. Salters (300) writes, the shift indicates that this chapter is meant to function as a drama. The reason for the disjointedness is to "convey in the drama the disturbed mind of the weeping figures" (32). The first-person voice is used to represent the community in biblical Hebrew poetry [*Communal Lament, p. 114; Hebrew Poetry, p. 116*]. This means *I* or *my* does not necessarily mean an individual. It may refer to the entire community, as it does in this poem.

Violation 1:10-11

Using the imagery of rape, the violation of the city is graphically described in verse 10. The narrator notes that enemies, the foreign nations whom God had forbidden to enter the community (Deut 23:3-6), have done so. The implication is that God did not or could not stop them. The disruption of normal trade and business has triggered an internal famine in the city. It is not that there is no food anywhere. It is that they have no access to it.

The word *treasures* in the phrase *they trade their treasures for food* (v. 11) may refer to temple treasures or it may refer to children, as Provan suggests (47). The treasures of Israel are its children. The female imagery in this chapter, however, implies that the treasures bartered away are virtue. Following up on the theme of rape in verse 10, Judah barters her virtue for food, a not uncommon occurrence in times of war and other catastrophes. The reference to worthlessness confirms this. It is a value judgment, not a reference to wealth and poverty. It is not poverty that is distressing to Zion but a feeling of worthlessness. Zion's voice is again heard in an appeal to God to see how *worthless* she has become. This imagery is easier to understand when one considers the context being a society where women were often blamed for being raped and their value diminished because of it. Raped women internalized the violence done to them because society forced them to do so. This violent imagery is meant to cause the reader to sympathize with Zion.

The Charge against God 1:12-17

In this next section, a list of charges is leveled against God. It is God, these verses declare, who has inflicted pain on Zion. God set it on fire and entrapped it. God left the city weak and vulnerable. God prevented the city from protecting itself. God crushed the young warriors. God commanded Jerusalem's neighbors to become enemies. And God has no response to the charges.

Kathleen O'Connor (1998: 189) understands verses 12 to 22 to be a description of an abused woman. O'Connor notices that Zion personified in female imagery accepts blame and therefore participates in her own abuse. Moreover, God is the abuser. She therefore concludes that the female imagery in chapter 1 "symbolically blames women alone for the destruction of the city, and it teaches disdain for women and for their bodies." O'Connor (190) also points out a positive function of the imagery. In it, the abused woman "articulates her own pain and ultimately demands that God redress what seems to be divine injustice." Another interpretation of the former statement suggests that because women in traditional patriarchal societies are more vulnerable, Lamentations uses female imagery and highlights the suffering of women and children in order to garner sympathy for the city, which includes a population of both males and females. It is the collective that is being blamed, not just the women.

The language in this chapter is not exclusively feminine. Masculine imagery in these verses includes rejected powerful men (v. 15, translated *warriors* in NIV and NRSV but probably referring to the elite), young men (v. 15), and Jacob (used as a synonym for Israel) as the target of God (v. 17). In verse 18, both (young) women and men have gone away into exile. There is also a mixture of male and female language in this passage.

The meaning of the first part of verse 12 is unclear. NIV and NRSV have *Is it nothing to you?* NJPS has *May it never befall you.* In either case, the overall message of the verse is likely the same. Provan (48) suggests that God has inflicted Israel in the presence of others so that they may learn from its mistakes.

Human nature demands that suffering be unique. *Look and see if there is any sorrow* [lit. *pain*] *like my sorrow"* (v. 12 NRSV). The NIV reads, *Look around and see. Is any suffering like my suffering?* Both of these translations are pointing to psychological pain rather than physical pain. Neither suffering nor sorrow is entirely unique. They are universal realities that come with being human and caring about what happens to yourself and others. On the other hand, because each relationship and culture and society is unique in some way, every experience of suffering has elements that are unique. Most people will experience the death of a parent, for example, but the relationships that individuals have with their parents differ; therefore the way they experience that death is unique.

Fire from above is an image of God's judgment. Here is the notion of being trapped and unable to escape. The image of God spreading a net in order to entrap people is common in the Old Testament (see, e.g., Jer 50:24; Ezek 12:13; Hillers: 89). Verse 14 reshapes the image. The transgressions themselves are what weigh the poet down and prevent escape or fighting back, not God; but God takes them in their helpless state and hands them over to the enemy.

Several names for God are used in the book of Lamentations. In this chapter, the divine name *Yahweh* first appears in verse 5. Yahweh is used as a personal name specifically for the God of Israel in the Bible *[Yahweh, p. 118]*. It was particularly appropriated by the southern tribe of Judah. Here and in verses 12 and 17, Yahweh is the one who makes Judah suffer. The name also appears in verses 9, 11, and 20 in the appeal by Zion to God to notice her pain. In verse 18, Yahweh is declared to be righteous (or *in the right*, as the NRSV translates). In verses 14 and 15 (three times), the word *Adonai*, a generic phrase that is usually translated as *the Lord*, appears as the one abusing Israel.

In verse 15 the *Daughter Judah* phrase is modified by the word *betulah* (an unmarried young woman), often translated *virgin daughter Judah*. The latter phrase refers to the city as a whole, not to the young women in the city. However, *young men* (*baḥur*, an unmarried young man) appears to be not a metaphor but a reference to the human young men.

The imagery in verse 16 transports the reader back to the imagery in the first verse, the city as a weeping widow. Notice the continuing reference to the lack of a *comforter*, a dominant theme in chapter 1.

Provan (52) understands verse 17 to be a narrator's insertion between the first and second speeches of this first chapter. It seems to be reiterating a moral lesson made before. Earlier the enemies stretched their hands over Zion. Here Zion is stretching out her hands: probably the reader is meant to infer that these are stretched to God. Hands can be used to destroy or to beg for life or comfort. In this verse there is an interesting pivot from the female Zion to the male Jacob. Jacob is used as a synonym for Israel. A Targum provides an alternate interpretation to verse 17: "Zion spreads out her hands in pain, as a woman spreads out over the birthstool" (Levine: 65) *[Targum, p. 118]*. That imagery, however, anticipates the birth of a child, which is usually a good thing. And the woman giving birth would have had a comforter, a midwife or experienced woman who would have assisted and reassured her through the birth.

The last phrase in this verse indicates that Jerusalem has become a *niddah*, a ritually unclean woman. The NRSV translates the word as *filthy thing*, and the NIV reads *an unclean thing*. In Orthodox Jewish tradition, a woman is impure at certain times during her life, such as during menstruation or after childbirth (Greenberg: 120-36). In ancient times that meant that she could not participate in certain rituals until she had gone through a purification process; this involved immersing herself in a ritual bath, separating herself from certain activities and contacts for a period of time, and offering a sacrifice (Lev 15:19-30). There were similar rules for men who become ritually impure due to various bodily emissions and other reasons (Lev 15:2-18; Douglas). Because a woman is *niddah* for a limited period of time, the use of the word in this text is a hint that Jerusalem's pain can be expected to come to an end and that she will be restored.

Confession 1:18-21b

The LORD is right or *in the right* is a legal formula (Hillers: 90). There is a confession of guilt in this passage, but it is quickly passed over in favor of a description of the city's suffering. The young people have been taken away, threatening the very survival of the city, and the allies (lovers) deceived her. Judah had hoped that Egypt, one of her lovers, would come to the rescue, but it did not. There is a reference to the death of the priests and the elders by starvation. The loss of the priests represents a loss of the rituals of mourning, which help people to express their grief and publically mark the loss. Priests also perform the rituals that signal normalcy and ensure the favor of God. The elders provide direction and leadership. Without the guidance of the priests and elders, the people feel lost.

A final appeal to God to see the distress of Israel occurs in verse 20. There is no escape and no refuge since death is both in the streets and in the house. To make matters worse, the enemies all around know of the distress that Jerusalem is in. Israel was always concerned about its reputation, how it appeared before outsiders, even enemy outsiders. Notice that the enemies in this chapter also recognize the "Lord," Jerusalem's own god, as the one responsible for its plight.

Call for Vengeance 1:21c-22

As is typical in some biblical laments, toward the end there is a call for vengeance (see Ps 137). In light of the described distress, one might expect a request for help to remedy the situation, to stop the suffering, starvation, and pain. Instead there is only a request that the enemies experience the pain that Jerusalem is experiencing. The call for vengeance expresses how some people in Jerusalem felt while close to the time of the event. It is not a description of what actually took place. The poem ends with a statement of utter hopelessness *[Communal Lament, p. 114]*.

Verse 22 begins with the last letter of the Hebrew alphabet (*tav*). With no more letters, this alphabetic acrostic has come to an end.

THE TEXT IN BIBLICAL CONTEXT

The Source of Evil

Lamentations is not a historical account of what followed the conquest of Jerusalem *[Capture and Destruction of Jerusalem, p. 112]*. It is a theological reflection on the event in poetic form. For many, the most difficult theological idea in this chapter is that, in the thinking of the poet, God was instrumental in the suffering, death, and pain of innocent children and adults, as well as others who may not have been entirely innocent but who certainly did not merit the holocaust that ensued when Jerusalem fell to the Babylonian army in 587/586 BCE. This is a problem of monotheism. If there is only one God and one believes that God is good, forgiving, and powerful, how does one explain the presence of evil in the form of war in this context and the suffering that invariably accompanies it? In the Old Testament there is no evil being with independent power upon which one can place the blame. When things go wrong, there are only two possible sources: God or human beings. There is a third possibility, and that is that neither God nor human beings are responsible, that nature, for example, is functioning independent of human or divine will. But the Bible is a theological collection, and when bad things happen, it is primarily concerned with questions of human and divine agency [*Evil Spiritsm, p. 116*].

How to Prevent Evil from Happening

Throughout the Bible, human beings are instructed in how to live in such a way as to nurture good relationships with one another. "Do not kill," "Do not steal," "Do not commit adultery"—all are well-known examples of this from the Ten Commandments. Consequences of choosing a course in opposition to these instructions are listed and illustrated in the text. Jacob, for example, deceives his nearly blind father and is forced to flee and remain apart from his family for twenty years in a far country. Things that go wrong in the human community may be blamed on human actions. Sometimes in the thought of ancient Israel, God intervenes to "raise hell" in the human community. The story of the great flood that destroys all human beings and animals, except for a remnant by divine fiat, illustrates how Israel understood God to act from time to time. In the Old Testament, the Creator can also be the destroyer. Isaiah 45:7 reads, "I am the one who forms light and creates darkness, the one who makes shalom and creates evil" (AT).

Although a God of wrath is depicted in this poem and others in Lamentations, this is not the only image of God that one sees in the Old Testament. The third chapter of Lamentations speaks of another facet of God's character, that which expresses itself in compassion and steadfast love. Psalm 145 praises God for divine graciousness, faithfulness, mercy, and compassion. Amos understands God to be one who restores and plants people in their land (9:15). When God is depicted as punishing, there is usually a link to sin. God's wrath is not meted out arbitrarily. Moreover, most typically in the Bible, accompanying the language of doom are words of hope and restoration.

THE TEXT IN THE LIFE OF THE CHURCH

Lamentations and Anabaptists

In spite of a history of suffering, loss of homeland, and trial by fire because of some of their distinctive beliefs or just for being Christians, Anabaptists have not embraced Lamentations as a vehicle for expressing their grief. Perhaps they find a sharp dichotomy between those suffering for their faith and those suffering for their purported sins and therefore do not relate the two. Perhaps they are offended by the God-blaming language in the poems or the imagery of a God who acts violently. Perhaps the imagery is just too foreign. But because Lamentations is part of the Bible that they do embrace, they must come to terms with it. The book of Lamentations acknowledges that suffering is a reality even in the lives of people of faith. It affirms that expressing one's sadness, disappointment, confusion, despair, and anger has a role in the grieving process. It models a relationship with God that holds on and keeps the conversation going. Anabaptists would do well to make Lamentations a regular part of their devotional reading and teaching.

Opportunities to Grieve in the Church Year

The purpose of the book of Lamentations is to help people to grieve, not to make them feel guilty for expressing how they feel. It encourages mourning rituals. It suggests that people ought to feel free to articulate their feelings and thoughts in times of grief without censure. To this day, every year on the ninth day of the Hebrew month of Ab, which usually falls in July or August in the Western calendar, Jews commemorate the fall of Jerusalem and other disastrous events in the life of Israel by chanting the book of Lamentations while in postures of mourning. This holy day recognizes that loss is a part of the human condition and that God's people need to deal with it. In the Christian calendar, Good Friday serves a similar function. To this time, in some churches, Good Friday is a day of mourning. Some Christians attend church dressed in black, a symbol of mourning, seriousness, and respect. Noontime services, some of which stretch over three hours, commemorate the death of Jesus. In many communities a variety of denominations come together to hold joint Good Friday services, a witness to the common faith that is shared. More recently, the drama of the Tenebrae service has lured Christians back to church on Good Friday. During the Tenebrae service, candles and lights in the church are gradually extinguished as Scripture texts are read and hymns are sung. At the end of the service, the sanctuary is in total darkness. People need to mourn their losses. When they are denied that privilege, feelings of sadness and grief can be channeled into more destructive methods of coping, such as the acting out of vengeance.

Some scholars have suggested that the tight alphabetic structure of Lamentations was added later on, after the shock of the events of the day. During times of grief, when one's world appears to be falling apart, it is not unusual to find something that you can structure as a means of control.

Rabbi Harold Kushner, in his widely read book *When Bad Things Happen to Good People*, proposes that God cannot be simultaneously all-powerful, just, and loving. God can be any combination of two out of the three but not all three. Kushner chooses to reject the notion that God is all-powerful. He nuances that by suggesting that God is self-limited in power. Process theology has also assumed that God either is not all-powerful or is self-limited. It further suggests that God can beckon but not force humans to do the divine will. It is possible that God has chosen to limit divine power so that humans can learn to develop their own power and use it as a force for good.

Perhaps Christians can find some insight from 1 Corinthians 13:12, which indicates that human understanding will ever only be partial, like looking through an old-fashioned mirror rather than the clear glass we have today. Lamentations demands that we keep asking the questions and searching toward answers. We may not get entirely there, but we will make progress as we work at it.

Shame

In the first poem, Zion expresses feelings of shame in verse 11: she feels worthless. That is a common feeling among those who have been victims of sexual assault. Women, particularly, have been taught to blame themselves for being in the wrong place or wearing the wrong clothes or speaking to people that they should not have been speaking to, even when the rapist is standing over them with a gun to their head and even when the "woman" is just a child. That feeling of shame or embarrassment extends beyond the individual in community-wide traumas. Years after the Oklahoma City bombing, a young woman clerk in a hotel expressed dismay at the continued interest in the bombing by outsiders. She seemed to be embarrassed by it. She preferred to converse about the wonderful museums and other places of interest in the city. German theologian Eugen Drewermann thinks that shame drove the German people to choose National Socialism, which they thought could restore their pride after their defeat during World War 1 (Beier: 26, 144, 173). Sometimes people should be ashamed of what they have done or propose to do. But at other times, there is no basis for the shame.

Lamentations 2:1-22

The Lord Has Become Like an Enemy

PREVIEW

Like the others, the second poem in this collection stands independently. Theologically this poem is difficult. God is blamed for the suffering, and there is no hint that conditions will change or that relief will come.

Where the first poem focuses on Jerusalem personified as a grieving woman, this second poem opens with a hyper-masculine image. God as warrior is waging war against God's own people *[Capture and Destruction of Jerusalem, p. 112]*. Words and phrases, such as *swallow up, cut down, bend a bow, enemy,* and *throw down,* evoke an image of a battle scene. Several voices are heard: the narrator (vv. 1-10), children (v. 12), and those who deride the fallen city (v. 15). There may be even more voices. The complaint is directed against God, God's role in the destruction, and God's relationship to Israel. Of the six elements of laments by Craven's count (27), two are found here: an address to God is found in verse 20; a complaint is present throughout the poem (see the Introduction on "Structure"). The primary content is complaint: complaint about God's actions (v. 19) and complaint about the situation itself (vv. 10-12, 17, 14-16, 21, 22). There is no confession of trust. There is no petition, though there is a call for one in verse 19. There are no words of assurance. There is no vow of praise. The four missing lament elements suggest that the poet is still in the midst of pain and suffering. It is palpable in this chapter *[Communal Lament, p. 114]*.

Like chapter 1, this poem is an alphabetic acrostic; the first word of each line begins with a successive letter of the alphabet in order [*Acrostic, p. 111*]. In Hebrew, each verse is composed of three poetic lines (three bicola; each bicola = a pair of half lines) except for verse 19, which has four lines (four bicola). Structurally, the poem moves from a list of charges against the Lord, the God of Israel (vv. 1-9b), to the fate of the city's inhabitants (vv. 9c-12), to an address to Jerusalem (vv. 13-19), followed by an address to God (vv. 20-22) [*Hebrew Poetry, p. 116*].

In English Bible translations, the phrase "the Lord" in small caps with a capital *L* substitutes for the divine name *Yahweh*, which appears in the original Hebrew language. The use of this name (as in 1:5, 12, 15) adds a note of irony to the poem. The God who is known personally to Jerusalem by the divine name appears to have turned against it. This is why it hurts so much [*Yahweh, p. 118; Zion Theology, p. 119*].

OUTLINE

Charges against the Lord, 2:1-9b
The Fate of the City's Inhabitants Described, 2:9c-12
An Address to Jerusalem, 2:13-19
An Address to the Lord, 2:20-22

EXPLANATORY NOTES

Charges against the Lord 2:1-9b

The poem in chapter 2 begins with the same word as the first one, *’ekah* (*Alas! How!*), but its tone, mood, and content are different. The first poem appeals to the reader to sympathize with a personified Zion by stressing her isolation and need of a comforter. The second poem designates Yahweh, the God who loves Israel, as an enemy, and it pulsates with anger [*Yahweh, p. 118*]. A variation of the same phrase, *in (the day of) his* [God's] *anger*, appears twice in the first and once in the very last verse of the poem. In the next verse a slightly different phrase, *his fury*, is used. The third verse reiterates the theme in a reference to God's *burning anger*. The reader might ask, "Why is God so angry?" The poem never answers that question. That is the baffling part. Indeed, the only cryptic reference to a reason for God's anger and subsequent behavior appears later, in verse 14, where the prophets are blamed for not having exposed the iniquity of Zion.

The absence of a reasonable explanation for the anger of God was noticed in ancient times. Early scribes tried to remedy the problem by supplying answers. A Targum (an ancient Aramaic translation of the OT) lists sins that Israel engaged in, as imagined by the scribes, sins resulting in God's displeasure *[Targum, p. 118]*. It points to the execution of a person named Zachariah bar Iddo (II, 20), "the interrupting of the daily sacrifice (II, 19), not obeying the Sinai covenant (II, 9, 17), desecrating the temple (I, 19), and not frequenting the temple (I, 4)," and so on (Levine: 17). Many of these issues involve ritual behavior. Levine thinks that the catalog of sins flagged by the Targum points to "postbiblical concerns of the rabbinate" (17). This list does not reflect the view of the author of the poem but of a later theological interpreter.

In the text itself, the nature of Zion's sin is not named, and the focus on the prophets is not maintained. So, rather than searching for a reason, the poem in highly metaphorical language focuses on what God's anger looks like and how people and place are affected by it. In this chapter, the poet is assuming the role of a prosecuting attorney, listing the charges against God.

The first charge is that God is clouding over Daughter Zion in his anger (v. 1). The poet chose a rare verbal form as a nominative meaning "a dark cloud" (NRSV, *humiliated*; but better NIV and KJV, *covered... with... cloud*). This is the only place where the verb "cloud over" is found in the Old Testament. Therefore, we have to guess at the meaning of the phrase. A cloud prevents one from seeing the sky above. From the vantage point of being above the cloud (in symbolic space, one might think of God spatially as being above), it prevents one from seeing below. This image suggests that God at the moment is choosing not to look at Daughter Zion.

The verse continues: *God has thrown down from sky to earth the splendor of Israel* (AT). The phrase *splendor of Israel* is found only here in the Old Testament. Its position, in Hebrew at the end of the second statement in verse 1, places it parallel to the end of the first sentence in the same verse, juxtaposing *splendor of Israel* with *Daughter Zion*. In biblical Hebrew, "daughter" refers not just to human female offspring, but also to a town. It is safe to assume that Daughter Zion (Jerusalem) is the *splendor of Israel*. The remnant left in Jerusalem feel that the city has lost that privileged position *[Zion Theology, p. 119]*.

The next two-part phrase of verse 1 contains the puzzling term *footstool*. It reads, *He [God] did not remember his footstool on the day of his anger* (AT). In the context of this verse, the footstool would appear to be a good thing. It is something to be remembered. But Psalm 110:1 uses the same phrase to describe the positioning of the enemies of Israel. It reads, "Sit at my right side until I place your enemies as a stool at your feet" (AT). However, in Isaiah 66:1 the earth is the footstool for God: "The sky is my throne, and the earth my footstool" (AT). Psalm 99:5b demands, "Worship at his footstool," and Psalm 132:7b suggests, "Let us worship at his footstool" (NRSV). Both encourage Israel to worship before the footstool of God, which is a way of saying that the footstool is imbued with God's holiness. The last reference to a footstool appears in 1 Chronicles 28:2b, where it is implied that the ark of the covenant is God's footstool: "Listen my brothers and my people, I have in my heart [a desire] to build a place of rest for the ark of the covenant of Yahweh and for the footstool of our God, and I had decided to build it" (AT). The only reference that seems out of place is the one referring to the enemies being made a footstool. The other references understand the footstool to be something to be reverenced or a position of privilege or honor. There is a slight difference in the syntax in Psalm 110:1 that may supply the answer to the puzzle. The preposition represented by the Hebrew letter *lamed*, which can be translated as "to" or "for," appears after *stool* and before *foot*. In other places where "to" is used, it appears before *the footstool*. Further, in every other reference, the footstool belongs to God, while in Psalm 110:1 it belongs to the king. It is a stool before or toward the king's feet. The "to" is there to distinguish this stool from the others.

In Lamentations 2:1, Zion as God's footstool was in an appropriate and indeed good place. To be removed from being a footstool is to remove Zion from a place of honor or privilege, albeit a humble place.

The phrase *on the day of his anger* closes the first verse. The use of the word *day* and the verbal form indicate that the anger will not last forever. It will come to an end.

Verse 2 addresses the next series of charges against God. They involve the Lord swallowing the *pastures of Jacob* (AT), not having compassion, throwing down in anger the *strongholds of Judah*, and throwing down the *kingdom and its princes* (NIV). This is a destruction that involves the physical structures of defense (*strongholds*), the political structure (*kingdom*), and the leadership (*princes*). The downward movement suggested by the verbs here creates a great distance between these structures and God. Importantly, no example of throwing down in this verse involves the social fabric (such as the family) or the lives of the ordinary peasants, artisans, or workers. The anger of God is directed against the leadership and the structures that undergird that leadership.

The theme of tearing down continues in the third verse. What is torn down here is every *horn* of Israel (NRSV *might*). In ancient Israel, "horn" was a reference to strength or power. The turning back of the right hand from Israel means that Israel will lose to the enemy. In this verse, God's actions are clearly indirect. By withdrawing the hand of protection, God exposes the Israelites to danger. God is compared to an out-of-control fire that consumes indiscriminately.

As the diatribe continues in verse 4, no relief from the theme of God's anger is provided. God stretches out God's bow the way an enemy stretches out a bow in preparation for shooting an arrow. Here the killing is directly from God. God directs the bow. God kills all the delights of the eye and pours out the divine anger. It is critical to remember that God is *not the enemy of Israel* in these verses, but God is patterning divine behavior after that of an enemy. God is like an enemy. The language suggests that while God's behavior is like that of an enemy, God's motives or desired outcome is not the same. But the reader is not going to learn what those different motives or desired outcomes are in this poem.

Verse 5 twice uses the verb "swallow" in the negative sense of destroy. Again God is behaving like an enemy. Again there is a reference to destruction of fortresses. When fortresses (the walls and gates of a city) are destroyed, protective barriers are gone, and the enemy gains access. Mourning and lamentation are multiplied in Judah.

In this chapter, *Daughter (of) Zion, Virgin Daughter (of) Zion, Israel, Jacob, Jerusalem, Daughter (of) Judah,* and *Daughter (of) Jerusalem* are synonyms of the same real and symbolic entity Jerusalem/Zion.

The charges leveled against God continue in verses 6-9a. Three categories of leaders—king, priest, and prophet—have been spurned by God. These three represent the power structures but not the ordinary people. All suffer but in different ways. The elite are killed or sent into exile *[Elite, p. 115]*. The poor are left in the devastated city and suffer the consequences of war in the midst of the ruined city. The highly rhetorical language in the text would have evoked horror in the ancient reader: *The Lord has rejected his altar and abandoned his sanctuary. He has given the walls of her palaces into the hands of the enemy* (2:7a NIV). The notion of rejection and abandonment is found elsewhere in the Bible (cf. Pss 74:1; 77:7; 88:14; 89:38-46; Hos 5). God's threat to abandon the temple was issued as early as its dedication, during the reign of Solomon (1 Kings 9:1-9). The desire of God was to dwell, as an unseen presence, in the midst of people. The construction of a building, though it was meant to be a sign of God's presence, could deteriorate into an idol or a kind of talisman thought to guarantee God's blessing and protection. That is what happened. In the end, the city and the temple became a distraction rather than a vehicle for God's grace.

The second and third phrases of verse 7 clarify that God has used an agent (Babylon) to accomplish the divine purpose. In the same verse this is followed by the use of the third-person plural: *They gave forth a sound* (AT; *a clamor was raised*, NRSV). The simile in the last sentence of the verse provides an ironic image, a sound going out in the house of the Lord like the sound that goes out on a festival day. But this is no festival day. Sadly, it is a day of destruction.

In verses 7-9 are multiple references to the destruction of the fortifications of Zion. A destruction of physical, economic, religious, and political structures is indicated by words and phrases such as *the wall of her fortresses* (v. 7, *palaces* in NIV and NRSV), *wall of Daughter Zion* (v. 8), *rampart and wall* (v. 8), *her gates* and *her bars* (v. 9), coupled with the leaders of verses 6 and 9b and the festivals and Sabbaths of verse 6. In ancient Israelite cities, the marketplace and the courts were located in the city gate *[City, p. 113]*. In Hebrew, the generic term *the Lord* (*Adonai*, not *Yahweh*) appears in verses 1, 2, 5, 7, and 8. In verse 8, the personal name of God, *Yahweh*, appears in the phrase *Yahweh planned to wipe out the wall of daughter Zion* (v. 8a AT) *[Yahweh, p. 118]*.

It is significant that the Lord is pictured as the divine warrior, an angry male, in this poem, while Zion, as *daughter Zion*, is depicted as a young female. She is the object of the brutal attack. The imagery is disturbing. It is meant to be disturbing.

The Fate of the City's Inhabitants Described 2:9b-12

The last two bicola of verse 9 change the subject of the poem from the charges against God to a description of the plight of the people who are left in the city. The leaders are scattered about among the nations. There is no divine instruction (*guidance*, NRSV; *the law*, NIV). *Her prophets have not found a vision from the L*ORD (AT). The verse does not specify a lack of vision but that a vision has not been found, not found by the very people who ought to have a unique ability to envision what others cannot: the prophets. Without human or divine leadership, the ordinary folk are left to fend for themselves. Those remaining in the city are suffering unspeakable hardships, as described in the rest of the poem.

The response of the people to the destruction is both physical and psychological. The downward movement of the elderly, the young children, and the young women is noted. The elderly have not lost control of their physical movement. They sit on the ground in the posture of mourning. They clothe themselves in the attire of mourning: sackcloth. And they cover their heads with dust. The small children are not in control of their movements. They faint in the streets. They appeal to their mothers for bread and wine. Neither is available. As is true in the aftermath of most wars and situations of famine, the youngest children, being the most vulnerable, die first. But in this text they are not abandoned. They die in the arms of their mothers, where in their last moments they can at least know that they are cherished (v. 12).

The young women of Jerusalem put their heads to the earth (v. 10 AT). The emotional distress is manifested in physical symptoms felt in the stomach and in weeping (v. 11). Even outside of times of war, there is pain in the course of life. One expects the elderly to be able to put things into perspective for younger people. They have been through a lot. They ought to be able to draw parallels from past catastrophic events, thereby to reassure the young that this too is survivable. But the response of the elderly indicates that things are really as bad as they seem. They have no wisdom to share. They are silent.

An Address to Jerusalem 2:13-19

The voice of the poet calls out to Jerusalem, asking how the city can be comforted (v. 13). A series of four rhetorical questions appears, suggesting that Jerusalem's breach is unprecedented. There are disputes among scholars as to how to properly translate some of these questions. The NIV translates the questions as *What can I say for you? With what can I compare you? To what can I liken you? Who can heal you?* The expected answer to the first three of the questions is "Nothing." Nothing can be said. There is nothing to which the suffering of Jerusalem can be compared. It can be likened to nothing. The final question is the most disturbing. Given that God is the one who has caused the pain and suffering, the answer to that one must be "No one." No one can heal Jerusalem. This is the way they felt at that time.

It is the responsibility of the prophet to point out error and to teach (v. 14). The prophets did not do their job, and therefore they are responsible for the resulting devastation—a sobering thought. The people also bear responsibility because they chose to follow prophets who were preaching messages of peace and comfort. They ignored the words that they did not want to hear.

Israel is mocked by the surrounding people. The city used to be called *the completeness of beauty* (AT) and *the joy of the whole earth*, but no longer (cf. Pss 48:2; 50:2). Jerusalem was not the only city described in that language. In Ezekiel 27:3, Tyre, the arrogant island kingdom to the north of Israel, had proclaimed itself the "completeness of beauty" (AT). In Ezekiel 28:12, the God of Israel also proclaims Tyre to have been "a complete beauty" (AT). Although the phrases for Tyre and Israel appear in different books, they suggest that a certain ideology in ancient Israel understood God to see beauty not only in Israel but in other people as well. All the kingdoms of the world are God's kingdoms. This universalism is also found here in Lamentations 2:15, where the poet recalls that Jerusalem was described as *the joy of all the earth*.

According to verse 17, the destruction of Jerusalem had been promised long ago. One wonders, "How long ago?" In the thought of the poet, was this the envisioned outcome for Jerusalem from the time of David, who centralized and merged the political and religious life in his capital city (2 Sam 6)? Or his son Solomon, who in his political role as king demanded that the shrine at Jerusalem be privileged above all others in Israel (1 Kings 8)? Important to the theology of ancient Israel, the fall of Jerusalem is not to be interpreted as a chance occurrence. It was something that God intended to do. But why? Many scholars point to the many prophetic admonitions to Israel to reform its ways as the antecedent for this statement in verse 17 (see Westermann: 155; O'Connor 2002: 40). But given the way the statement is phrased, it sounds as though Jerusalem was doomed from the start. It may suggest that the seeds of its undoing were planted in the political elite's very choice to establish a religious center that was under their jurisdiction *[Elite, p. 115]*.

An appeal is made to the Israelites to cry out to God (vv. 18-19). According to the NRSV, the phrase is *Cry aloud to the Lord! O wall of daughter Zion!* Adele Berlin (75) thinks that, as an image, the wall is addressed because "the wall, the protector of the city, . . . has not been able to provide protection." "Crying out" to God is supposed to result in improvement in the life situation. In the book of Judges, when the Israelites are in trouble, they cry out to God, and God responds by raising a deliverer who leads the Israelites into a successful battle against the enemy. Notice that there is no call for repentance here or in Judges. Rather, they call to let God know what they are experiencing. They expect God to respond to their pain because God responded to their pain in the past. Israel is advised to cry out at the beginning of the watches. One in such pain should not be able to sleep through the night. Let God know the pain. Appeal to God for the sake of the children. The expectation is that God will respond, heal, and restore.

An Address to the LORD 2:20-22

Verse 20 is a plea to the LORD to look and consider the appalling situation of the people. Ironically, this is a hopeful note in this bleak text. God is clearly the one who is causing the suffering of the people of Jerusalem. A human enemy is referenced in verse 22, but that human enemy could not have been successful without God's permission. Therefore, God is the one to whom the community appeals, not the human enemy. The appeal itself suggests that the Israelites are holding on to a belief that God's compassion will overcome God's anger. If there were no hope that God could be moved, there would be no need for an appeal to God. God is reminded of who is actually suffering in the city: not the people who caused the problem in the first place, nor the warriors who took up arms. Rather, it is the innocent: women, children, and those set apart for divine service. This is abnormal, and it causes abnormal behavior on the part of the city dwellers, such as cannibalism (v. 20). This is not right. But it is the way of war—every war.

This chapter is particularly critical of prophets but still considers it a disgrace that they along with the priests are killed in the holy place that itself should offer some protection. The death of the priests and prophets not only leads to a void in religious leadership; it also defiles the sanctuary where they died. The implication is that without religious leadership and a functioning sanctuary, worship will cease. Priests appear twice in the chapter, once coupled with kings (v. 6) as a focus of God's anger, and once coupled with prophets as those killed in the sanctuary (v. 20).

Not only have people been slaughtered in the streets; their bodies even remain there. The sight and odor of decaying bodies make life in the city unbearable; in addition, the unburied dead defile the entire city and prohibit the souls from finding rest. The death of the young means there will be no future, or the future will be bleak as a generation is skipped.

The destruction of Jerusalem provided a great day of festival for the enemy. Was this the intent of God? No one in the city was unaffected by the fall of the city. In most situations of distress, those not personally affected may assist those who are. But in Jerusalem, everyone was deeply affected by the tragedy.

This second poem, like the first, ends with the last letter of the Hebrew alphabet (*tav*). It ends on a note of despair. There is no real comfort here. It is purely an expression of anger and grief.

THE TEXT IN BIBLICAL CONTEXT

God's Anger

The God of Israel, driven by anger, is behaving in an extremely harsh and destructive manner, perhaps too harsh, according to the sentiment expressed in Lamentations 2. Christians are often uncomfortable with the idea that God gets angry. Yet there are many references to the anger of God in the Bible: "The anger of Yahweh burned against Moses" (Exod 4:14 AT), and "the anger of Yahweh burned" (Num 11:10 AT). The imagery of God's anger also appears in the New Testament, though it is sometimes obscured in translations. Stephen H. Travis (998), for example, points out that the Revised Standard Version "preserves the archaic word 'wrath' with reference to divine *orgē* while using 'anger' when the human emotion is at issue."

Romans 1:18 reads, "For the wrath [*orgē*] of God is revealed from heaven against all ungodliness and wickedness of those who by their wickedness suppress the truth." In the Bible, God's anger is not only destructive and not only for punishment. It also liberates. In what is perhaps the oldest poem in the Bible, the Song of the Sea, it is God's anger that frees the Israelites from bondage (Exod 15:7). In Romans 12:19, it is the anger of God that will see to any vengeance that is called for as a result of the persecution of God's people. To speak of God's anger is to use anthropomorphic language. Humans really cannot know or understand the emotional life of God. People interpret phenomena that appear to them to have their source in God based upon their own understanding of how they react in particular situations. Hence, God's anger functions to liberate as well as to punish in the Bible (Exod 15:7; Rom 12:19). While recognizing that, humanly speaking, God could become angry, Israel also understood God to be loving and compassionate (Ps 136) as, of course, did the early church.

Prophetic Blame

The prophet Ezekiel (ch. 34) shares with Lamentations 2 much disappointment in the leaders of ancient Israel. Ezekiel also blames the plight of the kingdom on its weak leadership. The shepherds, as he calls them, have enriched themselves while neglecting people placed in their care.

Prophecy was a confusing phenomenon. The story found in 1 Kings 22 shows prophets pitted against prophets. One set of prophets encourages the kings to go to war. One prophet stands alone in stating opposition to war. First that true prophet lies before telling the truth. How can anyone know which prophet to believe or when to believe a prophet? Deuteronomy 13 suggests that the test of prophecy is consistency with Torah (God's instruction). The role of the prophet is to contextualize Torah in a particular place and time in history. Providing insight into the events of the day, the prophet speaks God's word to the people.

Ezekiel's accusations against the leaders of Judah were consistent with the teaching of the Torah. Kings and others placed in leadership were to protect widows, orphans, and strangers and to provide for them. They were not to use their office for their own aggrandizement.

Concern about the Perception of Others

In Lamentations 2 is a concern for how other people see Israel. When the Israelites sin and God announces their destruction, Moses appeals to God, saying that if God permits the destruction of the people, then the other nations will say that God brought them into the wilderness for an evil purpose, to destroy them (Exod 32:11-14). God has to protect God's own reputation. The point seems to be that other nations too must eventually acknowledge that God is God. If God's behavior, from the outsider's point of view, is dishonorable, they will never come to a point of recognizing who God is. Therefore, God must be merciful, compassionate, and kind to God's own people.

Suffering of the Innocent

In the book of Judges, Exodus 2:23, the book of Job, and Psalm 107, "crying out" to God for help is not necessarily preceded by repentance. The concept of repentance is present in the Old Testament, but there is also the idea that God hears and responds to those who cry for divine help whether they repent or not. Indeed, in the situation depicted in Lamentations 2, there may have been no sin committed that required repentance on the part of most of those who suffered. Here and in other texts, much of the blame for Jerusalem's fall is placed on the leaders of ancient Israel. Those leaders are gone, either into exile or to the grave. The people whose voices are heard in the poem are likely largely innocent peasants, children, lower-class individuals, and others who posed no threat to Babylon and therefore were left behind. The word "innocent" does not mean "sinless." The innocent are those who are not responsible for the war. This reflects the truth of suffering. So often, the people who bear the brunt of war are the innocent.

THE TEXT IN THE LIFE OF THE CHURCH

Waves of Grief

In times of war or natural disasters, entire communities may be affected. Such events can cause a community to disintegrate, or it can make the bonds stronger, depending upon the nature and extent of the disaster. In chapter 2, it is too early to tell which direction Jerusalem will go. The city is eventually rebuilt and reinhabited. But that time has not yet arrived.

After a war, people are angry. They are angry because no matter who won or lost, the end result—deaths, separation, destruction of homes and infrastructure, psychological and physical trauma—were far more devastating than they could have imagined before the first shot was fired. They ask, "Who is to blame for getting us into the war in the first place? Was the cause worth the cost? Why did we let it continue for such an extended period of time? Why did we not try harder to find a peaceful solution through negotiation and compromise? Why did the world community fail to intervene to protect the innocent?"

People do get on with their lives, but the anger is just below the surface. Unfortunately, the church too often has silenced people by telling them that being angry is wrong and that they should forgive and let go. It would be healthier spiritually and psychologically if congregations would acknowledge and engage the anger, thereby helping people to work through it.

Mental health professionals emphasize that it is healthy to express anger. Problems arise when anger is expressed in an unhealthy way or toward those who have not done the harm but who are convenient targets. Often these are family members, subordinates, or those we deem to be significantly different from us. Ephesians advises, "Be angry but do not sin" (4:26a).

Wrestling with the Origins of Evil

This text sends many Christians scurrying to their New Testaments to find a God with whom they are more comfortable. They are confused and offended by the imagery of an angry God who functions as an enemy of God's people (cf. Ps 6; Amos 2–3). They have been taught that God is good and does not harm people. Therefore they conclude with Marcion (an early Christian teacher who was labeled a heretic by the later church) that the God of the Old Testament is a different God than the God of the New Testament.

One must bear in mind that this poem is a theological interpretation of the events of 587/586 BCE. It was the army of the king of Babylon that invaded and destroyed the city, exiling some and leaving the rest in despair and misery. The poem, however, accuses God of actively fighting against God's own people.

So from where does evil come? In many strands of Christian theology, the enemy is another being who goes by names such as *Satan*, the *Devil*, or *Lucifer*. This figure—modeled on a theological concept in a Persian religion that posited a good god and an evil god who battle it out until the end time, when the good god triumphs—is not consistent with the description of the *saṭan* ("adversary") that appears in the Old Testament. The former imagery may be more comfortable because it transfers evil to another being, but it strays from the monotheistic ideal *[Evil Spirits, p. 116]*. In ancient Israel, the belief in one God meant that all things we experience as good or bad emanate from that one God. Isaiah 45:6b-7 reads, "I am Yahweh and there is no other, [the] former of light and creator of darkness, maker of shalom and creator of bad. I, Yahweh, do all this" (AT). The last phrase in this text is frequently translated into the archaic language of "weal and woe" (NRSV), which obscures the literal meaning of the text. The NIV has "prosperity" and "disaster." None of these words carry the moral-theological overtones that the Hebrew words *shalom* (*šalom*) and *raʿ* convey.

Abraham Heschel (85-86), a twentieth-century American rabbi, suggested that the language of emotion—anger but also love—in relation to God is a way of conveying that God cares about humans. Heschel (224) contrasts the concepts of passion and pathos: passion is when irrationality rules; "pathos was understood . . . as an act formed with intention . . . the result of decision and determination." God's anger is focused and functions to change the negative behaviors and practices of humans because God wants humans to be better. In human terms we might say that God gets angry because God loves.

Another difficult image is that of God as an angry male abusing a young female (*Daughter Zion*). This image is meant to be disturbing. It is meant to arouse feelings of anger and sadness. In the church our tendency has been to stifle feelings of anger and sadness when we see them rising as a result of a tragedy or normal loss. But that is not the function of these poems. The function of literature such as the poems in Lamentations is to help stir up feelings that are within real human beings when they experience loss. People really do feel that they are being assaulted by God. They feel helpless. The poem is meant to encourage mourners to "let it out," to express their own feelings of anger and loss. This is not the only model of grieving in the Bible (see 2 Sam 21:10; Ezek 24:15-18; Ps 137:1-4), but it is one that should not be dismissed.

Limits to God's Responsibility

Transferring anger from persons directly responsible and placing it on God is the result of a theology insisting that God is directly involved in everything that happens. This theology promotes the idea that bad things do not happen to good people. Therefore, if something bad happens to a person, it is because the person did something wrong. God is punishing her or him through other people or through a situation set up to cause distress. Another way of looking at it is that anger gets transferred to God because God is not hurt by anger. God understands anger. God knows that persons are angry at situations, other persons, or themselves, but they cannot see that at the moment. People may feel safer in directing their anger at God rather than at the actual source because they know that God can take it and accept it for what it is. God knows what is in the heart and mind and makes a distinction between that and outward expressions of anger.

Christians emphasize the need for repentance, but there is neither repentance in this poem nor a call for it. Even if people have done wrong and "deserve what they get," it may be that people need to be showed love, mercy, and forgiveness before they can come to the point of understanding the role that they played in the bad outcome. That middle step can also disrupt a pattern of wrongdoing.

Lamentations 3:1-66
The Lord Will Not Reject Forever

PREVIEW

This third chapter of Lamentations finds many voices arguing back and forth about how to understand God's role in suffering. There are voices expressing despair, testimonies of God's goodness, wisdom sayings, and calls for judgment. It runs the gamut from conventional theology to near heresy. This is a community trying to come to grips with pain and suffering.

The opening voice of this poem is that of a lone individual who feels that he has been under a sustained attack. The unnamed attacker is usually presumed to be God. The attacker is accused of vicious acts of physical and psychological torture. The Old Testament has a number of examples of venting of anger and sorrow. Sometimes it is chastised by a voice espousing a conventional theology that affirms the goodness of God. That is what happens in this poem. The middle section of the poem departs from the prevailing tenor by affirming the kindness and compassion of God. But the complaint continues, this time with a communal voice rather than that of a lone individual.

Although the book of Lamentations is thought to be a reflection on the aftermath of the Babylonians' conquest of Jerusalem in 587/586 BCE, the reality may be more complex than that. There is no specific reference to that particular city in the third poem. There is a reference to a "city" in verse 51. It certainly could be Jerusalem, but it could also be another city undergoing a similar experience during a different time period. The reference to the *destruction of my people* in verse 47 likely refers to the conquest of the southern Israelite kingdom by the Babylonians, but again it is not specific. This poem has elements of both a personal lament (similar to those found in the book of Psalms) and a communal lament enmeshed in a greater tragedy *[Communal Lament, p. 114]*.

A structural change occurs in the third poem of Lamentations that is reflected in the number of verses contained in the chapter. Like chapters 1, 2, and 4, this poem is an alphabetic acrostic: the first word of each line begins with a successive letter of the alphabet in order. However, here it contains a threefold (triad) repetition of each letter in the Hebrew alphabet, yielding sixty-six rather than twenty-two verses *[Acrostic, p. 111]*. Although there are more verses in the third poem, each verse contains only two cola (= one line) rather than the six per verse found in Lamentations 1 and 2. Thus there are the same number of cola as in those chapters, and chapter 3 is about the same length as the poems in the first two chapters. Chapter 1 has 376 words, 2 has 381, 3 has 381, 4 has 258, and 5 has 145 *[Hebrew Poetry, p. 116]*.

The structure of the chapter is not clearly visible in English translations except for the presence of the 66 verses. The reader of English-language Bibles will also not be aware of the sounds of words, wordplays, and other features of the language that are not translatable. For example, the word *tob* ("good") is the first word in verses 25, 26, and 27. The preposition *ki* appears at the beginning of verses 31, 32, and 33. The NIV translates *ki* as *for* in verse 31, *though* in verse 32, and *for* again at the beginning of 33. A reader of an English Bible will not be aware that the exact same word appears in each place. But the ancient reader of this text would know it and appreciate the reinforcement of the idea expressed by the repetition.

If this poem were not an acrostic, it would be hard to believe that it is a single poem because of the dissonance in the sentiments expressed. Claus Westermann (168–69) is likely correct in suggesting that this single poem was once a collection of poems that later were placed together and set into an acrostic frame. It may be helpful to think of the poem as either a liturgical piece where different voices speak, adding their perspective to the question at hand, or as a dialogue, as Nancy Lee proposes (2002: 168–81). Imagine a responsive reading where one voice expresses anger and bewilderment, followed by another voice expressing a word of comfort and hope.

This is the kind of order that exists in this poem. The poem moves from despair to hope and back to despair again, with a cry for vengeance at the end.

The poem contains five of the characteristic elements of a lament as described by Toni Craven (27) in her study of Hebrew poetry: address to God (vv. 55, 58-66), complaint (vv. 1-20, 43-54), confession of trust (vv. 21-33), petition (vv. 64-66), and words of assurance (vv. 22-25, 31, 57). The only element missing from her list is the vow of praise (see the Introduction on "Structure").

OUTLINE

Complaint, 3:1-20
Turning Point, 3:21
Affirmation of God's Trustworthiness, 3:22-39
Self-Examination, 3:40-41
Complaint Addressed to God and Response, 3:42-60
Call for Vengeance, 3:61-66

EXPLANATORY NOTES

Complaint 3:1-20

The poem opens with a complaint: *I am the man who has seen affliction by the rod of the LORD's wrath* (NIV). The word translated *man* in some English versions (*one* in the NRSV) is *geber* in Hebrew. *Geber* is not the word most typically used in the Bible to indicate an ordinary man or an ordinary person. Usually *geber* indicates a man of accomplishment and distinction, a highly respected person in the community. The word is used to describe David's "mighty warriors" (NIV) in 2 Samuel 23:8. F. W. Dobbs-Allsopp (1993: 108) notices that the phrase "I am" is associated with royal inscriptions. This strengthens the argument that the man in question is a member of the elite *[Elite, p. 115]*. The NRSV's generic *I am one* ... is not adequate here. Contrary to what Hillers (109, 122), Dobbs-Allsopp (109), and many other scholars suggest, this is not an "everyman." The choice of language in Hebrew points to a man who ought to be a hero, in control of himself and his situation, and respected among men in a hierarchical and patriarchal society; but this *geber* is not. The reader might ask, "If a *geber* can be depressed and defeated, what hope is there for the ordinary person?"

The man describes himself as the sole victim of a merciless force whose design is to inflict the greatest pain possible, allowing no room for assistance from any source. Adele Berlin (85) points out that the description of the suffering man is similar to that of Job. Yet, as she writes, "this is not a poem about the suffering of the righteous; it is a poem about the suffering of the guilty." The poem does not, in fact, focus on guilt. The words themselves (vv. 1-20) do not confess sin, either generally or specifically. The poem begs sympathy from the reader, not judgment.

The pain of the *geber* is described in physical terms, what suffering feels like to the body. It is like being slapped around, having one's bones broken, being walled in, being torn apart, like being shot with an arrow. The response to the attack is also physical: the man's teeth grind; he cowers in the dust. The subject complains of being driven into *darkness* and being forced to sit in *dark* places like the dead. In the thought world of ancient Israel, the dead abide in a place known as *Sheol*. Characteristically *Sheol* is dark (Ps 88:6). At a time when evening lighting was poor and predators both human and animal were known to lurk about under cover of darkness, going out at night was a frightening undertaking, to be avoided unless absolutely necessary. To be in a dark place meant to be unsafe and alone, literally or figuratively. *Sheol* is not to be associated with "hell," a place of punishment. That is a later conceptualization of what happens after death. In ancient Israel, all of the dead, no matter what their virtues or lack thereof on earth, were thought to descend to *Sheol*. That conception begins to change only toward the very end of the Old Testament time period. In the book of Daniel, for the first time the notion appears that there will be a different fate for the righteous (Dan 12:2-3).

In verse 14, the *geber* complains of being a *laughingstock* (*śeḥoq*), someone who is ridiculed. He has become the subject of their songs. These shaming mechanisms point to some sort of behavior that is unacceptable to the community. However, not all behavior unacceptable to a particular community is morally objectionable or sin. Not conforming to community norms may lead to rejection by the community. The goal of shaming mechanisms is to force a straying person to conform to community expectations. Prophets were sometimes subjected to shaming rituals because they preached against behavior and practices in their communities that led to, for example, the oppression of the poor. In the book of Jeremiah, the prophet complains of being an object of laughter: "I have become a laughingstock all day long; everyone mocks me. For whenever I speak, I must cry out, I must shout, 'Violence and destruction!'" (Jer 20:7b-8a).

Who is the force that is attacking the *geber*? The NRSV inserts the word *God* in verse 1, *God's wrath*, and the NIV has *the Lord's wrath*, but the Hebrew only has *his wrath* (so NIV 1984). Daniel Grossberg (1595) specifically names God as the one inflicting the pain: "The LORD is the implied subject of the actions." Even Nancy Lee (2002: 167) assumes that the attacker is God, but adds, "The heavy use of *accusations* against the Lord [is] heretofore unprecedented in the Old Testament." Virtually all scholars agree with them. The text itself, however, is not clear as to who the assailant is, and the obvious intent of the author was to protect the mystery. "He" or "his" language is used throughout the first twenty verses without specifying who the "he" is. The name of God, Yahweh, appears only once in this section (in v. 18), where there is juxtaposition between the one who destroys glory and the hope that comes from the God of Israel *[Yahweh, p. 118]*. The malevolent force appears to be distinct from Israel's God and not one and the same. In verse 8, the being stops prayers, presumably from reaching God, who would help if only God knew that divine help was being requested. Again, this may suggest that the "he" is a being other than God *[Evil Spiritsm, p. 116]*.

In Hebrew poetry, an individual voice may represent the collective voice of the community. Some have suggested that the *geber* is therefore a representative of the community, the community of Israel. Verse 14 implies otherwise: *I was a laughingstock to all my people, their mocking song all day* (AT). The man in this verse is set over against the community. The community is laughing at him. Therefore he is not meant to represent the community.

Grossberg (1595) understands the *rod* mentioned in verse 1 to be a shepherd's rod. Likely Grossberg is correct, but the shepherd in this case is cruel. He is tormenting the sheep, not protecting them.

The enemy is metaphorically compared to a bear and a lion (v. 10). Bears always appear as predators in the Old Testament, where they tear apart misbehaving children (2 Kings 2:24) or hapless adults (Hos 13:8). The one exception is in Isaiah 11:7, where the cow and bear rest together in the "peaceful kingdom," contrary to their behavior in the natural world. Lions are also depicted primarily as predators (1 Kings 13:24), but lions may also be positively portrayed as symbols of power and bravery (2 Sam 17:10). The use of animal metaphors for God (if the enemy is assumed to be God) is present in the Bible, but they are not common. This is because of a theology that distances God from the natural world to reinforce the notion that God is not a created being and is not to be worshiped through objects of nature. In contrast, worship outside of Israel involved items such as trees, the sun, and rivers. A text where God is described using the imagery of a bear is in Hosea 13:8, where God as bear attacks a disloyal Israel.

As in English, certain letters of the Hebrew alphabet are used less frequently than others to form words. Very few Hebrew words begin with the sixth letter of the Hebrew alphabet, *vav* (pronounced like the English *v*). Because the poem is an acrostic, this letter must be used three times and is so used in verses 16, 17, and 18. A *vav* prefixed to a word, however, is not unusual. It represents a conjunction that is most often translated *and*. Unlike English, Hebrew often attaches conjunctions directly to a word. Sometimes the *vav* is left untranslated, as here in most English Bibles. These verses indicate that the poet is moving from bewilderment at the poem's beginning to utter despair. He no longer remembers how it feels to be at peace or experience goodness.

Verses 19-21 begin with a continuation of the complaint, then switch from complaint to hope in the last line. This final verse of the triad may, in fact, represent a second voice, interrupting and countering the monologue presented in the first 20 verses. The words of the *geber* end with verse 20. What does this new voice suggest? It calls the despairing *geber* to remember. Remembering is what causes Jonah's change of attitude when he is in the belly of the fish (Jon 2:7). In ancient Israel, remembering is what ought to cause the Israelites to be faithful to God—remembering what God had done for them in Egypt. Verse 19 begins with the word "remember" in Hebrew cast as an imperative. *Remember my misery!* (AT). It may be an appeal to God or a call to the reader to sympathize. The second line (v. 20) reads, *Remembering, you remember*, a Hebraic expression best translated, *Surely, you remember!* Three times the Hebrew word "remember" is repeated in two verses. As in this case, repetition of the same word is not always visible in English translations because English style prefers the use of synonyms to avoid monotony. Hebrew style, however, is different. It frequently uses the very same word over and over again. The NRSV omits the imperative and instead translates "remember" as *The thought of* (v. 19) and *thinks* (v. 20). The NIV translates the command "remember" in the first person as *I remember* and *I well remember*.

Turning Point 3:21

This is a transitional verse that changes the direction of the poem from the theme of despair to hope. But it is merely a digression, not a climax, because the poem returns to despair and complaint after verse 33; even before that are ominous warnings of suffering to come. This interlude of hope and affirmation is the part of Lamentations that is best known. It expresses optimism that waiting and hoping will be rewarded. The Israelites are encouraged to take heart because their own history confirms that God will take pity on God's people. The next two stanzas of the poem, verses 22-24 and 25-27, express confidence in God's kindness and goodness.

Affirmation of God's Trustworthiness 3:22-39

The stanza composed of verses 22-24 contains words of affirmation of God's love and mercy. It is striking that these reassuring verses that appear in the Old Testament are absent from the Septuagint (an early Greek translation of the Bible). They may have simply dropped out in the transcribing of the text, or they may have been deliberately omitted. The absence of these verses means that in the Greek translation an entire letter of the Hebrew alphabet is missing! That suggests that the error was on the part of the translators of the Septuagint. Such errors sometimes occurred when a scribe, while copying a word or phrase in handwriting, looked away from the master text for a moment, turned back, and continued from a second place where the same word or phrase appeared later in the text. In this reading, the end of verse 21 is almost identical to the end of verse 24.

The phrase that opens this stanza is *the loving-kindness of Yahweh* (v. 22 AT). This exact phrase appears several times in Scripture, such as twice in the Psalms (89:2; 107:43) and once in Isaiah (63:7). Variations on it are frequent, and it is a central element of the theology of ancient Israel. God's loving-kindness is never exhausted. There is no end to God's compassion. God's mercies are new every morning. Even though one may experience the wrath of God one day, there is hope that God's love and mercy will prevail the next day.

The word ḥeleq in verse 24, *Yahweh is my ḥeleq* (AT), is often translated as *portion*. However, the English word *portion* falls short of the meaning of the Hebrew word, which is "a possession," often in the sense of an "inherited possession." An inherited possession is one that is bequeathed from generation to generation with the hope that each recipient will treasure it and pass on to the next; and not only the possession, but the knowledge of its value. An "inherited possession" is not one that is earned or deserved, and it may not be sold and alienated from the family. One obtains it by virtue of being a member of a particular family. The possession connects one to the past and to the future. *The LORD is my inherited possession* (AT) is a poetic expression found also, for example, in Psalm 119:57 and Psalm 73:26 (using *Elohim,* "God," rather than "the Lord").

The central verses in the third chapter are a reflection on the goodness of God. Because they come near the center of the middle chapter, they are often used as an interpretive key to the book, but that may be placing too much weight on these words. A variety of perspectives are being engaged in this chapter. Some of the voices are despairing, some are hopeful. They do not all express the same sentiment. Within a community at any particular time, various individuals and groups are experiencing the highs and lows of life. The value of having a community is that those who are "up" at a particular time can help those who are feeling depressed. That is one reason why community was so important to the ancient Israelites, as expressed in this liturgical piece.

The three verses 25-27 all begin not only with the same letter of the Hebrew alphabet but also with the same word, *ṭob. Ṭob* means "good" in Hebrew. What is good? The Lord is good to those who seek and wait for God and the deliverance that will come. It is also good for a man to lift (carry or bear) a yoke in his youth. This phrase "to bear a yoke" is idiomatically used to indicate that one places oneself under divine sovereignty. Delbert Hillers (129) suggests another interpretation of the reference to bearing the yoke: the yoke is a metaphor for trials. By bearing such trials as a youth, one grows into a man of distinction, a *geber.*

The reference to bearing the yoke in youth seems awkwardly placed. It is a wisdom saying in the midst of the lament. A wisdom saying is one that instructs people in appropriate behavior and modes of thinking. When adults instruct youth to bear the yoke, they do not do so without ulterior motives. Adults want youth to learn but also to pay their dues, so to speak, and to discipline themselves to wait until adults are ready to give up positions before they seek them. If youth get out of line, powerful adults can put them back in their places. This portion of the poem suggests that if youth are disciplined while they are young, they will develop into the kind of adults that they ought to be.

The second set of three verses in this group, 28-30, continues the theme of being patient. It appears to be a reflection on the *geber.* The person reciting these words suggests that there is still hope for him. The *geber* sits in silence, putting his mouth into the dust (v. 29). This suggests lying prostrate before one who is greater than one's self. The text implies that this is not unusual or unexpected. Therefore he must put up with it until there is a change in his situation.

The triad of verses 31-33 is an apologetic, a defense of the actions of God. It introduces the idea of divine rejection. Divine rejection does occur, according to this text, but such rejection is temporary, not forever. The theological notion that God causes grief is present in verse 32. But in what sense does God cause grief? Verse 33 indicates that God does not *willingly bring affliction or grief* (NIV). The word translated *willingly* in most English Bibles is the Hebrew phrase "from his heart." In ancient Hebrew, the heart was the seat of thought and will. Today we would say "mind." This almost suggests that, rather than the result of targeted acts of God, grief is a by-product of being human in a natural and social environment that from time to time brings suffering. Does this mean that there is suffering outside of the will of God? Most scholars think that the first third of the chapter (3:1-18) blames God for directly causing the suffering. As in a number of other biblical texts, when the rhetoric becomes too strident, a voice espousing conventional wisdom enters. That is the case here. The reader is reminded of God's compassion and love.

Using a series of infinitives, the apologetic continues as verses 34-36 highlight the poet's belief that God is concerned about human rights and matters of justice. Surely the ancient Israelites were ahead of their time in their concern for proper treatment of prisoners (lit. *the ones that are bound*). They were not to be crushed underfoot. Perverted justice before God does not go unnoticed. In ancient times, the elite controlled the justice system *[Elite, p. 115]*. The laws and statutes were written by the elite for their own benefit. The phrase in verse 35 is *justice of men (geber)* or *human justice*. It is not God's justice that is in question. God is aware of these perversions of justice. The implied question that is not answered is that if God is aware of injustice, why does God not act to restore justice? There is no response to this implied question.

These next three verses, 37-39, are also an apologetic, a defense of divine justice in the face of what appears to be injustice. Only God has true power, the ability to command and it is done. Therefore, whatever happens is the will of God. From God come both good and evil; there is no secondary source of power in the universe. People should not complain about the evil that comes as a result of their sin when they gladly receive good from the same source *[Evil Spirits, p. 116]*. Although biblical Hebrew did not originally use punctuation, the use of interrogative words such as *who?* and *what?* indicate that these three verses are meant to be understood as a series of rhetorical questions. Therefore, the theological assumptions made in these verses would have been accepted by those who read or heard them recited. The assumed answer to verse 38 is "Yes": from God comes what people experience as both good and bad.

Self-Examination 3:40-41

Beginning with verses 40-41, other voices enter. There is a change to "us" language for seven verses. *Let us examine our ways* (NIV). The poet calls for collective self-examination. Rather than complaining to or about God, the question that the human community ought to be asking is "What are we doing to cause this to happen?" The lifting of the heart as well as the hands may reflect a particular theological notion about prayer as well as the question of sincerity. Lifting the hands is a physical act that can be seen. Lifting the heart is not seen but reflects the sincerity of the repentant.

Complaint Addressed to God and Response 3:42-60

Verse 42 belongs to the letter triad (*nun*) that includes verses 40-41, but the topic has changed and its complaint properly belongs to what follows. The complainer has done his job, transgressing and rebelling, but God has not forgiven. What a strange saying! But actually, it is quite logical. God has no need to forgive those who do not sin. Therefore sin must precede forgiveness. The text does not indicate whether those complaining also confessed or repented as a prior step to expecting God to forgive.

Another perspective enters the conversation. This collective voice speaks in opposition to the presentation of God as being endlessly compassionate. God is accused of killing *us* and not having compassion. According to this voice, God prevents prayers from reaching the divine self. God seems very distant. God is impenetrable. The reference to being *in the midst of the peoples* (v. 45 AT) is a reference to exile, and it accuses God of having placed them in that position. The language of this passage is not God but *you*. It is direct address.

An odd thing happens in this triad. An expected letter of the Hebrew alphabet, *ayin*, is skipped. The seventeenth letter of the Hebrew alphabet, *pe,* has its triad where *ayin* is supposed to be. *Ayin* then appears after *pe*—equivalent to placing the *q* before *p* in the ordering of the English alphabet. This reversal also occurs in the second and fourth chapters of Lamentations. The first chapter, however, has the expected order. This may suggest that the order of these letters was not yet set, or that the poems may have been composed by persons with different orderings of the alphabet.

Israel was ever concerned about what other people, even enemies, thought about it. In verse 46, the complaint is that the enemies are speaking against it. This complaint implies that God should defend Israel for God's own sake. If God's people are being verbally attacked, God is also being attacked.

Another abrupt change occurs in verse 48, where the language reverts from the collective *our* to first-person singular *my*: *Streams of tears flow from my eyes because my people are destroyed* (NIV). The phrase translated *my people* is literally *daughter of my people* in Hebrew. The phrase *daughter of my people* in verse 48 appears solely in Lamentations and Jeremiah (Lam 2:11; 4:3, 6, 10; Jer 4:11; 6:26; 8:11, 19, 21, 22; 9:7; 14:17). However, quite often parallels to this phrase appear, naming a specific ethnic group, such as daughter of Edom or daughter of Judah. The use of common phrasing causes some scholars to support the traditional notion that Jeremiah was the author of some of the poems in the book of Lamentations. Most often the phrase *daughter of my people* is used to elicit sympathy. Verse 48 ends the triad with eyes weeping because of *the destruction of my people*.

The next verse (v. 49) begins a new letter of the alphabet (*ayin*) and continues the same theme. The weeping will not stop until God responds. The thinking here is that God is far away and does not care. Yet the voice continues to appeal to God until God responds. The *fate of all the young women* (v. 51) may be a reference to rape, but it may also be a general reference to destruction. The phrase is more literally *daughters of my city*. This language is sometimes used to refer to the villages that surround a city and are economically tied to it [*City, p. 113*].

The eighteenth letter of the Hebrew alphabet (*tsade*) fronts verses 52-54 and returns the subject to "they" language for the enemy. The victim is *me*. The enemy is clearly not God in these verses. The complaint that the enemies hunted him *without cause* suggests that the enemies in these verses are not a foreign nation but personal enemies. Like the brothers of Joseph (Gen 37:19-20), the enemies threw him into a pit. But unlike Joseph, he is covered with stones. They have buried him. He is invisible and beyond human help. The water imagery in this verse is reminiscent of Jonah: as he sinks into the sea, he notices the water closing in over him (Jon 2:5). Jonah and the *I* in this verse both cry out to God. And God responds each time.

The nineteenth letter of the Hebrew alphabet (*qoph*) is the first letter of the three different words that appear first, respectively, in verses 55-57. They are single words in Hebrew but must be translated into phrases in English: *I called, my voice, you drew near.* A voice calls out for divine help, recalling that, in the past, God heard and said, *Do not be afraid.* Again, one hears echoes of Jonah's poem from the belly of the great fish: "I called . . . to the Lord, and he answered me" (Jon 2:2 AT).

Six verses in a row (vv. 55-60) testify that God has been known to see, hear, and respond to those who call out for divine help. This statement is powerful testimony to God's help and comfort in a past time of need. The poet's own life witnesses to God's willingness to respond to those who cry out to him. Moreover, the testimony expresses confidence that God is on the side of the one in distress. However, the person is not content with personal redemption. In light of all of the trouble that the enemies have caused, the complainant wants them to be punished so that the cause of justice is served.

Call for Vengeance 3:61-66

When God is aware of injustice, God must respond by punishing the perpetrators of the injustice. God should destroy the enemy. Justice demands it! The enemy should get back what it gave.

The concept of vengeance is present in several places in the book of Lamentations, including 1:21-22 and 3:64-66. Wayne Pitard's study (786–87) of vengeance in the Bible found that most often the idea is for the wrongdoer to receive a "just punishment." The call for divine vengeance comes, according to Pitard, when the person or group is not confident that human justice will prevail. Pitard understands the call for divine vengeance to be a call for justice to "restore the balance." Certainly there were many occasions when the superpowers of the day, such as Babylon and Assyria, caused great pain for Israel: killing and exiling its leading citizens, causing famine and disruption for those who remained behind. Tiny Israel could never hope to get even or to see that justice was served. Its only recourse was to call on God to do so on its behalf. Confidence that God would execute justice in this way would be "encouragement to the oppressed" (Pitard: 787).

In ancient times, many matters of justice were settled between families. If kin groups could not cooperate and find a mutually satisfactory solution to their dispute, and if the local court system failed, they sometimes resorted to violence. An example of this is found in the story of the rape of Dinah in Genesis 34. After their sister is raped, Dinah's brothers kill not only the man who committed the act but also all the men in the town. The father of the clan,

Jacob, is angry, observing that this will lead to a blood feud. He does not have the resources to fight all of the Canaanites. Given the prevalence of blood feuds in the ancient Near East, it may be that calling on God to take revenge on one's enemies was a way of rejecting human vengeance and the continuing bloodshed that usually occurred on both sides of the dispute. If God would take the revenge, neither side could blame the other, thereby avoiding continued feuding. In addition, one could be assured that only the appropriate amount of punishment would be meted out for justice to be served.

THE TEXT IN BIBLICAL CONTEXT

Acrostics and Repetition

Acrostics are found in several books in the Old Testament *[Acrostic, p. 111]*. However, the triple acrostic structure of this poem is unique in the Bible. (Psalm 119 has an even more complex eightfold repetition of each letter of the Hebrew alphabet, but no other poem has exactly three repetitions of each letter of the Hebrew alphabet.) Brug (4) suggests that the alphabetic acrostic form is meant to appeal to the eye and not the ear. But the alliteration caused by the triple acrostic would catch the ear, especially in cultures that are more aural than visual in learning patterns.

Is there a special significance attached to threefold repetition in the Bible? In the book of Amos (chs. 1-2), three transgressions are noted, but the punishment is not carried out until a fourth transgression. In Deuteronomy (16:16), all of the males are to appear before the Lord to celebrate certain festivals three times each year. When David is told to pick a punishment, he is given a choice of threes: three years of famine, three months of losing battles, or three days of contagious disease (1 Chron 21:12). Jonah spends three days and nights in the belly of the fish before being expelled and sent on his mission (Jon 1:17-3:2). The number three and its multiples appear quite often in the Bible in a variety of texts. Its usage in texts varies widely. The threefold repetition of each letter in the acrostic appears to have no particular theological or practical significance beyond aesthetics, its value as a mnemonic device, and traditional practice.

Lament Metaphors

Many of the metaphors in the chapter and the book are found in other poems of lament in the Bible. Some of the phrasing and images are stock in lament poetry. Suffering is associated with being in darkness in 3:2, 6 and Psalm 88:18. References to crushed or broken bones (3:4) are also found in Psalm 51:8 (Heb. v. 10). References to affliction and pain appear in Psalm 69:29 (Heb. v. 30).

Expressions of hope and confidence in God are characteristic elements of laments. After a series of complaints against God, the author of Psalm 38 states that he is waiting for God and expects God to respond (v. 15 [16]). Psalm 73 begins with a general statement of the goodness of God and then enters into a tirade of complaints about the lack of fairness in life before returning to a statement of confidence in God at the end of the poem. Expressions of grief that proclaim no words of hope rightly belong in the category of dirge rather than lament (Ps 88) *[Dirge, p. 115]*.

THE TEXT IN THE LIFE OF THE CHURCH

Liturgical Use of Lamentations

The part of the book of Lamentations with which most Christians are familiar is verses 22-26 of this chapter. It expresses confidence in the unending goodness of God and the inexhaustible supply of God's kindness and mercy. It encourages the reader to exercise patience because the Lord will deliver. These words are beautiful and comforting. In the Christian tradition, however, these words are frequently read outside of their larger context within a chapter and a book that includes suffering, protest, and complaint. It is like celebrating Easter while ignoring Good Friday. In the book, the intensity of God's loving-kindness and goodness is known against the intensity of the felt experience of the absence of love and goodness in life.

This poem enters the liturgical life of the church through the well-known hymn "Great Is Thy Faithfulness" (based on 3:22-23), by Thomas Chisholm (1923).

In Jewish synagogues, the book of Lamentations is chanted in its entirety, and in order, every year on the ninth day of the Hebrew month of Ab, a summer month that often coincides with late July. The ninth of Ab is the day when the suffering of the Jewish people throughout the ages, from the fall of Jerusalem to the Holocaust, is mourned. In Christian circles, the book appears less frequently in reading cycles. In the Roman Catholic and mainline Protestant lectionaries, brief selections from Lamentations appear (*Lectionary: Rev. Lect.*). In Protestant denominations that use the International Sunday School lessons, Lamentations is presented for study in some of the six-year adult cycles but not all. During the period 2001-7, selections from Lamentations appeared as the printed text for the day on two Sundays. One use focuses on 1:12-26 and 3:22-24, 31-33 (the entire book was assigned for background reading), and the second use focuses on 3:25-33, 55-58.

Searching Oneself

Self-examination has always been one of the spiritual disciplines taught and practiced in the church, both in the monastic traditions and in the Anabaptist traditions. Until fairly recently, in Anabaptist denominations during the weeks before communion, elders visited with individual members of the congregation to guide them in the process of self-examination, to prepare for participating in communion. The purpose of the exercise was primarily to make sure that one was right with God and the community before participating in the ritual that symbolizes that. Sometimes this process focused on trivial matters rather than spiritual matters, and the practice has died out in many congregations. Other congregations remind their members and participants to do their own self-examination in preparation for the rite. In addition to individual reflection, some congregations do collective self-examination in formal and informal ways, asking themselves questions such as these: "What are we as a community doing right? What could we do better? Where have we missed the mark?"

Lamentations 4:1-22

War Changes Behavior and Social Structures

PREVIEW

The fourth chapter of Lamentations, similar to chapters 1 and 2, begins with the anguished exclamation *How*! (*'ekah*; NIV, NRSV), followed by a graphic description of the situation in the city of Jerusalem after the war *[Capture and Destruction of Jerusalem, p. 112]*. This chapter has a feeling of immediacy. To elicit sympathy from the reader, the suffering of children is highlighted in the opening verses. Then the focus shifts to the elite, and finally to Israel's cousin kingdom, Edom, that thus far had escaped the wrath of the Babylonian invading force.

This poem and the last one (ch. 5) describe the suffering of the elite *[Elite, p. 115]*. There is no mention of the plight of those who had always been poor. Prior to the last century and a half, the vast majority of earth's people lived at a subsistence level. At the top of more developed societies was a small group of elite who had acquired wealth and power. In smaller and more traditional societies, the wealth spread was not great, and social mechanisms ensured that the more prosperous members of society did not get too far ahead of everyone else. During the period of the monarchy, ancient Israel was like the former. The excesses of the wealthy are named in prophetic books such as Amos (2:6-8; 5:10-13). The focus on the leaders and the plight of the elite suggest that this poem was composed by a member of the upper classes. It is written from that point of view, and it sympathizes with them *[Elite, p. 115]*.

Lamentations 4:1-22

This chapter is the last of those structured as an alphabetic acrostic in Lamentations: the first word of each line begins with a successive letter of the alphabet, in order *[Acrostic, p. 111]*. Dianne Bergant (109-10) notices that the first three chapters of Lamentations have longer verses. The last two are shorter. This mimics the pattern of the lament meter, where longer lines of poetry are followed by shorter ones, mimicking progression and regression in the grieving process *[Hebrew Poetry, p. 116]*.

Of the six elements of the lament as outlined by Toni Craven (address to God, complaint, confession of trust, petition, words of assurance, vow of praise), in this chapter we find only a complaint (see the Introduction on "Structure"). The primary complaint is about the grievous suffering of those who should not have suffered because of their status (as a member of the elite)—*those who were brought up in purple, . . . those who feasted on delicacies*—or because of their innocence (such as children). The blame for the devastation of the city is explicitly placed on God and the shoulders of the prophets and priests (but notice, not the political leaders) who failed in their leadership roles. There is no confession of trust, no petition, and no word of assurance except for a statement assuring punishment for Edom (4:22). Two other characteristic features of laments are also absent: a vow of praise and address to God. There is no overwhelmingly male or female language in this chapter *[Communal Lament, p. 114]*.

OUTLINE

Starvation in Jerusalem, 4:1-10
The Reason for the Deprivation, 4:11
The World Looked On in Disbelief, 4:12
The Fate of the Prophets and Priests, 4:13-16
No Help Arrived, 4:17-20
Next, It Is Edom's Turn, 4:21-22

EXPLANATORY NOTES

Starvation in Jerusalem 4:1-10

This chapter, like 1 and 2, begins with the cry of lament, *How!* The complaint in the first and second verses concerns that which is most precious, the children of the city, who are being treated as commonplace as a piece of pottery. Adele Berlin (105) thinks that the phrase translated *children of Zion* in verse 2 may be referring to all of the Israelites and not just the children. She rightly points out that the phrase is used in other parts of the Bible to refer to all of the Israelites (Ps 149:2; Joel 2:23). However, if in this chapter the phrase refers to all of the people, the statements about the people being cruel in verses 3 and 4 seem ill placed. There the children are called *sucklings*. Clearly the text has young children in mind. In verse 3, the people are compared to wild animals in relation to their offspring. The first comparison is to a jackal. Predators like jackals, who kill and devour the young and weak of other species, are good to their own young. Ostrich mothers were thought to be negligent because they sometimes leave their eggs exposed in a shallow pit. Observing this behavior (which does not endanger them because ostrich egg shells are very hard and protected), the Israelites may have concluded that ostrich mothers were cruel.

Great tragedy sometimes causes people to behave in perverse ways. Children depend upon their parents or, in the absence of parents, other adults to feed, protect, and take care of them. They are not responsible for the war and the situation that they are now in. They are bewildered by the treatment that they are receiving. They do not have enough knowledge or skills to help themselves. They turn to their parents, who are not responding to their needs. It is not natural for parents to leave their young unfed as the Jerusalemites are doing. But, of course, they cannot feed their children if they have nothing to give them. The situation, not their mind-set, forces them to be cruel. The famine in Jerusalem is an aftermath of war, a humanly created catastrophe. The phrase *daughter of my people*, sometimes just translated *my people* (as in NRSV, T/NIV), is an expression of endearment. Its use in verse 3 expresses the pathos of the situation.

Verse 5 empathizes with the plight of the wealthy. It focuses on those who were used to eating dainties and those who wore purple. Purple was only worn by the wealthy because the process of creating the color was expensive, coming from marine mollusks living in the ocean off the coast of Phoenicia. The elite have lost everything and are forced into the world of reality, where life is difficult *[Elite, p. 115]*. This is the first of several verses in the chapter decrying the losses that the privileged experienced when the city fell. Downward mobility was their lot.

The comparison to Sodom in verse 6 is unexpected. Sodom was destroyed because of its sin (Gen 18:20). The sin, according to Ezekiel 16:49-50, was failure to aid the poor. The punishment of Sodom was meted out directly by the Lord, who rained fire and brimstone from the sky (Gen 19:24). No human had a hand in its destruction. The complaint is that there is an imbalance in the punishment meted out to Jerusalem when compared to Sodom. In Sodom, all of the people sinned; but in Jerusalem, according to this chapter, solely the prophets and priests sinned. Jerusalem's suffering was deemed greater than that of Sodom because Sodom was destroyed in an instant; but men, women, children, and the elderly of Jerusalem—those not taken into exile—experienced the famine, which brought about a prolonged period of agony before death (Hillers: 147).

Verse 7 contains another reference to the elite. Those who had been protected from hunger and other suffering are now experiencing it. The contrast motif, comparing past and present situations, is a common literary device in the poetry of lament and funeral songs, and it is found here (Hillers: 147). Although a contrast is clearly intended, the object of the contrast is not as clear. The word translated *princes* (NRSV, T/NIV) is not the usual term for a prince, though it is a possible word for a prince. The verse could also refer to a priest (one who has been consecrated) or a Nazirite (one who sets himself aside for a period of religious devotion). Another interpretation, taking an alternate meaning of the word and translating it as *crown* or *special head band* as a symbol of an office, suggests that it is pointing to princes (*nezer, HALOT*). Moreover, the word translated *white*, as in *whiter than milk* (NRSV, NJPS, NIV), is not the color white. No color terminology appears in the first half of the verse. It is better translated *bright* or *clear* or *fine*, as in *Her consecrated ones were brighter than snow, smoother than milk. They reddened more intensely than coral; lapis lazuli was their court* (AT). This may be a reference to priests who were living lives of comfort and luxury. Later in the chapter, priests are singled out for their iniquities. Their life circumstances have undergone a sharp decline as a result of the destruction of the temple and, hence, their livelihood.

According to verse 8, *Their appearance has become darker than dark. They are not recognized outside. Their skin contracts on their bones. It dries up like wood* (AT). This is an image of starvation. Cannibalism is a last resort option during times when no other food is available. Children usually die first in times of deprivation. The image in verse 10 is that of women eating children who had already died (cf. Lam 2:20). A similar incident is recounted in 2 Kings 6:24-31. There the city of Samaria is also suffering from a famine caused by war. Two women agree to cook and eat the son of one of them one day and the son of the other the next day. The account in Lamentations 4 may be a metaphor describing the lack of a future for Israel rather than a factual description of what happened. There will be no future because the hope of the future has been consumed in the present. The unnatural behavior of the women is highlighted.

The Reason for the Deprivation 4:11

In this verse the God of Israel is charged with having poured out his anger on Judah. But, importantly, that anger has been spent. It has come to an end. The theology in this verse states that God acted against God's own people. This belief was also present among the people surrounding Israel. We have an example in an ancient inscription called the Moabite Stone. On it the king of Moab says that the Israelites were able to "humble" the Moabites because the Moabite god, Chemosh, was angry with his people (*ANET* 320). Similarly, the Babylonians were understood to be the agents of God's wrath.

The World Looked On in Disbelief 4:12

There was a faction in Judah who thought that Jerusalem, being the home of the temple and therefore the place where God lived, was inviolable. They assumed that the whole world understood this. God would protect God's city no matter what the people did, for God's own sake. This thinking is also written in the statement attributed to Solomon given at the temple's dedication in Jerusalem (1 Kings 9:3). God's response to the edifice at that time was that God is more concerned about faithfulness than impressive structures: "If you turn aside from following me, . . . then I will cut Israel off from the land that I have given them; and the house that I have consecrated for my name I will cast out of my sight; and Israel will become a proverb and a taunt among all peoples" (1 Kings 9:6-7). When Jerusalem fell, so did the theology of its permanence.

The Fate of the Prophets and Priests 4:13-16

The prophets and the priests are accused of having poured out the blood of the righteous. These two categories of religious leaders were given the responsibility of keeping the people on the right track. The job of the prophet was to warn people when they were straying from what God commanded. Most of the genuine prophets challenged the establishment; their particular target was kings, as in 2 Samuel 12, when kings functioned only according to the status quo and did not call the status quo itself into question. The prophets were particularly concerned about matters of justice. Priests were religious functionaries who carried out the rituals and sacrifices in the temple that symbolized the connection that the people of Israel had to God. When things got out of order due to sin and failure on the part of people, they could make it right again and symbolized that in the temple rituals. The priests also served as teachers of Torah (religious instruction) in the ancient world (Deut 24:8; 31:9-13).

According to verses 13-15, something has gone terribly wrong, but exactly what is unclear. The sentence *Blindly they wandered through the streets, so defiled with blood that no one was able to touch their garments* (v. 14) could mean that the priests and prophets are actually killing people; but more likely, they are being accused of destroying the righteous by their mistreatment of them. Such mistreatment might not have been visible, but it is made visible in the imagery of blood.

Ritual uncleanness was thought to be contagious. A person who was ritually unclean could transfer the uncleanness to someone else, but a ritually pure person could not transfer purity to anyone else. The driving away of the priests and the prophets who have become unclean is like the isolation of those with diseases thought to be contagious, as in the book of Leviticus (13:45-46). In Leviticus, the person with the disease calls out "unclean" to warn people to stay away. In Lamentations, the townspeople declare the priests and prophets to be unclean. This represents a reversal of responsibility. Normally it is the priests who determine who or what is ritually clean or unclean, but in this verse it is the people. The ordinary people recognize and make judgments as to what is right behavior and what is wrong behavior. They no longer leave it to the priests.

The priests and the elders have become outcasts, no longer respected members of the community. The social structures of society have broken down. The religious leaders have been rejected.

No Help Arrived 4:17-20

According to the prophet Ezekiel, as the war machine of Babylon approached, the people of the southern Israelite kingdom of Judah appealed to Egypt for assistance (Ezek 17:15-17). The help never came. So people were forced to flee from the city into the surrounding countryside; but even there they were not safe.

The reference to *Yahweh's anointed* in verse 20 is likely a reference to one of the last rulers of the southern kingdom, perhaps Jehoiachin, who was taken to Babylon and imprisoned for many years before he was released (2 Kings 25:27-30). The Hebrew word that is translated *anointed* (*mašiaḥ*) is sometimes transliterated as *messiah*. A messiah is one who is anointed. In the Bible, the title *mes-*

siah is given to kings, even of foreign lands (Isa 45:1). Priests were also anointed (Lev 4:3, 5) as were prophets (1 Kings 19:16; 1 Chron 16:22; Ps 105:15). The *breath of our nostrils* (v. 20) was a known expression of the day. In Egyptian writings the pharaoh is referred to as "the breath of our nostrils" (Hillers: 151). Hence we might understand it to be a phrase used to describe rulers. Ironically, Egypt served as both a place of enslavement (Exodus) and sanctuary for Israelites over the centuries (2 Kings 25:26; Jer 43–44). At various times Abraham and the descendants of Jacob and his four wives migrated to Egypt to find food and a safe haven during famines (Gen 12 and 46). The people had hoped to live *under the shadow* (that is, protection) of their king among the nations (cf. Isa 32:1-2). But now they are scattered among the nations (1:3).

Next, It Is Edom's Turn 4:21-22

In verse 21, Edom is directly addressed. Edom was a small kingdom south and east of Israel. According to Israel's account of its own origins, the Edomites were descendants of Esau (also called Edom), the brother of Jacob (Gen 25:29-34). Jacob was the ancestor of the Israelites. The Israelite poet suggests to Edom that they should rejoice now because soon they too will suffer just as the Israelites suffer now. The sins of Edom will be exposed for the entire world to see. Why did the poet issue this warning to Edom? The chapter itself provides no clue. A possible explanation, however, lies elsewhere in the Old Testament.

According to Israelite historiography, there had been tension and conflict from time to time between the Israelites and the Edomites in spite of, or perhaps because of, their common origins [*Historiography, p. 117*]. The book of Numbers tells a story about the Israelites being refused passage through Edomite territory on their way from Egypt to the land of promise (Num 20:14-21). A king of the southern Israelite kingdom of Judah killed ten thousand Edomites for an unspecified reason (2 Kings 14:7). The seldom-read, one-chapter book of Obadiah records that when Jerusalem was attacked, the Edomites stood by and let it happen; they participated in the looting of the city, and they prevented Jerusalemites from escaping to safety (Obad 12-14). The writer of the fourth chapter of Lamentations is perhaps remembering that story when condemning the Edomites. Although Edom may have been able to aid fleeing Judeans, it is unlikely that it would have been in a position to support Jerusalem militarily. Edom was never a major player in the ancient near East, and the Bible makes note of its lack of political leadership at one point in its history (1 Kings 22:47). Even while it is condemning and blaming Edom, the text is issuing a word of encouragement to Israel. Israel's exile will come to an end.

In verse 22, both Zion and Edom are addressed as *daughter*: *Daughter Zion* and *Daughter Edom*. The use of the language of kinship suggests equality of affection for Israel and Edom even while punishment is being meted out.

THE TEXT IN BIBLICAL CONTEXT

Children and the Poor

In spite of its massive content, the Old Testament gives surprisingly little direct attention to children and the poor. To be sure, there are many statements about justice and the need to provide for the poor and the needy, the widows and the orphans. However, few stories actually focus on the lives of the poor or children. Most of the biblical stories focus on and are told from the point of view of leaders: kings, priests, prophets, and clan leaders such as Abraham, Isaac, and Jacob. That focus continues in this poem about those who are suffering from the aftermath of war. The exception is the attention given to the plight of children. Children who never do anything to provoke a war or call for it are always its victims. They lose those who love, protect, and care for them. They succumb to disease and lack of food and water. Yet the death counts provided, such as in the book of Judges, usually only count adult men who were directly involved in the battle (Judg 20:21, 25, 31, 35). They do not include what some euphemistically refer to as "collateral damage." Hints that others died, however, are suggested. At the end of the book of Judges, after a horrific civil war during which the tribe of Benjamin is nearly wiped out, it is reported that there are not enough women left for the surviving men to marry. The death or displacement of women is not specifically mentioned in the text, until their absence is reported (Judg 21). No mention is made of children.

THE TEXT IN THE LIFE OF THE CHURCH

Serving Those Affected by War

The reality of what happens in war and to those trying to survive in places that have been devastated by war—all this is often hidden from those who are removed from the situation. Neither the winners nor the losers have anything to gain by revealing the real cost of war in human lives and human misery. Following most wars, there are parades to honor those who fought. Soldiers in their uniforms march down the streets of the major cities and towns. Those who cannot march because their legs or their minds were blown away rarely participate in such events because they are still in hospitals, recovering from their injuries. The dead whose remains are recovered are in their graves. They are not visible during the parades. Lamentations is entirely about those who survive war, but with their bodies, minds, and spirits sorely wounded.

Persons who have not been in the midst of violent conflict often do not realize how disruptive wars are to the social fabric and mental and physical well-being of those who survive. The end of the war does not mean that everything returns to normal. Homes, schools, municipal buildings, shops, hospitals, power stations, and libraries are damaged or destroyed. Many people do not know what happened to their fathers, brothers, mothers, sisters, children, and other family members who disappeared. Some survivors will never learn their fate. Women or children who had not previously been primary breadwinners must seek ways to earn a living. This can be particularly challenging in countries where work opportunities for women are restricted because of custom and lack of education and where they earn significantly lower wages than men. The family may never return to economic stability.

Children go through the same trauma as the adults, yet with fewer resources for coping. When there is no food, they too live for days without eating, feeling the pain and emotional distress of hunger. Their bodies may never reach their full height, and their minds may never be as sharp because they are not receiving the nutrients that they need for full development. Without proper shelter, they are exposed to the elements, and they succumb to flu, pneumonia, malaria, and typhoid much quicker than adults. Children miss years of schooling that they may never be able to recover. During wars, people get out of the habits that directed everyday life. And how can anyone ever banish from one's mind the picture of a sister, mother, or child gang-raped, beaten, and left dead? Broken minds, spirits, bodies, families, and communities are the legacy of war.

Some religious traditions do better than others in theologically and psychologically assisting those who have survived war and other catastrophes. Requiem masses in the Roman Catholic tradition were originally designed to mourn an individual who died and comfort those who remained. The requiem tradition has been picked up by other Christian traditions and even secularists as a way of helping people to grieve and find hope, not just as individuals but also as communities. Benjamin Britten's *War Requiem* (1962) is one example. Requiems use biblical texts, statements from church history, and music to bring healing to wounded souls.

Anabaptists have been opposed to war from the beginnings of the movement in the sixteenth century, but until the nineteenth and twentieth centuries, most of their energies had focused on avoiding personal or communal involvement with war. More recently, Anabaptists have tried, through their peace and justice work, to mediate and train people in techniques to mitigate situations of conflict. They have also assisted persons affected by war. They have aided refugees and created resettlement programs. And Anabaptists have become involved in removing the remnants of war that still kill and harm, such as bombs and other munitions and equipment that armies leave behind. Denominational colleges and universities offer programs and degrees that educate persons whose countries and communities are or recently have been involved in violent conflict. This is done under the assumption that persons within cultures are the ones best equipped to nurture their communities toward shalom.

How Communities Bring Healing to Those Affected by Mass Traumas

Somasundaram and Sivayokan, in their article titled "Rebuilding Community Resilience in a Post-War Context," note that the individualistic methods of counseling that were developed in the West are not sufficient for communities that have undergone massive trauma, where everyone is affected. Moreover, those Western methods assume the autonomy of the individual and do not take into account the larger social context. They write, "In collectivistic societies, family or community members may join together in *collective coping* to pool resources, act cooperatively [by] sharing the burden to resolve a single or common problem at the family (extended family) or community levels. . . . Similarly, firm traditional and religious beliefs and social support have been shown to be a protective factor against the effects of trauma" (Somasundaram and Sivayokan: 2, with original emph.). After war, they write, it is important to restore family units. Family members who have been separated need to be found and reunited. They should be permitted to return to their homeplace. Even if their own homes no longer exist, just being in the area helps. Communal grieving rituals must take place as well as the usual festivals and commemorative events that mark normalcy in a society. Art forms, including "dramatic forms, *laments*, poetry, writings and drawing," foster the healing (21, with original emph.).

Lamentations 5:1-22

Restore Us to Yourself

PREVIEW

The fifth poem in the book is dramatically different from all of the others in several ways. The first, and most obvious to the reader of Hebrew, is that it is not an alphabetic acrostic *[Acrostic, p. 111]*. However, it does have twenty-two lines. Brug (3) refers to the structure as a "line-count acrostic." Without the constraints of the tight alphabetic acrostic structure, the poet focuses on a unity of meaning.

Another way in which this poem differs from the others is that each of its twenty-two verses consists of a single line bicolon (two phrases or sentences). This makes the entire poem significantly shorter than the other four, which have either three bicolon pairs (chs. 1–3) or two bicolon pairs (ch. 4) for each of the twenty-two letters of the alphabet *[Hebrew Poetry, p. 116]*.

The language of the poem is simpler than the others, and the grammar and syntax are more regular. The poem also differs in terms of the voice that emerges from it. While reading the poem aloud or hearing it recited, one is immediately struck by the very frequent repetition of the morpheme *nu* *[Morpheme, p. 117]*. When attached to a noun, *nu* is translated as "our." When attached to a verb or preposition, it can mean "we" or "us." It appears an astonishing thirty-two times in the twenty-two verses of the poem (eleven times in the first six verses). In this poem (ch. 5) the use of *nu* conveys a strong sense of a communal voice. This is not an individual reflecting on one's own experience or the fate of other people. It is the voice of a community pleading with God to hear and respond to their pain.

The voice, however, is not the voice of the entire Israelite community. It is the voice of a select elite *[Elite, p. 115]*. The voice complains about being reduced to the chores and vulnerabilities that the masses of the impoverished, women, workers, and enslaved people face every day. The poem conveys no sense of an "Aha!" experience: "Now we know what our servants go through every day." Perhaps, it is too soon in the grieving period.

Some ancient Greek manuscripts classify this chapter as a prayer. Indeed, it does have a defining characteristic of a prayer in that it addresses God directly several times (vv. 1, 19, 21). It opens with *Remember, O Lord, what has happened to us. Look and see our disgrace* (AT). This poem, like the others, is focused on complaints about the situation in which the upper-class people left in Jerusalem find themselves *[Capture and Destruction of Jerusalem, p. 112]*. Other characteristics of the lament form outlined by Toni Craven are also found here. The primary content of the poem is a description of the suffering in Zion (Jerusalem) and the cities of Judah. The intent is to appeal to God to remedy the situation by intervening on behalf of those who suffer (petition). There is no confession of trust. There is a petition in the form of a call for God to remember them in verse 1 and a call for God to restore them in verse 21. Instead of words of assurance, there is a suggestion that perhaps God has completely rejected the people. There is no vow of praise (see the Introduction on "Structure") *[Communal Lament, p. 114]*.

This is the last poem and the last chapter in the book of Lamentations. Therefore, the book ends with words of utter dejection, which is unusual for a biblical book. In Jewish liturgical practice, verse 21 is repeated after verse 22 so that the reading does not end on a note of despair.

OUTLINE

The Request, 5:1
A List of Grievances, 5:2-5
The Cost of Survival, 5:6
The Sins of the Ancestors 5:7
Roles Have Been Reversed, 5:8-13
No One Has Fun Anymore, 5:14-18
Appeal to God, 5:19-22

EXPLANATORY NOTES

The Request 5:1

This poem is the only one of the five in Lamentations that opens with a direct address to God. The divine name *Yahweh* (which appears as LORD in most English translations) was favored in the southern Israelite kingdom and is used consistently here (cf. vv. 19, 21). Three verbs with the force of imperatives order the Lord: Remember! Look! See! "Remember" is a theological term of some significance in the Bible. The Israelites are instructed to remember the Sabbath day (Exod 20:8-11; Deut 5:12-15), to "remember now your Creator in the days of [their] youth" (Eccl 12:1 AT), and to remember that Israel is God's servant (Isa 44:21). To remember, one must return to the past. It involves awareness plus a disposition to act upon it. As expressed in the Bible, God's claim on Israel is frequently based on God's favorable actions toward Israel in the past. God freed Israel from slavery in Egypt. God brought Israel into the Promised Land *[Yahweh, p. 118]*.

Not all remembering is pleasant or beneficial. In the first verse, God is implored to remember what happened and to take notice of the shame (or disgrace) of the people. Honor and shame are social mechanisms by which people are forced to conform to societal norms. Those who do what society expects are honored. Those who go against the norms are shamed in order to bring them back into conformity. By pointing to their shame or disgrace rather than ignoring or excusing it, the Israelites are showing the Deity that they have accepted the chastisement.

A List of Grievances 5:2-5

Although this poem is describing the aftermath of the Babylonian conquest through its references to *strangers* and *foreigners* having the possessions (including land and resources) of local people, the primary concern of the poet lies in the social and economic reversals that have occurred. The situation in which the people find themselves is similar to that of the poor, the orphan, the stranger, and the widow. Orphans and widows lack a protector. They are vulnerable to exploitation. They cannot rest when they are tired. For the wealthy in a given traditional society, water and wood are free because they own the land and resources, and they control access to them. In cases where the resources are not owned by them, they can still afford to purchase them. If the poor want to collect water or gather wood, unless there is a public well or commons, it is done on someone's property. The owner can request payment either for these commodities or for access to them.

In verse 4, the wealthy, for the first time, are having to experience what the poor do every day: pay for access to what ought to be freely available to all (water, natural products of the land). They do not have guaranteed access to resources, and they need to pay for what used to belong to them. The poet does not acknowledge that the current situation represents a reversal of the fortunes of Israel when they entered the land and possessed houses that they had not built and enjoyed the fruit of olive groves and vineyards that they did not plant (Deut 6:10-11). Now others have invaded their land and taken over their houses, vineyards, and olive groves. This is a cycle that has occurred over and over in human history.

Daniel Grossberg (1601) observes that in this chapter the central social institutions of Judean society have collapsed. They have collapsed for Israel, but other people are benefiting.

The Cost of Survival 5:6

Egypt was a location of settlement for some of the refugees from Judah and Jerusalem (2 Kings 25:26; Jer 43-44). The Elephantine papyri witness to that *[Elephantine Papyri, p. 115]*. These papyri are an extant series of letters and documents written by members of a flourishing Jewish community in Egypt in the fifth century BCE. Assyria is an unexpected reference (Lam 5:6). Assyria conquered the northern kingdom of Israel in 722/721 BCE. But by the time of this book, Assyria was no longer a superpower in the ancient Near East, and neither was Egypt. The text reads *We have given a hand to Egypt, for bread to satisfy, Assyria* (v. 6 AT). To "give a hand" means either to help or to reach out for help; the latter is the case here in verse 6. A similar expression, though with the alternate meaning, is found in 2 Chronicles 30:12. There the hand of God is given to create one heart among the people of Judah. Likewise in 2 Kings 10:15 (the text has difficulties), Jehu helps Jehonadab by giving him a hand to enter his chariot. In both of these cases, the ones giving the hand are in the superior position. However, in Lamentations 5:6, it is the weaker party that is giving (or holding out) the hand in hopes of having it filled. Both Assyria and Egypt may be inclined to help since they also felt the sting of Babylon. Another possibility is that the appeal is to Jews in Egypt and the former Assyrian Empire for help. Although the Jews in those areas were initially refugees, not all were destitute.

The Sins of the Ancestors 5:7

In this poem the communal voice places the blame for the community's suffering squarely on the shoulders of the ancestors. Yet the poem lists no sins of the ancestors and certainly none of their own generation. They cannot think of anything specific that their ancestors did to merit the treatment that they are now receiving. Therefore there are no requests for forgiveness in the poem. In ancient Israel there was a theological notion that children suffered for the sins of their parents (Exod 20:5). Sometimes this is interpreted to mean that God actively punishes children and grandchildren for the sins of their parents and forefathers, but it likely is simply an observation that children and grandchildren do suffer because of the sins of their forebears. The language in the King James Version is "visiting the iniquity of the fathers upon the sons." That antiquated language is closer to the Hebrew and expresses something short of punishing. In the later literature of the Bible, it is stated that children should not be punished for the sins of their parents (Ezek 18:20), or alternatively and more accurately, that guilt should not accrue to a child because of the sins of the parents. In ancient Israel and many traditional societies, families functioned as units, not as individuals. Children could be sold or put to forced labor to satisfy the debts of the parents. Because the parents and children were one unit, this was not seen as a punishment of the child. It was a loss to the family but necessary for the survival of the family as a whole.

Roles Have Been Reversed 5:8-13

In verse 8, to describe the new rulers, the poet chose the Hebrew word ʿabadim, which means "workers," "slaves," or "servants." The complaint is not that they are foreigners or conquerors but that they are beneath them socially and economically. This is an early hint that the people represented in this poem are not the poor or "people of the land," but the aristocrats who now are forced to live the lives of the poor. There is no one to rescue them from these uppity rulers, just as the poor have no one to rescue them from their poverty. The poor have always acquired their food and their livelihood by risking their lives in farms, mills, factories, mines, and quarries.

The phrase *sword of the wilderness* (v. 9 AT) appears only here in the Old Testament. Its meaning is therefore uncertain. The translations *sword in the wilderness* (NRSV) and *sword in the desert* (NIV) are not accurate. The phrase may be suggesting that sporadic fighting was still going on in the environs of Jerusalem. People need to tend their fields, get water, and bring in the harvest in spite of danger. In the story of Gideon found in Judges 6:11, Gideon is "beating out wheat in the winepress, to hide it from the Midianites" who were raiding Israelite towns. Normally wheat is beaten out on a threshing floor that is elevated and catches the wind. It was dangerous to be outside the city walls in an exposed place. In Joshua 8:24, the inhabitants of Ai are killed in a field, in the "open wilderness." During times of conflict or when nomadic raiders are in the area, people stay inside the city gates [City, p. 113]. But at some point they must come out to tend their fields, even at the risk of their lives, to put bread on the table or fetch water. Another possibility is that the phrase is meant to be understood metaphorically. Second Samuel 18:8 reports a battle between the forces of David and the forces of his son Absalom. They fought in a forest, and the text records, "The forest claimed more victims that day than the sword." The forest functions as a sword because of the dangers and pitfalls within it. It kills as surely as the edge of a sword. Perhaps the wilderness functions as a sword in Lamentations 5:9.

The poor have always been vulnerable in peacetime and wartime, having skin darkened not by melanin but by the sun, disease, or according to this text, by famine. Impoverished women have always been the most vulnerable to rape and abuse. What is different, as reported in verse 11, is that women who would have been protected in the past no longer can be safe.

In verse 12 the references to princes hung by their hands and elderly people who are not respected clearly express concern for an elite and respected group [Elite, p. 115]. The poet complains that young men are lifting millstones (see NJPS) and staggering under loads of wood (v. 13). In a premodern society, someone had to get wood every day, and someone lifted those millstones. That someone was likely to be a woman or girl, as Nancy Lee (2002: 193) has observed, and specifically a lower-class woman or girl. It is acceptable for women to stagger under loads of wood. It is not acceptable for upper-class boys to do so. In the Bible, women are often associated with millstones and grinding (Judg 9:53; Isa 47:2; Job 31:10; Eccl 12:3) but large-scale milling operations likely employed slaves (Judg 16:21) and animals to do the hard tedious work.

No One Has Fun Anymore 5:14-18

Early in Israel, some of the elderly may have had the leisure to sit in the gate, observing the comings and goings of the townsfolk and countryfolk (1 Sam 4:18) and functioning as judges and juries in court cases (Ruth 4:1, 2, 9). The elderly were usually put to lighter work in the household, and they watched over young children (Zech 8:4-5). Music is also a leisure activity, though one in which both poor and rich engage. The poem reflects that the usual pattern of work and celebration has been disrupted. Now there is only work.

Crowns are typically symbols of royalty, but they may also be used as a figure of speech referring to honor (v. 16). Honor is what publicly accrues to individuals who do well and are respected. The crown has fallen, and sin has been exposed. The brief confession suggests that the crown was misplaced from the beginning. Those who wore it were not worthy of it.

In these verses there is a surprising confession. The ancestors are not the only ones who sinned. They themselves have sinned, and their hearts are saddened (v. 16). They do not feel better for having vocalized the confession. The turn has not come.

Mount Zion is the location of palace and temple. It is desolate, and wild animals roam the streets (v. 18). This comment places the poem close to the time of the events reported in it. No restoration of the walls and city gates has taken place.

Appeal to God 5:19-22

Feelings of being forgotten and forsaken are expressed in the questions posed in verse 20. They are followed by a plea directed to God for restoration and renewal. The request indicates that the Jerusalemites believe that God still hears their prayers and can respond positively to them. Israel never lets go of God even when it feels that God has let go of it. This is because Israel knows that it possesses something more permanent than feelings; it possesses a relationship and a covenant that in the end is indestructible [Covenant, p. 114].

It is a custom in Judaism to never end a biblical reading on a negative note. Because Lamentations ends with the devastating thought that God may have rejected the people, the cantor of the synagogue returns to the penultimate verse and repeats it seven times, *Bring us back to yourself, O Lord. Let us return. Renew our days as at the beginning* (AT). The last phrase of the chant is the first half of the verse, *Bring us back to yourself, O Lord* (AT).

THE TEXT IN BIBLICAL CONTEXT
Inequities and the Poor

During antiquity, the vast majority of people were poor. There was a small middle class, consisting of successful artisans, traders, military officers, and midlevel administrators in the government; a tiny elite lived in luxury and controlled the lives of everyone else *[Elite, p. 115]*. Slavery was an accepted part of the social and economic system. Enslaved people were often outsiders who were captured in war. Sometimes natives of a land sold themselves or family members to relieve a debt. Usually this type of slavery was closer to the indentured servanthood of colonial America, because the slaves would be released once the debt was settled. On a theoretical level in ancient Israel, institutions such as the Sabbatical and Jubilee Years were meant to even things out economically so that over a period of time some did not become too rich at the expense of others who became too poor (Lev 25; Deut 15). But we do not know whether or not the Jubilee was ever instituted. Outside of the legal texts, other possible references to the Jubilee and Sabbatical Years in the Old Testament are found in Jeremiah 34:14-15 and Ezekiel 46:17, and maybe Jeremiah 25:11-12; 29:10; and Daniel 9:2.

Israel's account of its own history begins with a mixed group of enslaved people in Egypt, some of whom traced their ancestry back to Abraham and Sarah (Exod 12:38). Those descendants of freed men and women made their way to Canaan and settled there. Eventually they were able to gain political power in the land. After a succession of kings, they lost the land and found themselves under the hegemony of other people. Reversals were their own collective experience in life.

Inequities in society and a dream of a reversal of fortunes appears in Hannah's song (1 Sam 2:1-10) and Mary's song (Luke 1:46-55). In each of these, a time is envisioned when the poor are lifted up and the powerful are brought down. In Genesis, one of the common motifs is that of the younger son (Jacob, Joseph) or daughter (Rachel) who is preferred. This is another type of reversal. In ancient times, the older children were usually more highly valued because they were the ones who would take care of the parents in their old age. The older children would receive a greater share of the inheritance along with the responsibility to care for the parents and dependent siblings. In Genesis, however, frequently the preferred child in the stories is the younger one who strikes out on his own and makes something of himself that eventually benefits the family as a whole. The social and power structures needed to be reversed in order for social and religious change to occur.

In Lamentations 5, the voices of the powerful brought low are heard. But they seem not to have learned a lesson. They still feel that they ought to be treated better because they are the elite. But the reader knows that the pain they experience after the fall of Jerusalem is the pain that the poor experience every day.

THE TEXT IN THE LIFE OF THE CHURCH

Women in War

In Lamentations, rape and the sexual abuse of women are noted in metaphor (in ch. 1) and in fact (5:11). Rape and sexual slavery have always been a part of war, a part on which the media rarely report. And rape does not stop when the war is over. The winners, whoever they may be, take advantage of a vulnerable population of females who have no one to defend them. One might wonder what political or military purpose rape could possibly serve in war. The function of rape is to destroy individuals and communities. In patriarchal societies, women and girls, even when gang-raped at gunpoint, are often blamed for being raped and then are ostracized from whatever is left of their families and communities. Many of those women and girls will give birth without proper medical attention, and many will die along with their babies. Those who survive will be forced to raise children that they did not choose to bear, without an income, without nutritious food, without a secure home environment, and without educational facilities, guaranteeing that many of those children will never reach their full potential. In some cases, the brutal rapes will render women and girls infertile. Many will become infected with sexually transmitted diseases. The psychological trauma that results from rape is as destructive as the assault upon the body. And sexual abuse is not limited to women and girls. Men and boys are also subjected to such abuse even within their own militaries by fellow soldiers as well as by enemy soldiers. The church, in its writings on war and peace, has rarely given attention to the prevalence of rape and sexual abuse in war and the sexual slavery of women and girls. The book of Lamentations has not been silent about these issues, and neither should the church.

Moreover, after the war, things do not go back to normal for these women. The phenomenon emerges of war widows, young women with small children. These women are unlikely to ever marry again because the war has killed so many young men. There are parts of Vanni (where the final battles of the civil war took place in Sri Lanka) where the adult female to adult male ratio is seven to one. The patriarchal cultures in which these women live do not permit them free and open access to society. This is because their cultures expect men—husbands, fathers, adult sons—to work in and to negotiate with the outside world on behalf of the family. But the women have no husbands, fathers, or adult sons (in the case of middle-aged and older women) because they were killed during the war. In some cases even their young sons were taken to be child soldiers. Women who actively seek help from government offices or aid agencies are ridiculed and labeled as prostitutes—as a means of controlling them and keeping them in their place. When women ask how they are to feed their children because the war has taken away jobs, they are told that they can become prostitutes for the soldiers who are occupying the territory. Mennonite women faced the same issues when they were driven out of Russia (Ukraine) after the Second World War. Some immigrated to Paraguay, where they had to clear land, build houses, cook food, plant both gardens and cash crops, and raise their children, without the help of men who had been killed during the war. Needless to say, children, too, were forced to do work that normally would be handled by adults. One settlement became known as "the women's colony" because of the absence of men in it.

Reading on Two Levels

In affluent societies, biblical texts are read from the point of view of the affluent. It takes greater effort to look at the text through the eyes of the poor, the suffering, and those who are oppressed if one is not in that situation. The collective voice in Lamentations 5 is that of people who were affluent in the past but have suffered a reversal of fortunes. The church needs to learn to read this poem from the point of view of both the affluent and the poor. The affluent are now suffering. They deserve a response of compassion and indeed help. They are human beings and children of God. But the text should also sensitize the affluent to the daily plight of the poor. They also deserve a response of compassion and indeed help. They are human beings and children of God.

Remembering and Forgetting

Relationships are built on remembering and forgetting. Remembering the things that brought the group together, that nurtured the relationship, that made life better—and forgetting the gaffes, thoughtlessness, and slights that are not worth fretting over. This poem begins with a request that God remember, and it ends with an expression of fear that God has not remembered. Rituals of remembering have always been a part of the life of the church. Every Sunday we remember the resurrection. Every Christmas we remember that Jesus came into the world. In our Sunday schools and sermons, we remember the teachings of Christ. During Lent and each Friday of the year, we remember the suffering and death of Jesus. These times of remembering are built into the church calendar. While we do not build in times of forgetting as such (we do not want to forget everything lest we do not learn from past experiences), we do have times of confession and repentance to restore relationships that have been bruised.

Healing and Hope

Throughout the thousands of years since this text was written, civilizations have come and gone. Wars, natural disasters, or rumors of resources in other places have caused migrations and emigrations. But humans have stubbornly rebuilt and re-created community life whenever and wherever it has been disrupted. Ultimately, there are voices that remain, such as the ones that speak in and through these poems. That in itself is a sign that life goes on and that hope remains.

This is the last poem in the book of Lamentations. This and the other poems are meant to assist in the mourning process. They affirm that expressions of anger and grief are appropriate and even necessary for healing, restoration, and growth. These poems are meant not only to be read and studied but also to be incorporated into the worship life of the community.

Fr. S. D. P. Selvan composed the following poem after the end of the civil war in Sri Lanka. Vanni is the region that experienced the brunt of the last years of the war (2006–9). The poem was originally written in the Tamil language. In Tamil, it is an alphabetic acrostic and has a 3:2 beat [Acrostic, p. 111]. Fr. Selvan also produced the English translation that appears below.

Lamentation: A Rereading of Vanni in the Perspective of Underside History

01. Woe of Vanni

    1. Oh see how we have fallen to a pathetic state of woe.
       We are in a stage of destruction.
       We are in agony and distress.

    2. Oh see how there was no availability of *six-feet land*
       even after a continuous search to bury one of our own dead.

    3. Oh see how we lost everything
       and dispersed and scattered from place by place
       due to awful violence.

    4. Oh see how we have stopped and silenced
       the funeral rites of our own loved ones.
       We were not allowed to taste any improvement.

    5. Oh see how our feelings and emotions were frozen
       due to the unavailability of simple food, clothes, and sleep.

    6. Oh see how we have forgotten our lives,
       which were once full of enthusiasm and excitement.

    7. Oh see how we have controlled our usual responses
       and buried our inner spirit.

    8. Oh see how we have come together
       and engaged in mocking and humiliating our own past
       and history of hopeful times.

    9. Oh see how we buried ourselves
       in fear and doubt deeply
       due to the sorrowful situation
       we were forced to face.

    10. Oh see how we loudly praised
        our oppressors for our own survival.

11. Oh see how we went here and there,
    looking for persons who were snatched
    by unidentified persons, and cried without stopping.

12. Oh see how we became a community of destruction
    who think, plan, and speak evil
    for survival and passive existence.

02. Reasons for the Suffering of Vanni

1. The reason for the suffering
   was the act of harm and crime by those who made us live
   always with death fever.

2. The reason for the suffering
   was doubt and suspicion
   that led to the death of equality,
   that changed our land to graveyards.

3. The reason for the suffering
   was selfishness
   that said "bye" to us
   and whose act was shouting for their rights
   at the very cost of our lives.

4. The reason for the suffering
   was patriotism
   that determined that they were born to die
   with love for their motherland
   through bloodshed and destruction to us,
   without love for human lives.

5. The reason for the suffering
   was the ones who praised war and arms traders,
   and we became consumers of war and their armaments
   in Vanni, the war market.

6. The reason for the suffering
   was political parties
   who like rubber change according to the conditions,
   without any principles,
   to dictatorship and unjust laws and governance.

7. The reason for the suffering
   was betrayal in the name of brokenness in their relationships,
   divisions, and different interests.

8. The reason for the suffering
   Was the rule of Guns and praising of violence
   as peak of wisdom in human history of cosmos.

9. The reason for the suffering
   was greediness over land
   that created many wars through which we lost
   all basic rights, basic needs, and basic structures.

10. The reason for the suffering
    was deserters who acted as good committed lovers in the past
    and turned to evil for us to suffer
    as aliens with loneliness in our own land.

11. The reason for all their suffering
    was the militarization,
    which destroyed the human existence totally.

12. The reason for all their suffering
    was the intoxication of racism and pride of mother tongue,
    which created disunity, envy, and fights.

13. The reason for all their suffering
    was the idea of "whoever reigns is not our matter, let us live,"
    which made sure their existence here and abroad,
    at the sacrifice and cost for us.

14. The reason for the suffering
    was the ones who gave armaments and war strategy,
    which killed and destroyed us.

15. The reason for the suffering
    was felling of trees and destruction of jungles
    to make sure
    the poverty prevails,
    which made us to live as beggars.

16. The reason for the suffering
    was economic low profile and poverty
    through killing of youngsters,
    which made us to suffer in chaos.

17. The reason for the suffering
    was raping and killing of women and children,
    which made us to suffer within.

18. The reason for all their suffering
    was the introduction of machines
    to replace the work of human labor in paddy fields for the cultivation,
    which made us to suffer with hunger.

03. Repentance

    1. We died without repentance because we accepted divisions.

    2. We died with dependence because we trusted foreigners and foreign powers.

    3. We died by our votes because of our situation.

    4. We died by guns because we did not follow nonviolence.

    5. We died of greediness over land because we rejected humanness.

    6. We died by our irresponsibility because we accepted and followed selfish politics.

04. Will Vanni Restore? An Optimistic Search

    1. Destructed grasses are growing.
       Will destructed Vanni grow?

    2. Shoot is coming up from the stump.
       Will broken Vanni sprout?

    3. Cried child laughs.
       Will weeping Vanni laugh?

Lamentations 5:1-22

4. Destructed grasses grow
   due to the unity.

5. Stumped tree sprout
   due to the optimism.

6. Cried child laughed,
   due to the humanness.

7. If there be unity,
   definitely destructed Vanni will grow.

8. If there will be optimism,
   definitely broken Vanni will sprout.

9. If there will be humanism,
   definitely weeping Vanni will laugh.

10. Unity, optimism, and humanism
    are essentials for the life of Vanni.

11. Divisions, pessimism, and demolition
    cause the destruction of the cosmos.

12. Woe to those who sow divisions.
    They will become solitude.

13. Woe to who share pessimism.
    They (walking dead bodies) will get demolished.

14. Woe to those who plant destruction.
    They will certainly be wiped out.

15. Oh People of Vanni,
    Come together for the birth of Vanni.

16. Oh People of Vanni,
    Plan out for the life of Vanni.

17. Oh People of Vanni,
    Engage in action for the resurrection of Vanni.

18. Through the resurrection of humanness
    only world would get restoration.

05. Restoration of Vanni: A Dream

    1. Cultivation of violence is destruction.
        Therefore Vanni is in woe.
        Let humanness blossom in human hearts.
        Let holiness blossom in the world.

    2. We live as selfish people.
        Our land was captured by violence.
        Our land was full of land mines.
        We got militarized.

    3. Our selfishness ruled us.
        Our children got killed.
        Our sons disappeared and lost.
        Our daughters wounded and raped and severely injured.

    4. We lived as selfish people.
        Our babies suffered in poverty.
        Our children died of disease.
        Our students lost education.

    5. Our selfishness ruled us.
        Our economy declined.
        Our sea resources were robbed.
        Our children became unemployed.

    6. We lived as selfish people.
        Our environment got polluted.
        Our land got filled with polythene and plastics.
        We eat and drink poison.

    7. Our selfishness ruled us.
        Our land ruled by selfish farmers.
        Our soil exploited by egotistic damagers.
        Our fundamental rights were violated.

    8. We lived as selfish people.
        War has taken place in our land.

Conflict was created in our soil.
Armaments were purchased in our territory.

9. Dictatorship of our selfishness is enough.
Destruction in our land is sufficient.
Violation of our rights is adequate.
Destruction taken for and in us is enough.

10. Let humanness rule us.
Let holiness encircle us.
Nonviolence is our breath.
Love is our conscience.

11. Let humanness rule us.
Let holiness encircle us.
Equality is our heart.
Sharing is our action.

12. Let humanness rule us.
Let holiness encircle us.
Good governance is our dream.
Reign of people is our wish.

13. Let humanness rule us.
Let holiness encircle us.
We do not want war.
Let war armaments get frozen.

14. Let humanness rule us.
Let holiness encircle us.
Let women sleep in peace.
Let children live and rule with rights.

15. Let humanness rule us.
Let holiness encircle us.
Justice is our mind.
Peace is our chest.

16. Let humanness rule us.
Let holiness encircle us.
Let wounds of victims get healed.
Let relationships develop deeper between the ones who still live.

17. Let humanness rule us.
    Let holiness encircle us.
    Let there be sustainable development.
    Let the decisions of victims be carried out.

18. Let humanness rule us.
    Let holiness encircle us.
    Let the voice of Vanni live long.
    Let Vanni get restoration soon in the reality beyond dreams.

Outline of Lamentations

There Is No Comforter for Zion	**1:1-22**
A Lonely City	1:1-2
Exile	1:3
Zion Mourns	1:4-6
Jerusalem Remembers	1:7
The Charge against Jerusalem	1:8-9
Violation	1:10-11
The Charge against God	1:12-17
Confession	1:18-21b
Call for Vengeance	1:21c-22
The Lord Has Become Like an Enemy	**2:1-22**
Charges against the Lord	2:1-9b
The Fate of the City's Inhabitants Described	2:9c-12
An Address to Jerusalem	2:13-19
An Address to the Lord	2:20-22
The Lord Will Not Reject Forever	**3:1-66**
Complaint	3:1-20
Turning Point	3:21
Affirmation of God's Trustworthiness	3:22-39
Self-Examination	3:40-41
Complaint Addressed to God and Response	3:42-60
Call for Vengeance	3:61-66

War Changes Behavior and Social Structures — 4:1-22
Starvation in Jerusalem — 4:1-10
The Reason for the Deprivation — 4:11
The World Looked On in Disbelief — 4:12
The Fate of the Prophets and Priests — 4:13-16
No Help Arrived — 4:17-20
Next, It Is Edom's Turn — 4:21-22

Restore Us to Yourself — 5:1-22
The Request — 5:1
A List of Grievances — 5:2-5
The Cost of Survival — 5:6
The Sins of the Ancestors — 5:7
Roles Have Been Reversed — 5:8-13
No One Has Fun Anymore — 5:14-18
Appeal to God — 5:19-22

Essays for Lamentations

ACROSTIC The type of acrostic that is found in the first four chapters of Lamentations is based on the Hebrew alphabet. In such poems, the first word of each line begins with a successive letter of the alphabet in order. The Hebrew alphabet has twenty-two consonantal letters. Vowels are not counted as letters in Hebrew. Vowels were added to written texts over a long period of time, beginning late in the biblical period. They appear as dots, crosses, and lines in medieval texts. In Lamentations, each verse of chapters 1 and 2 begins with the next letter of the alphabet. If the first and second chapters of Lamentations were structured as alphabetic acrostics using English letters, they would look like this (though the lines would vary in length from line to line):

v. 1   A_____ _____ (one line, a bicolon pair)
        _____ _____
        _____ _____

v. 2   B_____ _____
        _____ _____
        _____ _____

v. 3   C_____ _____
        _____ _____
        _____ _____

and they would continue to the letter Z.

The third chapter would look something like this:

v. 1   A_____ _____
v. 2   A_____ _____
v. 3   A_____ _____

v. 4   B_____ _____
v. 5   B_____ _____
v. 6   B_____ _____

v. 7   C_____ _____
v. 8   C_____ _____
v. 9   C_____ _____

The fourth chapter would look something like this:

v. 1   A_____ _____
        _____ _____

v. 2   B_____ _____
        _____ _____

v. 3   C_____ _____
        _____ _____

The last chapter, which is not structured as an alphabetic acrostic, would look something like this:

v. 1   G_____ _____
v. 2   N_____ _____
v. 3   J_____ _____

Chapters 1, 2, and 4 of Lamentations have twenty-two verses and are alphabetic acrostics. The third chapter has sixty-six verses. It is a triple acrostic. Each letter of the Hebrew alphabet is repeated three times. Verses 1, 2, and 3 of chapter 3 begin with the first letter of the Hebrew alphabet. Verses 4, 5 and 6 begin with the second letter of the Hebrew alphabet. Acrostics also appear in the Psalms. Psalms 25 and 34 are structured as alphabetic acrostics. Psalm 119 is an acrostic that repeats each letter eight times, which is why it is so long. Psalms 9 and 10 together are structured as an acrostic. The first half of the alphabet appears in Psalm 9 and the second half of the alphabet appears in Psalm 10, indicating that these two were originally one psalm. The capable woman portion of Proverbs (31:10-31) is also structured as an acrostic. The use of the alphabetic acrostic form was to aid in the memorization of the poem. It is also thought that the form was used in laments to indicate that grief must be fully expressed and then end. One should not grieve forever. One should reengage the community and return to normal life.

CAPTURE AND DESTRUCTION OF JERUSALEM The capture of the city of Jerusalem began over ten years before its final destruction, when the empire of Babylon seized control of the city, imprisoned the reigning king (Jehoiachin), raided the temple, and carried away into exile all of the officials and affluent people. The king of Babylon set Mattaniah, an uncle of Jehoiachin, on the throne, hoping that he would be a docile puppet of Babylon. Mattaniah's name (meaning "gift of Yahweh") was changed to Zedekiah (meaning "righteousness of Yahweh") to symbolize his new subordinate position. Both are exalted and appropriate names for an Israelite. Changing names throughout the course of a lifetime was not unusual in ancient times. Personal names often changed to reflect qualities of that person that were not known or developed at birth. Abram is renamed *Abraham* by God to reflect his new reality. He will be the ancestor of many people. However, Mattaniah is renamed by a Babylonian king, not by God or his own people. The king uses naming as a device to promote Mattaniah in the eyes of the people of Jerusalem and to indicate his control over him. The one who has the power to name has the power to control. This is why Daniel and his friends are renamed in the Persian court. In that case, they are given Persian names. The king of Babylon does not want to alienate the people of Judah and Jerusalem by giving Mattaniah a Babylonian name, but he does want to change the name to indicate that he is in control of the new king of Israel. So he gives him an Israelite name of his own choosing.

Zedekiah, however, began to chafe against the boot of Babylon and rebelled during the ninth year of his reign by withholding tribute to Babylon. The rebellion was stayed, and Zedekiah was blinded and taken captive to Babylon. The last thing that he saw was the slaughter of all of his sons by Babylonian fighting men. The Babylonians dispensed with kingship in Israel and appointed a governor named Gedaliah over the land. He in turn was killed, not by Babylonians, but by his fellow Judeans because they saw him as a traitor. Thus the last remaining Israelite kingdom came to an end. The year was 587/586 BCE.

People remember that Judeans (now called Jews because they are descendants of the tribe of Judah) were sent into exile to Babylon, and some were scattered to other places. They often forget that many Israelites were left in the land to cope with the loss of their city and the political, social, and economic structures that undergirded them. The book of Lamentations is reflecting on those who remained in the city after its fall.

CITY The cities of ancient Israel were small. They were built primarily for defensive purposes. Cities were defined by walls and gates that surrounded them. The gates were more than a way to enter or leave the city. They housed chambers where a number of activities took place. Space around and inside the gate was used for marketplaces and courts. When the people of the city were called to assemble, it was usually to an area outside of the gate, where there was ample space. The city wall typically was a double-walled structure with space between the walls for storage and housing. Ancient Israelite cities were not planned. The spaces between buildings formed alleyways through which people could access their homes and businesses. A second wall within the city might separate the palace compound from the rest of the city. The palace was located at the highest and most protected place in the town.

In addition to the physical structures, a city was defined by its economic life. In contrast to today, many people in ancient Israelite cities had some connection to rural life. They or family members were farmers. But the city also housed a skilled labor class (artisans, traders), mercenaries who worked for the king or whomever held the highest rank in the city, priests, and a professional class. Because the market and court were in the city, it was a place that drew a diverse crowd of local people and foreigners, who rubbed shoulders on a daily or weekly basis, exchanging both material goods and ideas.

COMMUNAL LAMENT In his pioneering work on the Psalms, Hermann Gunkel (87) writes that in the communal laments found in the book of Psalms, the first-person language represents the leader of the community speaking on behalf of the community. In Lamentations, the "I" often refers to the personified Jerusalem. Gunkel further observes that Lamentations 1 contains characteristics of both the dirge and the communal lament form. A dirge is a secular poem that "normally concerns *the death of an individual*" (Gunkel: 95-95, with original emph.). Claus Westermann (117) lists two characteristics of the dirge form. They are "the mournful cry" and the "description of misery." In Lamentations, dirgelike material appears to mourn the death, not of an individual, but of the city itself *[Dirge, p. 115]*.

Toni Craven (27), drawing from the work of Gunkel and Westermann, identifies a sixfold structure that is characteristic of a lament. It begins with an address to God, followed by a complaint, confession of trust, petition, words of assurance, and a vow of praise. Some or all of the six are present in each of the poems in Lamentations *[Hebrew Poetry, p. 116]*.

COVENANT A covenant is an agreement between two parties. In ancient times, kingdoms signed covenants for mutual protection and support. Examples of covenants in treaty form that we have from the ancient Near East spell out the relationship between empires and smaller kingdoms. The relationship between God and Israel is also mediated through covenants, and a number of covenants are mentioned in the Bible. God makes a covenant with Noah and all living things in Genesis 9:9-17. The stipulations of that covenant are that God will never again destroy the earth by means of a flood. Genesis 17 and other texts refer to a covenant made between God and Abram. God promises Abram land and descendants. In exchange, Abram is required to circumcise all male members of his household, whether slave or free, as a sign of their place in the Abrahamic covenant. This covenant applies to descendants of Abram as well.

A covenant was also made between God and the Israelites at Sinai, which obligated the Israelites to follow the instructions that God gave to them. The Davidic covenant stipulated that there would always be a descendant of Israel on the throne (2 Sam 23:5; Ps 89:3-4). There are hints and references to other covenants as well. During the heyday of the Biblical Theology movement in the middle of the twentieth century, Walther Eichrodt (1961) proposed that covenant was a theological theme that guided and united the texts of the OT. Covenant is mentioned in many books of the OT but not all.

CREDO The *credo* is a name given to the brief statements of Israel's origins and the basis of God's claim on Israel (Deut 6:21-24; 26:5-9; Josh 24:2-13). Gerhard von Rad (1962: 121) isolated the statements that he considered to be credos and identified them as "confessional summaries of the saving history." Von Rad thought that the entire OT was shaped around the theology of the credos.

DIRGE A *dirge* is a funeral song. Like the lament, it expresses grief. Dirges from ancient Israel have certain common characteristics. They generally contain a word such as *Alas* or *Woe*. Dirges state the cause of the grief: the death of the beloved. They contrast the present situation of mourning with happier times in the past. Characteristics of a dirge and a lament overlap, but there is a significant difference. The situation that caused the rise of a dirge is irreversible, and the focus is on the past. Not so of laments. Laments look to the future and usually offer hope of change and amelioration of the situation that caused the grief (e.g., 2 Sam 1:19-27).

ELEPHANTINE PAPYRI The Elephantine papyri are a set of letters and documents written by Jews living in Egypt during the fifth century BCE. They provide a glimpse into the life situation of a Jewish community in exile and their attempts to maintain contact and to receive guidance from their compatriots in Jerusalem. From these letters we know that the temple in Jerusalem was not the only Jewish temple in existence in ancient times. There was also one in Egypt.

THE ELITE In ancient Israel, as in all of the kingdoms of the ancient Near East, there was a power center of wealthy and influential families and clans. This is in contrast to the vast majority of people, who were poor and had little say in the political, economic, or social structures that kept them poor and disenfranchised (Neh 5). Some books of the OT, such as 1 & 2 Samuel and 1 & 2 Kings, focus on the elite: the kings, the priests, the wealthy, and the privileged (see also Amos). The choices that they made affected the lives of everyone else. The frequent admonitions of the prophets to aid the poor, the needy, the orphans, the widows, and the strangers indicate that those to whom those admonitions were addressed were not the poor, the needy, the orphans, the widows, and the strangers.

When catastrophe struck, whether in the form of a war or natural disaster, it affected the privileged and the underprivileged in different ways. During a famine in Canaan, Jacob, for example, was able to send his sons to Egypt to purchase food because he had money (silver) and items to trade. One might ask, "How did the poor fare who did not have anything to trade and who could not afford to travel to a foreign country where goods were available during the famine?" Much worse, we can guess. War also affects different strata of society in different ways. That was particularly evident when the southern Israelite kingdom of Judah fell to the Babylonian army. The upper strata of society was targeted, just the opposite of what happens most often today. The king of Babylon killed and exiled the elite of Jerusalemite society (relatives of the king, the educated, the wealthy) because they posed the greatest threat to him. In the book of Daniel, Daniel and his friends are taken captive and educated in the king of Babylon's court because they are scions of the royal family (Dan 1:3-4). The king hoped to create loyal subjects of them as he had them molded into the culture and mores of Babylon. His eventual goal was probably to send the boys back, fully acculturated into Babylonian ways of thinking and loyal to the Babylonian king. The king did not care about the poor workers or small farmers or farm laborers left behind in Judah because they did not have the wealth, power, or influence to foment a rebellion against him or to be of much help to him in a positive way. Those people were negatively affected by the war but they were not the targets of it.

Some of the poems in Lamentations are clearly focused on the plight of the elite and not the poor because they complain about conditions that the poor live with every day. The elite think that they should not be doing things like gathering firewood or grinding flour (Lam 5). This study distinguishes between the voices of the elite and the voices of the poor in the poems of Lamentations. This is not to discredit the voices of either, but to point out that there are socioeconomic differences between the two, and how they experience the aftermath of war differs. Because both are human, it is easy to sympathize with them whether privileged or not.

EVIL SPIRITS In the OT, evil spirits were thought to come from God (see Judg 9:23; 1 Sam 16:14-16, 23; 18:10; 19:9). Although there are multiple references to idols and other gods, there are relatively few references to evil spirits. The *saṭan* figure that appears in Job is not an evil being; it is a "devil's advocate," which means one who presents an alternate viewpoint. Usually the word appears with *the* before it: "the adversary" (cf. Num 22:22). English translations typically drop the *the*, capitalize the *S*, and make it a name. The presentation of Satan as an evil being begins to appear in a couple of the latest books of the OT (see 1 Chron 21:1; Zech 3:1-2). In the OT, people believe that most of what they experience as bad comes from God or other humans.

HEBREW POETRY Hebrew poetry is primarily characterized by a pattern of two cola, or half lines (occasionally there are more than two cola), that are related to each other in some way. Robert Lowth, an eighteenth-century English scholar, used the term *parallelism* to identify the bicolon pair (see Alter: 3). He noticed that sometimes in biblical Hebrew poetry, the second colon repeats the basic thought of the first colon (synonymous parallelism). An example is found in Psalm 100:4:

> Enter his gates with thanksgiving
>   and his courts with praise. (NIV)

The second colon is repeating the thought of the first colon. Sometimes the second colon says the opposite of the first colon (antithetic parallelism). This is particularly a pattern in wisdom literature such as Proverbs, where the good behavior is contrasted with bad behavior. An example is found in Proverbs 22:3:

The prudent see danger and take refuge,
    but the simple keep going and pay the penalty. (NIV)

Sometimes, the second colon completes the thought of the first colon (synthetic parallelism), as in Song of Songs 1:9:

I liken you, my darling, to a mare
    among Pharaoh's chariot horses. (NIV)

The relationship between the first and second cola can be more complex than what Lowth describes. Robert Alter (ch. 1) rejects the notion that synonymous parallelism exists. He argues that when a second colon is repeating the first colon, the intent is to add intensification.

Another common structure in biblical poetry is the chiasm. A simple form of chiasm involves two half-line pairs. In the chiasm, a referent at the beginning of the first colon appears at the end of the second colon. A referent at the end of the first colon appears at the beginning of the second colon. It forms the Greek letter chi. In English, the letter X shows the structure. The bicolon pair below is taken from Psalm 29:10. The references to the Lord and to sitting alternate in the pair:

The Lord over the floods is seated.
He is seated, the Lord king forever. (AT)

Hebrew poetry has structures and characteristics that are not visible in English translation. These characteristics add to the aesthetics and complexity of the poem. They also aid in the interpretation of poetic texts.

HISTORIOGRAPHY The term *historiography* literally means "history writing." Ancient people did not practice the scholarly discipline of history that we know today. They did not diligently check their facts or always seek documents that would support their accounts of the past. They were writing the story of where they had come from as it had been passed down to them. That account of origins was shaped by their theological and cultural beliefs about who they were as a people. Scholars refer to this as *historiography* rather than *history*.

MORPHEME A morpheme is the smallest unit of language that has meaning. The noun *word* is a morpheme. *Love* is a morpheme. *Duck* is a morpheme. These words cannot be broken into a smaller unit that conveys meaning. An *s* added to the end of a word is a morpheme because it indicates a plural. The noun *words* has two morphemes, *word* and *s*. An *ed* at the end of a word that indicates a past tense is a morpheme. *Blessed* as a verb has two morphemes, *bless* and *ed*. In Hebrew, verbs and nouns have morphemes directly attached to the end of the verb or noun such as "our" and "their." "Our house" in Hebrew would appear as "houseour." In English, those morphemes stand alone.

ORALITY Until recently, scholars speculated that much of the OT existed in an oral form before it was written down. Priests, prophets, and ordinary people told the stories and passed down the ethical injunctions from one generation to another in word and song, in the context of formal rituals and within the family and community. In the case of Lamentations, the scholar Westermann (99) thought that from an oral beginning, the poems were later cast into their acrostic structure *[Acrostic, p. 111]*. He also thought that the presence of the tight acrostic structure indicates that they were originally "more apt to be read than heard" (99). The long tradition of singing Lamentations in the synagogue might challenge that notion. More recently, David Carr, in his book *Writing on the Tablet of the Heart*, examines the relationship between the oral and the written in ancient literature. He has proposed that there was more of an interplay between the two formats. Carr thinks that the OT was written primarily to provide an educational curriculum counter to that of the prevailing Greek culture.

TARGUM The OT, with a few small exceptions, was originally written in Hebrew. After the exile, for everyday conversation most Jews used Aramaic, a Semitic language similar to Hebrew. In the synagogues and the temple in worship services Hebrew continued to be used. Because the average person no longer understood Hebrew, translations were made of the OT (which in Judaism is referred to as the Tanakh) into the Aramaic language. Those translations are called Targums. Often the Targums contextualize the text by adding to it or paraphrasing. For example, *Targum Lamentations* (in the text of Codex Urbinates 1) inserts in Lamentations 5:11 that women were raped by Romans. Clearly this is a later addition to the text. Romans were not involved in the 587/586 BCE fall of Jerusalem to Babylon. Nevertheless, Targums are important witnesses to early biblical texts. That means, for example, that when the earliest Hebrew texts that we have (the Dead Sea Scrolls) and the earliest translations that we have (such as the Septuagint, which was written in Greek) have different versions of the same OT text, a Targum might help to determine which was the earlier or better reading.

YAHWEH The personal name of God, *Yahweh*, appears close to six thousand times in the OT. This is not obvious to people who read English translations of the Bible. Most of the time when the name *Yahweh* appears in the Hebrew text, the phrase *the* LORD appears in the English text. The reason for this is that during the period between the testaments, Jews stopped pronouncing this name for God. They feared that the name would be misused or blasphemed, either deliberately or by accident. Therefore when reading the text, they substituted another Hebrew word, *Adonai* (normally translated *Lord*), wherever the divine name *Yahweh* appears in the Bible.

Readers of Hebrew know that the divine name as it appears in Scripture is spelled with four consonantal letters that transliterate into English as YHWH. In ancient times, Hebrew was written without vowels. However, scholars who study the development of language think that the pronunciation would have been *Yahweh*. When vowel markings were added to the text, the vowels for *Adonai* were added to the consonants YHWH of God's name. This was done so that the reader would remember to read *Adonai* at that point. *Jehovah*, a familiar term from older English translations, results from combining the four consonants of one name (YHWH) with the vowels of the other (*Adonai*). According to Hartman and Sperling (675), early Christian writers preserved the original pronunciation of the name, which was similar to the English pronunciation *Yahweh*.

The problem with consistently substituting the phrase *the* LORD for *Yahweh* is that the meaning of the text is altered. LORD is hierarchical language. It is the language of patriarchy and domination. It is appropriate language for some texts, which is why *Adonai* (Lord) is used there. Sometimes the point is that God is Lord, King, Master, and so forth. But that language signifies difference and distance. The divine name *Yahweh* indicates intimacy, love, one with whom one can have a personal relationship. That can be lost when *the* LORD is used consistently where *Adonai* does not appear in the Bible.

ZION THEOLOGY Zion theology states that Jerusalem is given special significance and is set aside as a holy place (Pss 78:68; 132:13-14). At one point in Israelite history, Zion theology assumed the inviolability of Jerusalem, meaning that the city would never be destroyed because it was God's specially protected place (Pss 46:5; 48:3). Early on, Zion theology was a southern Israelite phenomenon. Most of the northern tribes did not subscribe to it because it fused politics and the religion of Israel. After the fall of the southern kingdom and the end of an independent Israelite state, Zion theology was reshaped to reflect a new reality. Zion, on the one hand, was synonymous with Jerusalem, a real city (or sometimes only the Temple Mount area), but more importantly, it transcended the physical city. It became a symbol and a hope of the Jewish people. Zion was a holy (set-apart) place imbued with holiness, God's grace. The last chapter of the book of Zechariah has a beautiful image of Jerusalem as a place of worship for all families of the earth. Jerusalem is a place so holy that even the bells worn by the horses will be inscribed "Holy to the LORD" and the ordinary cooking pots will be designated "holy" (Zech 14:16-21 NJPS). The nations will come to Jerusalem to pay homage to the true God and to have their disputes arbitrated (Ps 68:29; Isa 2:2-4). For further on this tradition, see Ollenburger; also see Roberts.

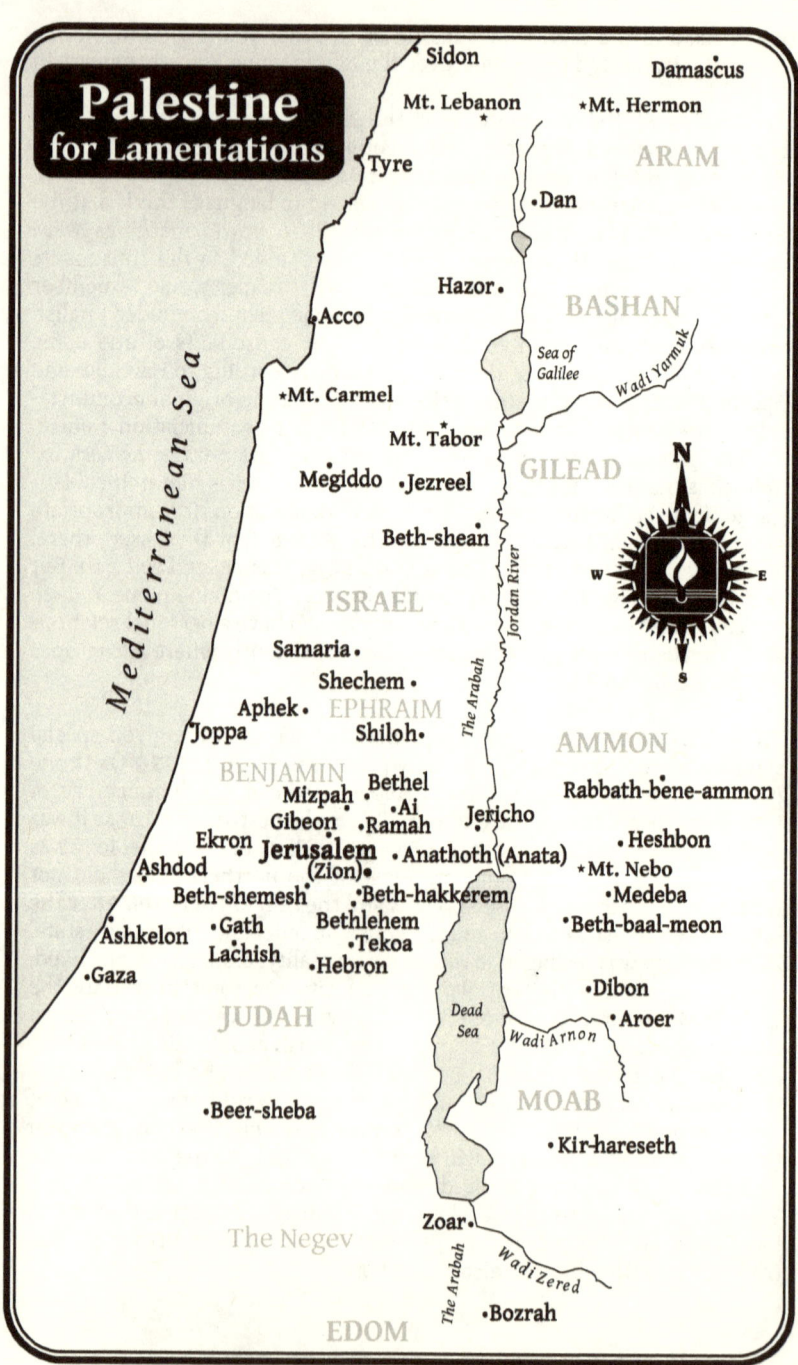

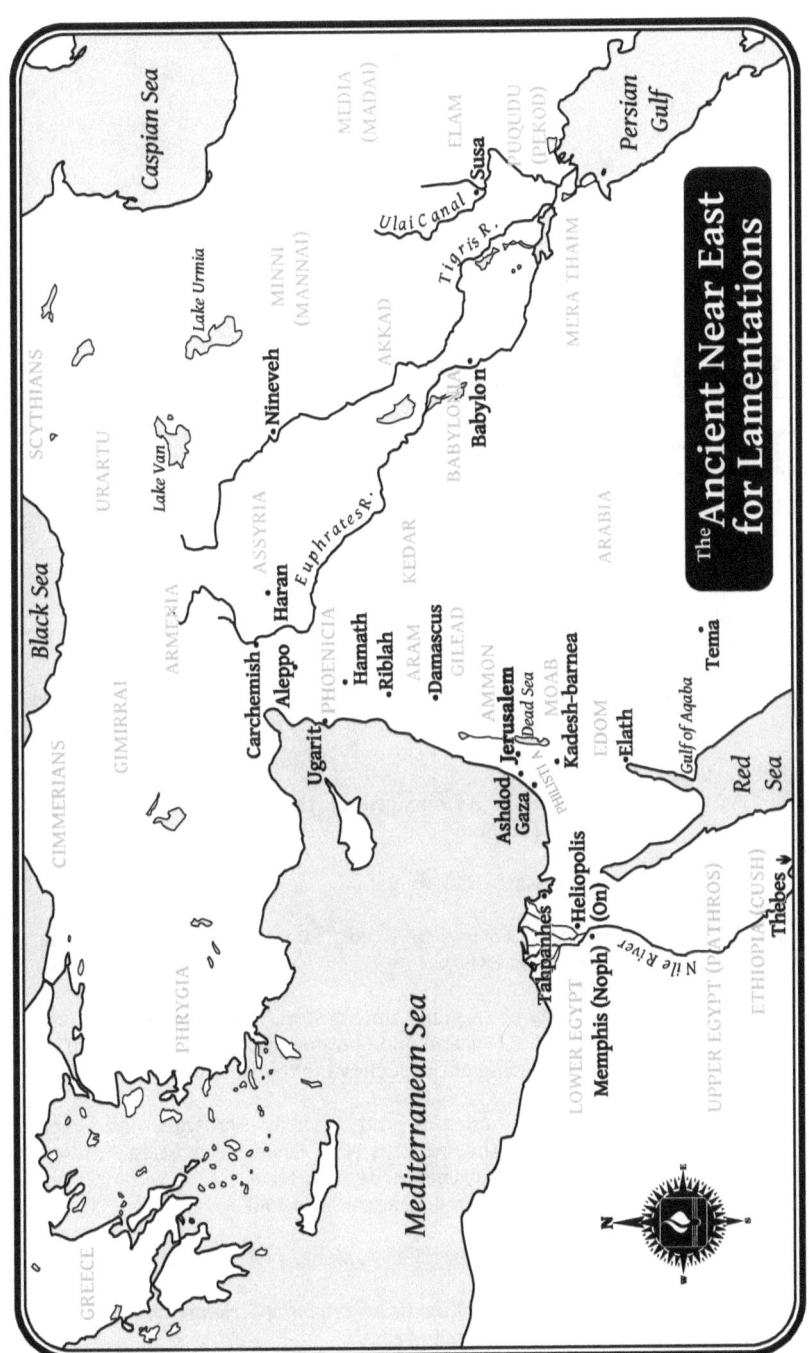

Bibliography for Lamentations

Alter, Robert
    1985   *The Art of Biblical Poetry.* New York: Basic Books.

Anderson, Gary A.
    1991   *A Time to Mourn, a Time to Dance: The Expression of Grief and Joy in Israelite Religion.* University Park, PA: Pennsylvania State University Press.

Beier, Matthias
    2004   *A Violent God-Image: An Introduction to the Work of Eugen Drewermann.* New York: Continuum.

Bergant, Dianne
    2003   *Lamentations.* Nashville: Abingdon.

Berlin, Adele
    2002   *Lamentations: A Commentary.* Old Testament Library. Louisville: Westminster John Knox.

Brady, Christian M. M.
    2002   "The Theology of Targum Lamentations." Paper presented in the "Lamentations in Ancient and Contemporary Contexts Group," at the Annual Meeting of the Society of Biblical Literature, Toronto.

Brug, John F.
    1997   "Near Eastern Acrostics and Biblical Acrostics and Their Relationship to Other Ancient Near Eastern Acrostics." 2nd ed. http://www.wlsessays.net/node/357. 1st ed., NEH Seminar: The Bible and Near Eastern Literature, Yale 1987.

Budde, Karl D.
    1898   *Die fünf Megillot.* Freiburg: J. C. B. Mohr.

Carr, David M.
    2005   *Writing on the Tablet of the Heart: Origins of Scripture and Literature.* Oxford: Oxford University Press.

Bibliography for Lamentations

Craven, Toni
    1992   *The Book of Psalms.* Collegeville, MN: Liturgical Press.

Dobbs-Allsopp, Frederick William
    1993   *Weep, O Daughter of Zion: A Study of the City-Lament Genre in the Hebrew Bible.* Rome: Pontifical Biblical Institute.
    2002   *Lamentations.* Interpretation. Louisville: John Knox.

Douglas, Mary
    1966   *Purity and Danger.* London: Routledge & Kegan Paul.

Eichrodt, Walther
    1961–67   *Theology of the Old Testament.* Translated by J. A. Baker. Vols. 1–2. Philadelphia: Westminster.

Greenberg, Blu
    1982   *How to Run a Traditional Jewish Household.* New York: Simon & Schuster.

Grossberg, Daniel
    2004   "Lamentations." In *The Jewish Study Bible,* edited by Adele Berlin and Marc Zvi Brettler, 1587–1602. Oxford: Oxford University Press.

Gunkel, Hermann
    1998   *Introduction to the Psalms.* Completed by Joachim Begrich. Translated by James D. Nogalski. Macon, GA: Mercer University Press.

Hartman, Louis F., and David Sperling
    2006   "God, Names of." *Enclyclopaedia Judaica,* 7:672–78. Edited by Fred Skolnick and Michael Berenbaum. 2nd ed. New York: Tomson Gale.

Heschel, Abraham
    1962   *The Prophets.* New York: Harper & Row.

Hillers, Delbert R.
    1992   *Lamentations.* Rev. ed. Anchor Bible. New York: Doubleday.

Horsch, James
    2007   Email interview. "Uniform Series." Aug. 17.

Kübler-Ross, Elizabeth
    1969   *On Death and Dying.* New York: MacMillan.

Kushner, Harold
    1981   *When Bad Things Happen to Good People.* New York: Schocken.

Lacey, Marc
    2004   "Nyala Journal: Singers of Sudan Study War No More." *New York Times,* under "World," July 12.

Lee, Nancy C.
    2002   *The Singers of Lamentations: Cities under Siege, from Ur to Jerusalem to Sarajevo.* Leiden: E. J. Brill.
    2010   *Lyrics of Lament: From Tragedy to Transformation.* Minneapolis: Fortress.

Levine, Etan
    1976   *The Aramaic Version of Lamentations.* New York: Sepher-Herman.

Linafelt, Tod
    2000   *Surviving Lamentations.* Chicago: University of Chicago Press.

Long, Thomas G.
    2009   *Accompany Them with Singing: The Christian Funeral.* Louisville: Westminster John Knox.

Mandolfo, Carleen R.
    2007   *Daughter Zion Talks Back to the Prophets.* Atlanta: Society of Biblical Literature.

Meyers, Carol
    2013   *Rediscovering Eve: Ancient Israelite Women in Context.* Oxford: Oxford University Press.

Mills, Watson E., gen. ed.
    1990   *Mercer Dictionary of the Bible.* Macon, GA: Mercer University Press.

Neal, Arthur
    1998   *National Trauma and Collective Memory.* Armonk, NY: M. E. Sharpe.

O'Connor, Kathleen M.
    1998   "Lamentations." In *Women's Bible Commentary: Expanded Edition with Apocrypha*, edited by Carol A. Newsom and Sharon H. Ringe, 187–91. Louisville: Westminster John Knox.
    2002   *Lamentations and the Tears of the World.* Maryknoll, NY: Orbis Books.

Ollenburger, Ben
    1987   *Zion, the City of the Great King: A Theological Symbol of the Jerusalem Cult.* Journal for the Study of the Old Testament Supplement Series 41. Sheffield, UK: JSOT Press.

Pham, Xuan Huong Thi
    1999   *Mourning in the Ancient Near East and the Hebrew Bible.* Sheffield, UK: Sheffield Academic Press.

Pitard, Wayne T.
    1992   "Vengeance." In *Anchor Bible Dictionary*, edited by David Noel Freedman, 6:786–87. New York: Doubleday.

Pritchard, James B., ed.
    1969   *Ancient Near Eastern Texts Relating to the Old Testament.* 3rd ed., with Supplement. Princeton: Princeton University Press.

Provan, Iain
    1991   *Lamentations.* New Century Bible Commentary. Grand Rapids: Eerdmans.

Rad, Gerhard von
    1962–65   *Old Testament Theology.* 2 vols. Translated by D. M. G. Stalker. New York: Harper & Row.

Robben, C. G. M., and Marcelo Suárez-Orozco
    2000   *Cultures under Siege: Collective Violence and Trauma.* Cambridge: Cambridge University Press.

Roberts, J. J. M.
    2006   "Zion Tradition." In *The New Interpreter's Dictionary of the Bible*, edited by Katharine Doob Sakenfeld, 5:987–88. Nashville: Abingdon.

Salters, R. B.
    2010   *A Critical and Exegetical Commentary on Lamentations.* International Critical Commentary. New York: T&T Clark.

Selvadurai, Shyam, ed.
    2013   *Write to Reconcile.* Colombo, Sri Lanka: Tharanjee Prints. Online PDF. www.writetoreconcile.com.

Selvan, S. D. P.
    2013   "Lamentation: A Rereading of Vanni in the Perspective of Underside History." *Sri Lanka Journal of Theological Reflection* 7, no. 1 (July): 1–9.

Bibliography for Lamentations

Somasundaram, Daya
    2014   *Scarred Communities: Psychosocial Impact of Man-Made and Natural Disasters on Sri Lankan Society.* Thousand Oaks, CA: Sage Publications.

Somasundaram, Daya, and Sambasivamoorthy Sivayokan
    2013   "Rebuilding Community Resilience in a Post-War Context: Developing Insight and Recommendations: A Qualitative Study in Northern Sri Lanka." *International Journal of Mental Health Systems*, 7/3. http//www.ijmhs/com/content/7/1/3.

Travis, Stephen H.
    1992   "Wrath of God: New Testament." In *Anchor Bible Dictionary*, edited by David Noel Freedman, 6:996–98. New York: Doubleday.

Westermann, Claus
    1994   *Lamentations: Issues and Interpretation.* Minneapolis: Fortress.

Selected Resources for Lamentations

Alter, Robert. *The Art of Biblical Poetry.* New York: Basic Books, 1985. Examines the aesthetics, structures, and functions of biblical poetry.

Berlin, Adele. *Lamentations: A Commentary.* Old Testament Library. Louisville: Westminster John Knox, 2002. A very good scholarly commentary on Lamentations from a Jewish perspective.

Dobbs-Allsopp, Frederick William. *Weep, O Daughter Zion: A Study of the City-Lament Genre in the Hebrew Bible.* Rome: Pontifical Biblical Institute, 1993. Compares the city laments found in the Bible with city laments found in other ancient Near Eastern cultures.

———. *Lamentations.* Interpretation. Louisville: Westminster John Knox, 2002. Part of a commentary series specifically designed to aid preachers.

Kushner, Harold. *When Bad Things Happen to Good People.* New York: Schocken, 1981. Rabbi Kushner, like the Israelites in Lamentations, tries to reconcile the theological notion of a loving God with the reality of human suffering.

Lacey, Marc. "Nyala Journal: Singers of Sudan Study War No More." *New York Times,* July 12, 2004. Examines the role of the wise women of Sudan whose songs of war and peace influence the direction in which the country is moving.

Lee, Nancy C. *Lyrics of Lament: From Tragedy to Transformation.* Minneapolis: Fortress, 2010. Compares laments from a variety of cultures, including the Bible.

Linafelt, Tod. *Surviving Lamentations.* Chicago: University of Chicago Press, 2000. Studies Lamentations as literature of survival and compares it to other literature written by those who survived great tragedies and witnessed to their survival in written forms.

Mandolfo, Carleen R. *Daughter Zion Talks Back to the Prophets.* Atlanta: Society of Biblical Literature, 2007. Often Zion is addressed in the prophetic literature, but there Zion does not speak. In Lamentations, Zion does speak, and Mandolfo uses her words as a response to the prophets as well.

Neal, Arthur. *National Trauma and Collective Memory.* Armonk, NY: M. E. Sharpe, 1998. Observes that national traumas shape particular generations and follow them through the rest of their lives.

Somasundaram, Daya. *Scarred Communities: Psychosocial Impact of Man-Made and Natural Disasters on Sri Lankan Society.* Thousand Oaks, CA: Sage Publications, 2014. On the effects of mass trauma on a community—the most comprehensive study I have found. The author is a psychiatrist.

Index of Ancient Sources for Lamentations

OLD TESTAMENT

Genesis
....97
9:9-17 114
12 86
17 114
17:5 113
18:20 82
19:24 82
25:29-34 86
29–30 24
34 76
36 42
37:19-20 75
37:34-35 30
42 115
46 86
49 24

Exodus 86
2:23 61
4:14 60
12:37-38 24
12:38 97
15:7 60
20:5 94
20:8-11 92
32:11-14 61

Leviticus
4:3 86
4:5 86
11–12 43
13:45-46 85
14–15 43
15:2-18 46
15:19-30 46
25 97

Numbers
11:10 60
20:14-21 86
22:22 116

Deuteronomy
5:12-15 92
6:20-23 41
6:21-24 .... 24, 115
13 61
15 97
16:16 77
23:3-6 43
24:8 85
26:5-9 .... 24, 115
26:5-11 42
31:9-13 85

Joshua
6:25 24
8:24 95
9 24
24:2-13 .... 24, 115
24:2-15 42

Judges 58
6:11 95
9:23 116
9:53 95
16:21 95
20:21 87
20:25 87
20:31 87
20:35 87
21 87

Ruth
4:1-2 96
4:9 96

1 Samuel 24, 115
2:1-10 97
4:18 96
16:14-16 116
16:23 116
18:10 116
19:9 116

Index of Ancient Sources for Lamentations

2 Samuel
.... 24, 115
1:19-27 115
6 58
6:2 38
7:12-16 24
12 84
12:15-22 30
17:10 69
18:8 95
21:10 64
23:5 114
23:8 67

1 Kings
.... 24, 115
6 38
6-8 .... 25, 39
8 .... 38-39, 58
9:1-9 55
9:3 84
9:3-5 25
9:6-7 84
13:24 69
19:16 86
22 61
22:47 87

2 Kings
.... 115
2:24 69
6:24-31 83
10:15 93
14:7 86
17:7-20 25
18:21 38
24–25 113
24:17 113
25:26 .... 86, 93
25:27-30 85

1 Chronicles
16:22 86
21:1 116
21:12 77
28:2b 54

2 Chronicles
30:12 93
35:25 28

Ezra
.... 32

Nehemiah
.... 32
5 115
7:3-5 40
11:1-4 40

Job
.... 61
31:10 95

Psalms
.... 42, 66, 114
6 62
9–10 112
25 112
29:10 117
34 112
38:15 78
46:5 119
48:2 58
48:3 119
50:2 58
51:8 78
68:29 119
69:29 78
73 78
73:26 72
74:1 55
77:7 55
78:63-64 41
78:68 119
78:68-71 24
88 78
88:6 68
88:14 55
88:18 78
89:2 71
89:3-4 114
89:38-46 55
99:5b 54
100:4 116
105:15 86
107 61
107:43 71
110:1 53-54
119 .... 77, 112
119:57 72
132:7b 54
132:13-14 119
132:13-18 24
136 60
137 47
137:1-4 64
137:7 42
145 48
149:2 82

Proverbs
22:3 117
31:10-31 112

Ecclesiastes
12:1 92
12:3 95

Song of Songs
1:9 117

Isaiah
2:2-4 119
11:7 69
17:12-14 24
32:1-2 86
37:33-35 24
44:21 92
45:1 86
45:6b-7 63
45:7 48
47:2 95
63:7 71
66:1 54

Jeremiah
4:11 75
4:28 40
6:26 75
8:11 75
8:19 75
8:21-22 75
9:7 75
9:10 28
9:17 28
9:20 28
12:4 40
14:17 75
20:7b-8a 68
25:11-12 97
29:10 97
34:14-15 97

39–42	28
43–44	86, 93
43:1-7	39
50:24	45

Ezekiel
12:13	45
16:49-50	82
17:15-17	85
18:20	94
24:15-18	64
27:3	58
28:12	58
32:16	28
34	25, 60
34:4	25
46:17	97

Daniel
1:3-4	116
1:7	113
9:2	97
12:2-3	68

Hosea
5	55
13:8	69–70

Joel
1:8-9	41
2:23	82

Amos
1–2	77
2–3	62
2:4	25
2:6-8	80
5:10-13	80
9:15	48

Obadiah
	42
10-15	42
12-14	86

Jonah
1:17–3:2	77
2:2	76
2:5	75
2:7	70

Zechariah
3:1-2	116
8:4-5	96
12:12	40
14:16-21	119

NEW TESTAMENT

Matthew
18:15-20	16

Luke
1:46-55	97

Romans
1:18	60
12:19	60

1 Corinthians
13:12	50

Ephesians
4:26a	62

1 Timothy
5	37

OTHER ANCIENT SOURCES

Dead Sea Scrolls 118

Elephantine papyri
.... 93, 115

Moabite Stone 84

Targums
.... 28, 40, 46, 53, 118

The Author of the Commentary on Lamentations

Wilma Ann Bailey is the Minnie Vautrin Professor of Christian Witness and Professor of Hebrew and Aramaic Scripture, Emerita, at Christian Theological Seminary in Indianapolis, Indiana. She grew up in New York City and attended public schools before entering Hunter College in the Bronx and graduating from Herbert H. Lehman College (same school, different name). She earned an MDiv from Goshen Biblical Seminary, now called Anabaptist Mennonite Biblical Seminary (AMBS); and an MA and PhD in religion, with a focus on Hebrew Bible and a minor in anthropology from Vanderbilt University.

Bailey's scholarly works and popular publications have usually focused on issues of peace and justice, women, and ecology. She has traveled widely in eastern and western Europe; Asia; Africa; North, Central, and South America; and the Caribbean. Her introduction to numerous cultures and languages has enriched her life immeasurably.

She currently lives in Indianapolis, where she attends Shalom Mennonite Church.

Song of Songs

Christina Bucher

Preface to Song of Songs

In this commentary, I hope to convince you to read the Song of Songs in two distinct but interrelated ways. First, I hope you will explore the love poetry in this book as an affirmation of human sexuality and the affective experience of being "in love." As Christians, we have inherited a tradition that both celebrates God's creation as good and struggles to understand what it means to be created as sexual beings. Within the Christian canon we have a book, the Song of Songs, which can help us reflect on this ambivalence regarding human sexuality. Second, I hope you will also consider reading this book as our spiritual ancestors did, viewing it as a guide for reflection on our relationship with the Divine. By reading this book as a mirror of our relationship with God, we come to know God as Lover and ourselves as Loved.

I have been living with the Song of Songs for a long time, moving back and forth between "simmer" and "boil" (and occasionally turning off the burner completely). As I reflect on the process of researching and writing about the Song of Songs, I am struck by how my assumptions have changed over the years.

When I began the project, I assumed that the book should be read only at the level of its literal meaning. I accepted a commonly held opinion (one that lacks evidence) that the church had covered up the obvious meaning of the book and supplied it with an allegorical interpretation because of its discomfort with the explicitly erotic nature of the poems when read literally. Before the twentieth century, however, few ancients read the book as modern readers do. For some two millennia, Jews have read the poems as describing

God's relationship with Israel, and Christians have read the book as a description of Christ's love for the church.

As I worked my way into this book, my assumptions were challenged. I found that nonliteral readings of the Song could open up new paths of spirituality for contemporary readers. Reading figurally, Jews and Christians have uncovered levels of meaning in the Song of Songs that relate to their experiences of the Divine. Across the centuries, poets, artists, and devotional writers have drawn upon the Song's language and imagery to express their understanding of the Divine Being as Lover. The influence of the Song on Christian tradition can go unrecognized today, but we continue to experience its influence on visual art and on music, especially through hymnody.

Other assumptions were challenged. Early in my research, I assumed the book chiefly relates the sexual experiences of the young couple who are the primary voices of the poems and describes, often using figurative language, what these two lovers do when they are together. When I analyzed the Song for a scholarly conference paper, however, I was struck by the book's emphasis on the experience of the *absent lover*. On the one hand, the book celebrates the joy of physical intimacy between two people who are in love. On the other, however, it expresses the lovers' deep despair when they are separated. This led finally to my understanding that this book has much to say about the *affective* experience of being in love. Even more than describing what lovers *do*, this book explores how lovers *feel*—how they are both overjoyed and overpowered by love. At a time when churches look for the Bible's prescriptive instruction regarding human sexual behavior, this book reminds us to pay attention to how love feels to those who are in love.

In the tenth century, Rabbi Saadia Gaon al-Fayyum wrote that the Song of Songs "resembles locks to which the keys have been lost." At the beginning of my research on this book, I hoped I would discover *the* key to the book. Now, however, I conclude that there is no single key and no single lock to this complex book. Rather, there are multiple locks and multiple keys to open those locks. My hope is that by using this commentary as a guide into the Song of Songs, you, as readers, will find a key that unlocks the book for yourselves.

Many people have contributed to this book. Some of them know that they have contributed; others do not. Through their publications on the Song of Songs, two scholars in particular have influenced my work on this commentary. Though her commentary and many scholarly papers, Cheryl Exum helped me appreciate the poetic beauty and the unifying features of the Song. By the time Stephanie Paulsell's commentary appeared in print, I had already completed much of the first draft of the commentary; however, Paulsell's theological approach inspired some of the book's final revisions. I heartily recommend her commentary to readers who are interested in a contemporary reading of the Song of Songs that reflects an embodied spiritual approach to the book. Given the nature of this commentary series, I have kept citations to a minimum. The bibliography gives evidence of the many scholars whose work has contributed to my thinking about this book. Any errors are, of course, my own.

Words of appreciation and acknowledgment are due to others who have supported my work in various ways. In 2001, as a faculty fellow at the Young Center for Anabaptist and Pietist Studies, I received released time from teaching and access to resources that supported my research into Anabaptist and Pietist interpretation and reception of the Song of Songs. In 2005, Elizabethtown College granted me a sabbatical leave to research the reception history of the Song of Songs in visual art and music. The librarians at Elizabethtown College supported my need for resources beyond those held at the High Library by quickly supplying me with books and articles through interlibrary loan. Members of the Believers Church Bible Commentary Editorial Council offered important critique and encouragement at several stages in the writing process. Elizabeth Huwiler provided helpful critique of a nearly final draft. David Garber's careful copyediting improved the manuscript in numerous ways. I am especially grateful for the guidance and support I received from Doug Miller, the Old Testament editor for the series.

Erika Fitz, Bob Neff, and Julia O'Brien read and critiqued drafts of early chapters. I am grateful to have them as conversation partners. Many students have listened and responded with critical questions and suggestions as I tested ideas in the classroom. I mention three former students who gave me additional opportunities to discuss the Song of Songs. Amy Milligan translated German poems by Johannes Scheffler. Randi Stanton Kennedy researched the Song's reception in the English literary tradition. In his senior honors thesis, John Mackey analyzed the nature of the couple's relationship. In addition to having conversation partners, writers need to spend a lot of time with the doors to their offices closed. For giving me time alone at my desk, I thank my family—my husband,

Ted; sons, Ted Z. and Matt; and brother, Loren—who have waited patiently (and sometimes not so patiently) for the completion of this project. Thank you for asking at regular intervals, "Is the book done yet?"

Christina Bucher
Elizabethtown, Pennsylvania

Introduction to Song of Songs

Let him kiss me with the kisses of his mouth! (Song 1:2). What a shock awaits the reader who opens the Bible to the first chapter of the Song of Songs (also known as Song of Solomon). Roughly two-thirds of the way through the Old Testament, we encounter eight chapters of love poems, written largely in the form of dialogues between a man and a woman. In these poetic dialogues, the unnamed man and woman express their admiration for one another and their desire to be together. Anyone handed this collection of poems without being told they are from the Bible would certainly take them to be a celebration of human sexual attraction and a poetic description of sexual desire. What is a book like this doing in the Bible? And why should we read it?

There are two primary ways of approaching the Song of Songs, and both are important. First, one can read the Song of Songs literally, that is, for the book's self-evident or plain meaning. At this level, the book has much to say about human sexuality. In fact, this little book of eight chapters has more to say about human sexual experience in all its dimensions than the rest of the Bible combined. It affirms human sexual desire as one significant element of creation. Additionally, the Song of Songs explores the human need for intimacy and the anguish that accompanies the loss of the beloved. From this little book, we gain insight into human sexuality and intimacy.

Second, one can search for a different level of meaning in the Song of Songs, one that explores the relationship between humans and the Divine. This is, in fact, the way the ancients read the Scriptures [*Allegorical and Figural Interpretation, p. 258*]. For centuries, Christian interpreters have read the Song of Songs as a celebration of divine-human love. Today, we can read the book on two different levels: the literal level (two lovers and how they relate to each other) and a second level (in which the man plays the role of God or Jesus, and the woman plays the role of Israel, the church, or the individual believer).

To appreciate the reading of the ancients, we recognize that they searched continually for deeper meanings in Scripture. Precisely because they valued the Scriptures so highly, they looked for what the Scriptures revealed about God (Barton: 2). An example from Jesus' teaching might be helpful. In Luke 15:11-32, Jesus tells a story about a man and his two sons. On one level, this is a story about family relationships; however, although the parable does not explicitly tell us to do so, readers often assume that the father in the story points to God and that the sons point to two differing human responses to the Divine.

If we read as our spiritual ancestors did, in the Song of Songs we find a way to reflect upon our relationship with God in terms of Lover and Beloved. Reading the Song of Songs with the ancients, we hear God's voice, desire God's kiss, and struggle through those dark nights when we feel God's absence most deeply. When we turn to our spiritual ancestors, we discover that the Song of Songs has inspired poets, musicians, and theologians through the last two millennia in creative ways. This commentary points readers to allusions and echoes of the Song of Songs that can be found in hymnody, visual art, and devotional writings [*History of Interpretation, p. 270*].

The remainder of this introduction offers an overview of the book by examining these areas: (1) major themes in the book, (2) background information on the book, (3) a brief overview of the Song in canonical context, and (4) an introduction to the use of the Song of Songs in Christian devotional writing and hymns.

Major Themes of the Song of Songs

An overview of the book's major themes may be a good place to begin. Although it is hard to discover a clear plot in the Song of Songs, several themes emerge from the poems in the book. These themes contribute to a sense that there is development or movement within the book, and this commentary suggests possible ways to understand the development of these themes within the Song of Songs.

Introduction to Song of Songs

Throughout the book, we read *expressions of admiration for the beloved*. This theme appears in four poems that have a similar structure (4:1-7; 5:10-16; 6:4-7; 7:1-7). Scholars often refer to these four poems by the Arabic term *waṣf*, meaning "description" *[Descriptive Inventories, p. 263]*. In three of the poems, the man describes the woman's body, using exaggerated metaphors. In the fourth poem, the woman does the same regarding the man's body. Elsewhere in the book, we find poems in which the man and woman express their admiration for each other in other ways (1:9-10; 2:2-3; 4:9-15; 6:8-10) *[Figures of Speech, p. 267]*.

Many of the poems express the interrelated themes of *the beloved's presence and absence* and *the lover's desire*. Although the poems of admiration often give the impression that the lovers are together, the man and woman speak more often about their separation and their desire to be reunited. The theme of the beloved's absence appears in poems that express desire (2:4-7; 8:1-4) and in poems in which one of the lovers invites the other to come away (2:10, 13; 4:8; 7:11; 8:14). Interestingly, the book ends on the note of desire and yearning, rather than satisfaction and fulfillment, concluding with the woman's request to her lover to *come away* (8:14).

A related theme is that of *seeking and finding the beloved*. This theme appears prominently in two poems in which it is unclear if the action occurs in a dream or in reality. In the first poem (3:1-5), the woman finds her beloved, but in the second poem, she searches but fails to find him (5:2-8). It can also be seen in questions in which the woman asks how she might find her beloved (1:7).

Lovers' relationships often encounter conflict, and the theme of *opposition to the lovers* appears in several poems. Conflict may be suggested already in the behavior of the watchmen in chapter 3 (v. 3), when they do not appear to assist the woman in her search for her beloved, but it becomes explicit in chapter 5, in which the watchmen beat the woman as she searches for her beloved (5:7). Opposition to the relationship also appears in the behavior of the woman's brothers (1:6; 8:8-9).

Throughout the poems we encounter expressions of *mutuality*. This theme appears most prominently in a refrain that occurs three times in the book, *My beloved is mine and I am his* (2:16); *I am my beloved's and my beloved is mine* (6:3); *I belong to my beloved, and his desire is for me* (7:10). Although somewhat formulaic, the refrain appears in a slightly different form each time it occurs, perhaps suggesting that a loving relationship cannot be packaged into a simple formula or that relationships can change over time.

The poems express a *celebration of human sexuality*. The lovers revel in each other's bodies, and they anticipate the pleasure of physical intimacy (1:12-13; 5:1-5; 7:12; 8:2-3). They refuse to give in to social pressures that seek to keep them apart (1:6; 5:7). They struggle to overcome their times of separation and return to each other (3:1-4; 5:2-7). Sexuality makes both the man and the woman feel vulnerable. She wonders about his constancy, and he feels overcome by his desire for her (4:9; 6:4-10). Nevertheless, they choose their sexual feelings for each other rather than deny them.

The overwhelming effect of the collection of poems communicates a sense of *the awesome power of love*. Although open to multiple interpretations, the refrain *do not arouse or awaken love until it so desires* (2:7; 3:5; 8:4) suggests that love is something dangerous and not to be treated lightly. This theme of the awesome power of love is expressed most straightforwardly in 8:6-7, which contains the twin claims that *love is as strong as death* and that *many waters cannot quench love*. The book's one possible reference to God appears at the end of 8:6, in a phrase that can be translated either *a mighty flame* or *like the very flame of the* LORD, which the NIV tries to capture by putting the second phrase in a footnote. In this verse the mysterious presence of the LORD underscores the awesome quality of love.

Lyric Love Poetry or Drama?

What kind of book is the Song of Songs? It might help to define the book if we look first at what it is not. Clearly the book has to do with love—but is it a story, a drama, or something else? Although we detect glimpses of a story line in the book, they are just that—glimpses. We notice fairly quickly that we are reading speeches and that the book has a dialogic quality to it. The majority of the book comprises speeches of a man and a woman to and about each other.

From this dialogic character, some readers have concluded that the book is actually a drama; however, the book does not well fit the category of "drama," at least as we understand drama today. First, the number of main characters is unclear. Some have suggested two major characters in the drama—a shepherd and the young woman who is the object of his affection. Others have proposed three major characters—giving King Solomon a speaking part in addition to the shepherd and the country lass. Second, the book lacks a clear plotline. Although readers may detect hints of a plot (e.g., in Song 3:1-5), the speeches, for the most part, are more akin to lyric poetry than to drama because they express the speakers' emotions and feelings. Could the speeches have been performed publicly? Yes, at least in the sense that reading in the ancient world meant reading aloud, including in the company of others. Do the poetic speeches in the book tell a story? No. Although the poems allude to conflict and its resolution, no clearly identifiable story line runs from chapter 1 through chapter 8. In order to read the book as a drama, the reader must reframe it as a drama by clearly identifying the speaking parts and providing a plotline that coherently reflects the speeches [*Dramatic Interpretations, p. 263*].

After eliminating story and drama, we are left with poetry—but what type of poetry? In the Western literary tradition, love poetry is most frequently cast as a monologue, in which an individual reflects on the nature of love or speaks about, or to, a lover. In many of the poems in the Song of Songs, however, a man or a woman speaks to the other, expressing admiration for the other. They also speak of their mutual desire to be together. Perhaps unexpectedly, the love poetry of the Song does not describe love in the abstract. We can find only one brief passage in which the woman makes an observation about love: *For love is strong as death, passion fierce as the grave* (8:6 NRSV). Even here, however, the statement appears within the young woman's speech to her beloved, so we do not entirely lose the conversational character of the poetry. If we examine the poetry of the Song within the context of the Western tradition of poetry, it is probably best described as lyric poetry, since lyric poetry expresses personal feelings and emotions, rather than telling a story. It emphasizes images and metaphors, rather than plot and characterization. Lyric poetry reflects on the inner life, rather than the outer world (Exum: 42–45; Dobbs-Allsopp 2005a; Linafelt 2005).

We can also examine the love poetry of the Song of Songs within the context of ancient Near Eastern love poetry. If we compare the Song and the approximately fifty known Egyptian love songs dating to the period 1300–1150 BCE, we discover both similarities and differences. In both Egyptian and Israelite love songs, the poems are in the form of speeches uttered by a young man and young woman of marriageable age. In both, the speakers express their admiration of each other and praise each other's appearance. Similarly, the young man uses "sister" as a term of endearment. And in both, the setting for the love songs is frequently the world of nature: gardens, fields, vineyards. Michael V. Fox (2014) concludes that, like ancient Egyptian love poems, the love poems of the Song of Songs were originally sung as entertainment (e.g., at banquets), and he observes that both collections of love songs create an imaginary world in which sexual love is idealized.

Who Are the Characters in the Poems?

The two main characters in the book are a young woman and a young man. They are likely quite young, perhaps in their early to midteens. Although we lack evidence for ancient Israel, it seems likely that women married while in their teens, but men may have waited to marry until they were in their twenties (King and Stager: 37). In biblical times, when people married, the young woman moved from the sphere of her biological family into the family of her husband. Because the Song connects the young woman with her brothers and mother, and because the two are not portrayed as married, it seems likely that they are both young, but of marriageable age. The precise nature of their relationship is left open to the reader's interpretation. In the poetry, the couple faces obstacles to their being together, and the young woman expresses some uncertainty about her lover's constancy. This suggests they desire an intimate relationship with each other but encounter resistance and experience doubt. What we know about social conventions in ancient Israel suggests that a young man and a young woman would not be permitted to engage in sexual activity unless they were married to each other (or possibly betrothed, although we have no evidence that a betrothed couple could engage in sexual intercourse). The betrothal stage is not always distinguished in the Bible from marriage and was considered binding upon the couple. Women, but not men, were expected to be virgins when they married (King and Stager: 54). Yet, some of the language of the poems is highly suggestive of sexual activity between the two.

We are left with a quandary. The evidence of the poems themselves seems to challenge what we know about the ancient Israelite social world. Are they betrothed to each other? If so, why does there seem to be so much uncertainty about their relationship? Why do the brothers (Song 1:6) and the city watchmen (5:7) appear unsupportive of the relationship? And why does the couple have to search for each other (1:7; 3:1; 5:6; 6:1)? But if they are not betrothed, how do we understand some of the references to their interactions? The poems employ ambiguous language to describe the couple's behavior, yet a few poems seem to describe intimate sexual activity between the two (5:4-6), whether real or imagined. Although suggestive, the poems nevertheless do not precisely describe the nature of their sexual intimacy. As Michael Fox (2014) observes, "The book's treatment of sex is subtle, but not too subtle."

In the Hebrew text, it is usually clear who is speaking because Hebrew has masculine and feminine pronoun forms that are lacking

Introduction to Song of Songs 145

in English. When we read "you" in the Hebrew text, we know if the speaker is addressing a man or a woman. Because this is not clear in English, many English versions aid readers by identifying the speakers (as you might see in a play script). The 2011 NIV identifies the two main speakers with the pronouns *he* and *she*, and refers to the group that occasionally interjects a comment with the noun *friends*. Other translations, including the NIV 1984, refer to *beloved, lover,* and *friends*. *The Message* identifies the two main speakers as *The Woman* and *The Man*. The NRSV and the KJV do not identify the speakers, but the NKJV does, using the term *Shulamite* (from 6:13) for the woman and *the Beloved* for the young man.

While these identifications can be helpful, readers should be aware that labels identifying the change of speakers do not exist in the Hebrew text. To further complicate matters, at some points, translators and interpreters do not agree on the identity of the speaker. Readers should also be aware that these labels have the potential to influence our reading. Some older editions used the labels *Bride* and *Bridegroom*; however, the poems provide no such indication of their marital status, and most recent versions avoid such language when identifying the speakers. The practice of the 2011 NIV is, perhaps, the best compromise. It helps English readers know who is speaking, but by using the pronouns *he* and *she*, the translators do not influence readers by defining the nature of the speakers' relationship with marital terms. Such terms are never used in the Hebrew text to identify the speakers; they reflect later traditions of interpreting the Song *[History of Interpretation, p. 270; Nuptial Imagery in the New Testament, p. 282]*. The NIV also avoids associating the passive term *beloved* exclusively with the woman and the active term *lover* exclusively with the man. In the Hebrew text of the speeches themselves, the young man and woman employ various terms of endearment. The woman refers to the man with a term translated in the 2011 NIV as *beloved*, but he never uses that term for her. If we analyze the *way* in which the two relate (rather than simply looking at terminology), each is at times more active than the other.

In discussions of the biblical text, this commentary will vary the terms used to identify the speakers. The female speaker will be identified as "she," "the young woman," "the lover," "the beloved." The male speaker will be referred to as "he," "the young man," "the lover," and "the beloved." Because the term "lover" implies a more active role than "beloved," this commentary avoids the practice of stereotyping the man as the active lover and the woman as the passive beloved. Both individuals will be identified with the terms "lover" and "beloved."

Most of the lines belong to the young man and the young woman; however, there is another group that occasionally chimes in. In the Hebrew text they are called "the daughters of Jerusalem." The role of this group of women is not clear. They may be friends of the woman, but at points, they seem to speak critically of her. That is, they don't sound supportive enough to be termed "friends" (although this is the term that NIV uses to identify the speakers). Some interpreters think they play a role similar to the Greek chorus in ancient Greek plays [Daughters of Jerusalem, p. 262; Dramatic Interpretations, p. 263].

One Poem, or Many?

Although the book is known by the singular word "song," it is not clear if the book was written as a unified whole or if it should be seen as an anthology of love poems. Those who view the book as an anthology of love poems point to the abrupt shifts in speakers, scenes, and subject matter, as well as the difficulty in identifying a unifying structure for the book. Scholars cannot even agree on the number of poems within the book. Those who view the book as a unified whole point to the repetition of phrases and refrains, the use of a common symbolic vocabulary, and a consistency in characterization, despite the fact that the book's organizational structure remains elusive.

The repetition of phrases and the use of refrains contribute to a sense of unity. In some cases, the refrain is repeated verbatim. In other cases, it is modified slightly when repeated.

> *His left arm is under my head,*
> *and his right arm embraces me.* (2:6; 8:3)

> *Daughters of Jerusalem, I charge you*
> *by the gazelles and by the does of the field:*
> *Do not arouse or awaken love*
> *until it so desires.* (2:7; variations in 3:5; 8:4; cf. 5:8)

> *My beloved is mine and I am his;*
> *he browses among the lilies.* (2:16; cf. 6:3 and 7:10)

> *Until the day breaks*
> *and the shadows flee,*
> *turn, my beloved,*
> *and be like a gazelle*

> or like a young stag
> on the rugged hills. (2:17; cf. 4:6 and 8:14)

In addition to the use of refrains, the poetry in the book shares a common symbolic vocabulary that also suggests unity (although it should be recognized that love poetry shares a common vocabulary even when individual poems arise from different sources or authors). In Song of Songs, the woman refers to her lover throughout the book (twenty-six times) as *my beloved*, and the man refers to her as *my darling* (1:9, 15; 2:2, 10, 13; 4:1, 7; 5:2; 6:4) and *my dove* (2:14; 5:2; 6:9). He calls her *most beautiful of women* (1:8; 5:9; 6:1).

Despite these unifying elements, the disparities mentioned above make it likely that the book brings together poems that were originally not part of a unified whole; however, the opening verse suggests that we *should* read the book as a single poem. The book's opening verse, *Solomon's Song of Songs*, with its singular "Song," promises unity. *The Song of Songs*, like the phrases "the king of kings" and "the holy of holies," expresses the superlative in Biblical Hebrew. With this title the author or editor of the book indicates that the entire book of poetry is both a single song and the best possible song.

The word "song" (Heb. *šir*) may suggest to modern readers something musical. Since we do not possess the musical scores, we do not know how songs were sung in ancient Israel. Many of the references in the Bible to "songs" mention musical instruments, including harps, lyres, tambourines, cymbals, and trumpets (1 Chron 13:8), which indicates that songs could have instrumental accompaniment. The term "song" appears only in the title of the book (1:1). Since we have the lyrics and not the music, the commentary will refer to the individual textual units in the book as poems, rather than as songs.

Did Solomon Write the Song of Songs?

Other aspects of the book's origin remain similarly elusive. Although many readers accept the opening verse of the book as an identification of the author, three bits of evidence encourage other ways of thinking about the reference to Solomon in the opening verse. First, although the Hebrew preposition *le*, which is attached to the name Solomon, can indicate authorship, it has other possible meanings. For example, the collection of poems may be dedicated "to Solomon" or written "concerning Solomon." Second, although the name Solomon also appears six other places in the book (1:5; 3:7, 9, 11;

8:11, 12), Solomon neither speaks nor is directly addressed in these texts. Finally, linguistic considerations suggest a date later than the tenth century BCE (Dobbs-Allsopp 2005b). For these reasons, it appears that the book should be attributed to an anonymous author or authors [*Authorship and Date, p. 261*].

Although Solomon may not be the book's author, there are clear connections between the book and traditions about Solomon. Solomon composed both proverbs and songs (1 Kings 4:32), and he had a knowledge and interest in flora and fauna (1 Kings 4:33). Throughout the poems, the Song refers to different types of flora and fauna. Solomon was remembered as a wealthy king whose court was known for its wealth and luxury (1 Kings 9–10). The Song of Songs refers to luxury items, such as nard (1:12; 4:13-14), and to jewelry and gemstones (1:10) and valuable metals (5:14)—objects that one might find in the court of a wealthy king (Munro: 35–68). Known to have had relationships with many women (1 Kings 11:1-3), Solomon may symbolize passionate love in the poems. A closer examination of the book's concluding chapter suggests, however, that the poet may use Solomon as a foil by which to make the points that (1) love cannot be bought (8:7b) and (2) an exclusive relationship between two lovers is better than multiple sexual relationships (8:11-12). Jill Munro (145) concludes, "If the wealth and splendor which accompany kingship are fitting metaphors for the lovers' splendor, they are also the foil against which love reveals its purity." Following this line of thinking, the opening verse of the book may represent either a dedication to the king ("the Song of Songs *for* Solomon") or a characterization of the poems through association with the king ("the Song of Songs *concerning* Solomon"). Katharine Dell (13) concludes that the Solomonic reference "may represent a deliberate attempt to associate this work, in a more integrated way, to wisdom's wisest patron, Solomon."

Noting the centrality of the female speaker in the poems, a few scholars have proposed that a woman wrote the poems. It can be observed that the female speaker appears to be present to readers throughout the book, whereas her male lover is notably absent at times. Even when she is not speaking, the woman appears to be listening to the speeches of her lover and others. We can also observe that a greater mutuality appears to exist in the relationship of the male and female lovers than can be seen in any other book of the Bible. Both express admiration for the other. Both issue invitations to the other. The woman explicitly describes their relationship as mutual: *My lover is mine, and I am his.* While these observations are significant in the interpretation of the book, none of this internal evidence definitively proves female authorship, although it might cause us to check our assumptions. At least for now, the question of the author's gender must remain open. The assumption in this commentary is that the poems in the book have been associated with Solomon in some way by an anonymous author writing sometime in the Persian period or later [Authorship and Date, p. 261].

Setting of the Poems

The poems of the Song of Songs are set within four primary contexts. These settings—which are often intermingled—usually relate in some way to the poems' content. (1) Many of the poems have a setting in the cultivated countryside—the gardens, orchards, and vineyards surrounding the village. These locations are frequently the settings for the expressions of love between the man and the woman. (2) Other poems are set "in the wild"—in the mountainous regions, where wild animals roam. In ancient times, the mountains and wilderness were hostile places for humans. In the poem, these settings suggest danger, but they also symbolize the elusiveness of love. These settings and the symbols associated with the wild—the gazelles and wild stags, for example—are often connected to the woman's beloved. The poet describes him as a gazelle or stag, leaping upon the mountains. It may be that the wild places, despite their dangers, offer opportunities for the lovers to be alone with each other. (3) A third setting is in the public squares and streets of the city or town. The young woman searches for her lover through the city streets and squares—hence, these areas symbolize the absence of the beloved. Here, too, danger is linked with violence. In the public areas of the city, the woman meets with disapproval, and it is there that the woman is found by the watchmen and beaten. (4) The fourth setting is in the interiors of buildings and other structures—for example, the king's chamber, the mother's house. The young woman appears most often identified with the interior settings and expresses a desire to draw her beloved into these settings.

Frequently the settings are juxtaposed, perhaps to suggest conflict, as in 3:1-5, where the woman leaves her bed to roam the streets, looking for her beloved. Once she finds him, they return to her mother's house. In 2:9, the woman's beloved is pictured as a gazelle peering in through the windows. In this way, the settings may serve to highlight threats to the woman and barriers to her love. They also geographically symbolize the separation of the man and the woman: he most naturally is located in the mountains, she indoors. They often meet in between those two settings, in the cultivated countryside—the gardens and vineyards, and the grazing grounds of the flocks.

Imagery of the Poems

The poems of the Song of Songs are rich in imagery drawn from various realms. Just as there are four major settings in the poems, the imagery of the poems is also drawn from a variety of settings.

Most common is agricultural imagery from the realm of the cultivated countryside. Here and elsewhere in the Bible, agricultural imagery symbolizes the blessings of this world. The poems are filled with images of wine, oils, and fruit, and of the cultivated spaces where these things grow: gardens, vineyards, and orchards. Domesticated animals complete this picture of well-being, with references to flocks, sheep, and goats.

Animals from the wild symbolize both danger and independence. As predators, lions and leopards suggest danger. Gazelles and stags imply speed and independence. Mountains, which usually impede human travel, provide no obstacle to the young man, who leaps and bounds over the mountains and hills, like a gazelle, although the mountains also appear as symbols of the woman's inaccessibility.

In the Bible, flowers often illustrate pride, beauty, love, or transience. In the Song of Songs, flowers most frequently symbolize beauty and love. English translations of the Song specifically name lilies and roses in connection with beauty and love; however, biblical scholars question the accuracy of these translations. It seems likely that the Song mentions the water lily, or lotus, which was associated with the decoration in Solomon's temple in Jerusalem [*Flowers, p. 268*].

In addition to the imagery already mentioned, we can find military imagery, often surprisingly linked to the young woman, such as when her neck is described as being like a tower that is hung with the shields of warriors. Other imagery contributes to the poems' sense of abundance. Jewelry and gems are associated with the young woman, and expensive oils and ointments, scented with myrrh and frankincense, evoke in readers the sense of the exotic [*Aromatics, p. 260*].

The poems of the Song of Songs appeal to the five senses to a degree unlike other biblical writings. Whereas most biblical narratives emphasize sight and hearing, the poems of this book appeal also to the senses of touch, taste, and smell. In the Song of

Songs, hearing the beloved's voice establishes a connection between the two lovers. Sight is frequently connected to hearing. For example, the young man says, *Let me see your face, let me hear your voice* (2:14 NRSV).

In addition to sight and sound, the reader is bombarded with other sensory perceptions. The sense of touch is important because the two lovers want not only to see and hear each other, but also to touch and to be physically close. She exclaims, *Let him kiss me* (1:1). When she finds him, she says, *I held him and would not let him go* (3:4). In an expression of her desire that they remain close together, she demands that he keep her as close to himself as if she were a signet on his arm or over his heart. The beloved also expresses his desire to touch his lover; however, he expresses his desires in more figurative language. He says, *I will hasten to the mountain of myrrh and the hill of frankincense* (4:6 NRSV); and after describing her as being *stately as a palm tree*, he exclaims, *I say I will climb the palm tree and lay hold of its branches* (7:7-8 NRSV).

Taste and smell together heighten our sense of abundance, prosperity, and blessing. Aromatic oils and specific scents are mentioned. In the Bible generally and in the Song of Songs specifically, eating and drinking refer metaphorically to the satisfaction of sexual desire. Foods and drinks are mentioned that suggest the pleasurability of love. Honey, milk, and wine all contribute to this understanding. Honey brings to mind the sweetness of love's kisses. The taste of milk lingers on the palate. Wine can make one feel giddy, as lovers often feel *[Figures of Speech, p. 267]*.

Song of Songs in the Context of the Christian Canon

Within the broader context of the Christian canon, the concept of love acquires a broad range of meanings. It can characterize interpersonal relationships, such as those between family members. Love also characterizes relationships between individuals and God. Both testaments of the Christian Bible affirm God's love of humankind, and both testaments offer instruction regarding love. In the Gospels, Jesus affirms the teachings found in the Torah to love God (Deut 6:5; Matt 22:37, with parallels in Mark 12:29-30 and Luke 10:27a) and neighbor (Lev 19:18; Matt 22:39, with parallels in Mark 12:31 and Luke 10:27b), and Jesus explicitly instructs followers also to love enemies (Matt 5:44; Luke 6:27). Love surfaces as a central motif in the theology of the apostle Paul (e.g., Rom 8:31-39; 1 Cor 13). The Johannine writings similarly emphasize the centrality of love (e.g., John 13:34; 1 John 4).

The concept of love pervades the Scriptures—but what about desire? For some people, the term "desire" is a synonym for "lust," and lust, we know, is one of the seven deadly sins. Although the two terms overlap in meaning, they are not synonymous. Philosopher Simon Blackburn (2) contrasts "love" and "lust," and the latter concept does not come off well. Among the catalog of contrasts Blackburn draws is this one: love pursues the welfare of others, but lust seeks self-gratification. But is all sexual desire to be characterized as lust? Although the Bible has relatively little to say about sexual desire, it does contain passages that affirm and celebrate sexual desire. Although other biblical passages enumerate the dos and don'ts of sexuality, the Song of Songs explores the experiences of human love and desire, only indirectly offering cautions about the misuse of sexual desire. If Phyllis Trible (144) is correct, the Song of Songs serves to redeem the "love story gone awry" that we read in Genesis 2–3 [Sexuality, p. 283; Love and Desire, p. 279].

The Song of Songs in the Life of the Church

If we look to the Song of Songs to understand what it means to be human, we discover that the book affirms sexual desire as one important aspect. Further, the poems in this book express a deep desire for connection, the longing of one person to be in an intimate relationship with another human being. Beginning in the mid-twentieth century, some Christians promoted the Song of Songs as a manual of instruction for husbands and wives, and for single Christians preparing for marriage (see, e.g., Nelson). Although this approach helpfully brings the discussion of human sexuality into dialogue with Christian life, the Song of Songs does not appear to be an instruction manual; it is a collection of lyric poems that powerfully and directly express what it means to be created a sexual being. Rather than instructing husbands and wives on sexual techniques, the poems of the Song of Songs explore the affective side of human sexuality by describing the conscious, subjective feeling of being in love and the accompanying desire for intimacy with one's beloved.

The historian Vern L. Bullough (Bullough et al. 100) argues that Christianity for much of its history could be seen as a "sex-negative religion." Augustine, the fifth-century bishop of Hippo in North Africa, helped set the stage for this, even though he was a moderating voice in his own time. Augustine held that while sexual intercourse that occurs within marriage and for the purpose of procreation is not sinful, celibacy is better. Keith Graber Miller (36) explains that

Introduction to Song of Songs

Augustine believed sexual arousal demonstrated the inability of the will to control the passions (a negative in Augustine's view) and that sexual intercourse was associated with human sinfulness. According to Bullough, Augustine's negative perspective on sexuality held sway for a millennium. Reformation views in the sixteenth century began to challenge it, but it was not until the twentieth century that Christianity began to develop a more positive understanding of sexuality. Yet there is more to learn and appreciate in this area. Rarely has sexuality been discussed openly within our churches. It is often not talked about until an issue arises. With regard to ethics, matters of sexual immorality are often treated more seriously than issues of economic injustice. Bullough might say this has to do, at least in part, with the sex-negative history of Christianity. Thus the affirmation of human sexual desire in the Song of Songs can help Christians today overcome the long history of "sex-negativity" in their background and contribute positively to the development of a healthy sexual ethic.

The Song of Songs also contributes to the development of a healthy spirituality (Bucher 2010: 226-34). The recognition that desire is at the heart of all spirituality helps to explain the attraction of theologians and spiritual writers to the Song of Songs. As the preeminent scriptural text on the subject of desire, the Song lends itself easily to spiritual interpretations. The longing of two persons to be united with each other expresses well the human longing for God and the corresponding desire to live in God's presence *[Allegorical and Figural Interpretation, p. 258]*. We are familiar with the Bible's images, or *models* (as theologian Sallie McFague terms them), of God as "father" and "king." A theological reading of the Song of Songs adds another model, that of God as Lover, a model that reflects a different way of understanding the relationship between God and humankind. In this model, humans respond to God out of love, not out of fear. Although some persons may find the model of "God as Lover" uncomfortable, the tradition of "Jesus as Lover" has been a central feature of devotional writing and hymnody, especially within traditions influenced by Pietism. In these traditions, Jesus is known as "lover of my soul," "my friend," and "my desire" *[History of Interpretation, p. 270]*.

The passion of the lovers in the Song is a mutual passion. *My beloved is mine and I am his*, the woman states (Song 2:16). She repeats the phrase in a slightly different form, *I am my beloved's and my beloved is mine* (6:3). Reading the Song spiritually, we reflect upon our own desire to draw closer to God, and we recognize that God desires our companionship as well. Like the woman of the Song who wants to be near her beloved, we long to be near God. When separated, we are filled with anguish and pain, as is the woman. The book's movement—from longing to joy and back again, to longing at the end of chapter 8—describes both the physical and emotional experience of human love and the human spiritual experience of love for God. In our relationship with God, we experience a similar ebb and flow: of presence and absence, joy and despair, gain and loss. We live our lives in anticipation of a spiritual intimacy with God that, if and when it occurs, is far too fleeting.

In the following commentary, the explanatory notes offer discussion of the Hebrew text of the Song of Songs. I offer my identification of the units and speakers and discussions of selected "thorny problems" of interpretation. While not proposing that the book has a single, clear plotline, I do offer a reading of the book that emphasizes linguistic threads and themes that unify the book. These threads suggest, if only vaguely, that the poems reflect the experiences of the same pair throughout the book and suggest development that occurs within that couple's relationship. The "Text in the Life of the Church" sections, in some cases, reflect on ways in which a plain reading of these love poems can illuminate our understanding of intimacy, love, and sexuality, thereby contributing to the development of a sexual ethic (also see the essays "Embodiment," "Love and Desire," and "Sexuality"). Other TLC sections examine ways in which the Song of Songs has been interpreted through the centuries. In particular, we will look at the rich stream of spiritual writers who draw imagery and language from the Song in their devotional writings and hymn texts. Still other TLCs offer theological reflections that connect the Song of Songs to our spiritual lives today.

This commentary pays most attention to the NRSV and NIV (2011) versions. All translations of Song of Songs are given in italics, including those of the author (AT). Unless otherwise noted, translations of the Bible will appear as NIV 2011 (not flagged). English versification of the Old Testament occasionally differs from that of the Hebrew (MT). Generally only English versification is indicated. When MT versification is added, it appears in parentheses or brackets.

Song of Songs 1:1-8
In Celebration of Love

PREVIEW

Love has a way of opening up all our senses. When we are in love, we become more attentive to our beloved's touch and scent. We long to see the one we love. The opening poem of the Song of Songs hits at least four of the five senses—touch, taste, vision, and smell—when describing a young woman's desire for her beloved. The poem also introduces us to three settings that will recur throughout the book: the palace, the vineyard, and the pasture where sheep graze. She then defends her own physical appearance. Finally, she longingly expresses her wish to find her beloved, a theme that is woven throughout the poems of the Song of Songs. In response, her friends reply somewhat teasingly, "If you don't know where he is, go look for him!"

OUTLINE

Title: The Most Beautiful of Songs, 1:1
In Celebration of Love, 1:2-8
    1:2-4   Her Expression of Desire for Her Lover's Kiss
    1:5-6   Her Self-Description
    1:7-8   A Dialogue about Her Lover's Whereabouts

EXPLANATORY NOTES

Title: The Most Beautiful of Songs 1:1

In English, this book is known by at least three different titles: the Song of Songs, the Song of Solomon, and Canticles. The Jewish tradition favors the title "the Song of Songs," the first words of the book in Hebrew. The title "Canticles" comes from *canticum canticorum*, the Latin translation of the Hebrew. Finally, the title "the Song of Solomon" picks up the identification of the book with King Solomon. This commentary follows the NIV in referring to the book by the title "The Song of Songs."

Solomon's Song of Songs (1:1) reflects a Hebrew construction that joins singular and plural forms of the word "song" to express the superlative. Although "the song of songs" is an accurate translation of the Hebrew words, it may fail to communicate the true meaning to some readers. As an expression of the superlative, the phrase means "the most excellent of songs," "the most sublime song," or simply "the best song." Some translations try to capture this meaning, as in the GNT, *the most beautiful of songs*, which is probably as good as any rendering. Other similarly constructed phrases appear in the Bible. The expressions "king of kings" (Dan 2:37) and "Lord of lords" (Deut 10:17) both express the superlative: the greatest king, the Lord above all lords. The same construction occurs in the term used to refer to the inner sanctuary of the temple: "the Most Holy Place" (1 Kings 8:6), sometimes translated as "the Holy of Holies."

The word "song" can refer to any type of joyful song. In the Bible it refers to songs of Zion (e.g., Ps 137:3) and Sabbath songs (Ps 92), but also to drinking songs (Amos 6:5-6) and love songs (Ps 45; Isa 5:1). In ancient Israel, songs could have been accompanied by an instrument, such as a lyre, flute, or tambourine. Interestingly, in the book the Song of Songs, the term "song" occurs only in the title. Biblical Hebrew does not have a word for "poem," but the Bible does contain poetry, and some of these poems are called "songs." Most likely that explains the choice of title for this book. In this commentary, the individual smaller units will be called poems rather than songs.

The opening verse associates this book with a famous Israelite king. Traditionally, the association is viewed as one of authorship: the songs, or poems, in the book are thought to have been composed by Solomon. According to biblical tradition, King Solomon composed three thousand proverbs and one thousand and five songs (1 Kings 4:32). Partly for this reason, tradition has viewed Solomon as the author of both Proverbs and Song of Songs. This commentary treats the poems as anonymous rather than accepting the traditional attribution of the collection to King Solomon [Authorship and Date, p. 261].

Poets often compose with an ear to sound as well as meaning. The opening verse of the book uses alliteration to emphasize a soft *sh* (*š*) sound: *šir ha-širim ʾašer li-šĕlomoh*. The consonant pronounced *sh* is repeated four times in this short verse. The *sh* sound recurs in the next verse, as well. Although we don't know the author's intention or how ancient people responded to the repetition of the *sh* sound, to modern ears, it is a soothing sound that fits love poetry.

In Celebration of Love 1:2-8

The Song of Songs contains a collection of poems, nearly all of which are in the form of first-person speeches. In the book's poems, the two main speakers are a man and a woman, both unnamed. In addition, several individuals speak as a group. Some translators in English editions of the Bible assist the reader by identifying the speakers throughout the Song. The NIV (2011) identifies the speakers with the terms *he, she,* and *friends*. In the NRSV, the speakers are left unidentified (for more on the identification of speakers, see the Introduction).

On occasion, translations disagree on the identity of a speaker or differ on where the shifts in speakers occur. In this opening unit, for example, it seems certain that the woman speaks first, but it is not clear how far her speech extends. Plural pronouns in verse 4 suggest that a group interjects a comment. Verse 8 also seems to be spoken by someone other than the woman, since she is addressed in this verse. These sudden shifts in speakers can prove challenging. Poetry—including ancient poetry—often displays this type of shift in speakers. Without becoming overly concerned, we need to read attentively, listening carefully for changes in speakers. Possibly the poet changes speakers rapidly and suddenly to express the spontaneity of emotion underlying this love poetry. This commentary follows the NIV's identification of speakers for 1:1-8, which attributes the speeches in 1:1-7 to the woman, except for a brief interjection by the friends in the middle of verse 4. The friends also deliver the speech in verse 8.

1:2-4 Her Expression of Desire for Her Lover's Kiss

As this passage opens, a woman expresses her desire for her lover. She both addresses her lover directly and speaks about him, using royal imagery as well as imagery that appeals to the senses. We immediately encounter a sudden shift from third person (*Let him kiss me with the kisses of his mouth*) to second person (*for your love is more delightful than wine*). Does she speak directly to her lover, or does she talk about him to herself or to others? The ambiguity of the text allows for different interpretations.

Some translators remove the ambiguity. In *The Message*, Eugene Peterson turns the woman's request into a direct command, *Kiss me—full on the mouth! Yes! For your love is better than wine*. Although Peterson's translation is dramatic, it dulls one of the main themes of the book, which has to do with the twin senses of longing for a lover from whom one is separated, and the joy of intimacy when that separation is overcome. For this reason, it may be better to retain the ambiguity of the Hebrew text, which could be translated, *How I want him to kiss me with the kisses of his mouth! For your love is better than wine* (AT).

The love poetry in the Song of Songs frequently evokes the different physical senses: touch, taste, smell, hearing, and seeing. The book abounds in descriptions of the beloved's appearance and of the physical world in which the lovers find themselves. The poems also appeal to our sense of smell, with references to the fragrant smell of flower blossoms and to the pungent odors of spices, such as myrrh, cinnamon, and spikenard—and to the sense of taste, with references to spiced wine and pomegranate juices. In this section, the poet appeals to the sense of touch (*Let him kiss me with the kisses of his mouth*), taste (*for your love is more delightful than wine*) and smell (*Pleasing is the fragrance of your perfumes*).

Touch. The expression *Let him kiss me with the kisses of his mouth* may strike us as odd. The noun "kisses" seems unnecessary. Could he kiss her with something other than kisses? Even more, we may wonder what kind of kisses they could be, other than "mouth kisses." She could state this more simply, "Let him kiss me," or "If only he would kiss me." The Hebrew text, however, is more complex, employing a verb (*let him kiss me*) and a noun ("kisses") that have the same root meaning. Most Biblical Hebrew words have roots of three consonants. The root of both the verb form *let him kiss me* and the noun "kisses" is *nšq*.

This type of wordplay occurs fairly frequently in the Hebrew Bible, but it is not always easy to translate into English. In this poem, the repetition of the root "kiss" expresses the intensification of the woman's desire. In English this intensification might be communicated by the expression *If only he would smother me with kisses*. In addition, the text's emphasis of the masculine pronouns ("him" and "his") suggests that it is not just any man's kisses she desires. She hopes that *he* will kiss her. This may lead us to ask, "But who is *he*?" Both lovers remain nameless in this book. Their names and identities are not important. What matters are the character of their relationship and the intensity of their feelings.

Taste. With the expression *For your love is more delightful than wine*, we encounter the sense of taste. In this verse the word translated *love* is a plural noun (*dodim*) that refers to all aspects of love, but perhaps more specifically to love as it is expressed physically through embraces or caresses. The term does not refer to an abstract concept of love, but rather to concrete expressions of love, and thus might be better translated as *lovemaking*. In a comparative statement, the woman rates the man's lovemaking as more delightful than wine.

In the Song of Songs, love and wine are frequently associated with each other (2:4; 4:10; 5:1; 7:9; 8:2), perhaps to suggest that love is intoxicating. In ancient Israel, wine was an essential part of life, and in the Bible, wine signifies God's favor. Thus the comparison of lovemaking to wine is favorable. Later in the Song, the man returns the woman's compliment when he says to her, *How much more pleasing is your lovemaking than wine* (4:10b AT). Wine is good and pleasant, but the woman rates the man's expressions of love better by comparison (see "Wine and Anointing Oils" in TBC).

Smell. We next encounter smell, with the woman's proclamation that *Pleasing is the fragrance of your perfumes; your name is like perfume poured out* (v. 3a). The word translated *perfume* is the word for oil in Biblical Hebrew (*šemen*). In ancient Israel, olive oil had multiple uses. It served as a cooking oil and as a fuel for lamps, but it also had both therapeutic and cosmetic functions. By adding spices, oil could become a perfume. As with hand lotions today, perfumed oils provide a pleasant scent and also soften dry skin. While some perfumed oils might have olive oil as a base, other scented oils might come from rare and expensive spices, such as oil of myrrh. The use of alliteration in Hebrew makes this verse pleasant to hear: the sounds *sh* and *m* occur three times within a sequence of six words.

The woman equates her lover's name with *perfume poured out*. It is not clear what the Hebrew word translated *poured out* (*turaq*) means in this verse. Most translations take it to be a passive form of a verb meaning "pour out," or "empty" (*ryq*), although a few translators think it refers to a special type of cosmetic oil (Pope: 300) or to an oil coming from a place named Turaq (Fox 1985: 97). Whatever the precise meaning of the word, the general sense of the verse seems clear. By proclaiming her lover's name to be perfumed oil, the woman suggests that he is as dear and as sweet as a precious, perfuming oil. The similar sounds of the Hebrew words for "name" (šem) and "oil" (šemen) contribute poetically to the association made between the lover's name and his scent. The woman concludes with the observation that since her lover has so many attractive features, other women love him too. It is not unusual for lovers to describe each other as desirable to other people.

Perhaps because she realizes that other women find her lover appealing, the woman now directly addresses her lover with two imperatives: *Take me away with you* and *let us hurry!* Suddenly the woman introduces a king into her expression of desire, saying, *Let the king bring me into his chambers.* The reference to Solomon in 1:1 might lead some readers quite naturally to assume that the king in this verse is Solomon. While this identification has its appeal, there are other ways to understand this verse. The poet's reference to royalty may be a poetic fiction by which the lovers express their mutual admiration and devotion through the use of royal language. The woman here honors the man (and, by extension, their relationship) by referring to him as a king *[King Fiction, p. 278]*. Although it is possible to take this as a past action (*The king has brought me into his chambers*), as the NRSV and some translations do, it seems best to take this as an expression of the woman's hope to spend time with her lover. The GNT expresses this well—also capturing the sense that she honors her lover by calling him a king: *Take me with you, and we'll run away; be my king and take me to your room.*

It is not clear who speaks in the rest of verse 4. The plural pronoun *we* suggests a shift in speaker. If we follow the NIV, the speech shifts to the woman's friends, who declare, *We rejoice and delight in you; we will praise your love more than wine.* Some interpreters propose that the woman continues to speak, perhaps referring to herself and her friends. Others think she may be speaking about herself and her lover. The masculine singular pronoun "you" in *How right they are to adore you!* suggests that somebody now addresses the man. Because of the plural pronoun reference "they," it seems right to accept NIV's suggestion that the woman speaks this line. One possible way to understand the movement of verse 4 is as follows. The woman expresses her desire to run away with her lover. The friends express approval. The woman agrees that others are right to love the man.

1:5-6 Her Self-Description

The poem next shifts to the woman's self-proclamation of her beauty to the group of women known in these poems as the "daughters of Jerusalem." Since the women do not respond, the passage is, in a sense, a soliloquy, in which the woman describes her appearance and comments on her brothers' actions *[Daughters of Jerusalem, p. 262]*.

Although there are several interpretive issues in these two verses, it seems clear that the woman asserts her sense of self-worth over against any negative evaluations of her appearance. Nowhere else in Song of Songs do we find negative statements about the woman's physical appearance. In fact, her lover repeatedly praises her beauty, expressing his positive evaluation of her in both direct statements (*How beautiful you are, my darling!*, 1:15a; 4:1a; *You are altogether beautiful, my darling; there is no flaw in you*, 4:7) and figurative language (4:1b-5; 6:4-9; 7:1-9). Why, then, does she sound defensive in this passage?

Before attempting to answer that question, we should consider two translation and interpretive issues. (1) The phrase *dark am I* and the word *lovely* are connected by a Hebrew word that can be translated either as a conjunctive: "Dark am I *and* lovely" or as a disjunctive "Dark am I, *but* lovely." The NIV chooses the latter route with its use of the word *yet*. The NRSV takes the conjunctive route and translates the woman's statement: "I am black *and* beautiful." (Both translations stand in line with early versions of the Hebrew text. The NIV follows the Latin Vulgate, and the NRSV follows the Septuagint tradition.) (2) We notice a second issue when we consider the NRSV. Does she describe herself as *dark* (NIV) or as *black* (NRSV)? With either term, contemporary readers should be careful not to read into this passage a racial or ethnic bias. There does appear, however, to be a bias based on socioeconomic status. Verse 6 implies that the young woman does not here describe her skin's natural pigmentation. Rather, she feels that people look down on her because her skin has been darkened by the sun. It seems likely that her self-description reflects a cultural bias for light-skinned women, perhaps because blackened or tanned skin indicates that the woman works outdoors and thus has lower status than light-skinned women who are privileged to stay indoors out of the harsh rays of the sun. As Stephanie Paulsell (198) observes, however, this young woman does not apologize for her appearance. Rather, she celebrates it.

> This passage is in no way an apology; rather it is the woman's assertion and celebration of her beauty. She delights in her body and in her

skin. Even held in a critical gaze by others who might see her skin not as beautiful but as a marker of lower-class status, the woman continues to view herself through the eyes of her lover, who, as he will soon declare, sees her as the "fairest among women" (1.8).

In describing her beauty, the young woman compares her darkness to the *tents of Kedar* and the *tent curtains of Solomon*. In the first simile, the *tents of Kedar* likely refer to tents made out of black goat hair (Keel: 47). Mentioned elsewhere in the Bible as well as in Assyrian records, Kedar was a nomadic tribe from Arabia, who lived in tents made of the skin of black goats—hence the comparison. The association with the *tent curtains of Solomon* is less clear. It may refer to luxurious tapestries hung either in Solomon's temple or in his palace. Poetic parallelism suggests that the woman may compare her dark complexion to the black tents of Kedar and her beauty to some type of tapestry located in the king's palace or in the Jerusalem temple: *I am dark like the tents of Kedar, beautiful like the tapestries of Solomon* (AT).

The young woman next tells the daughters of Jerusalem not to stare at her because of her dark skin. The Hebrew terms translated *dark* in verses 5 and 6 have the same root (šḥr), although they are not exactly the same word. The NIV uses the same word, *dark*, in both places. The wordplay might be better captured by translating the woman's command in verse 6 as this: *Do not stare at me because I am darkish*. The NIV uses another form of the word "dark" in the next line: *because I am darkened by the sun*. Here the Hebrew has a different word with a different root. A literal translation would be something like *because the sun has gazed upon me*. The poet employs a different type of wordplay based on the concept of "looking": *Do not stare at me because I am darkish, for the sun has gazed upon me*. A few translations capture this wordplay (NRSV, KJV, ESV).

If we return to the earlier question, why she sounds defensive about her appearance, we can speculate that she challenges a perspective on beauty held by urban elite, who remained indoors and out of the sun much of their lives. Although the book reveals little about the daughters of Jerusalem, to whom the woman directs her comments, their association with the capital city could lead us to conclude that they represent Israel's urban elite, whereas the young woman identifies herself with rural Israelites, who lived and worked out of doors. If this is the case, the young woman takes a proactive stance in asserting that by the cultural standards of rural Israel, she is, indeed, both dark and lovely.

The woman suddenly introduces her brothers into the conversation: *My mother's sons were angry with me and made me take care of the vineyards; my own vineyard I have neglected* (NIV 1984). The reason for the brothers' anger is not made explicit, but the second half of the verse offers some clues, if we assume there is a double meaning to the use of the term "vineyard." In the ancient world, families needed to guard their vineyards in order to keep out wild animals. The young woman may have been given the task of guarding the family vineyard (which would explain the reference to her darkened skin and the seemingly abrupt shift in her speech).

When the young woman refers to her vineyard, it seems likely she refers to her body, and perhaps by extension to her sexuality. If vineyard has this double meaning, she suggests that she has guarded the family vineyard, but not her own body (or her sexuality). The Hebrew text emphasizes the woman's possession with a doubling of the possessive pronoun (lit. *I have not guarded my vineyard that belongs to me*, AT).

Some interpreters suggest that this means the woman engaged in sexual activity with her lover, and it is this behavior that has angered her brothers (Bergant: 15-16). Others propose that she has not taken care of the physical appearance of her body (Longman: 98). The poetry is ambiguous. In some way, she has not guarded herself, but the precise nature of her behavior is unclear. The motivation for her brothers' anger is also unclear. Nevertheless, these few verses suggest that the woman's desires meet with resistance, coming from her family and from outsiders. Similar tensions will emerge in other poems within the book.

1:7-8 *A Dialogue about Her Lover's Whereabouts*

The love poems in this book have several primary settings: the royal court, the vineyard, and the pasture where shepherds graze their flocks. Thus far, the poetic dialogues have alluded to the royal court (with the references to Solomon in 1:4-5) and to the vineyard (1:6). The motif of shepherding a flock characterizes 1:7-8. The interconnected themes of presence and absence and searching and finding run throughout the book. The motif of searching for the beloved appears in this unit. Here the woman asks where her lover can be found. The reply, which comes most likely from her female companions, carries a tone of reproach. With their reply, the friends suggest that she should know the whereabouts of her lover, and if she doesn't know, she should search for him.

It appears that the young woman continues to speak in 1:7; however, the identity of the speaker, or speakers, is not absolutely clear in 1:8. It seems likely that the women (the daughters of Jerusalem) respond (although we cannot absolutely rule out the possibility that verses 7-8 are a playful interchange between the man and woman). First, we observe that elsewhere in the book it is the women who address the young woman with the expression *most beautiful of women* (5:9; 6:1). This suggests that in 1:8 it is the women who speak, addressing the young woman as *most beautiful of women*. Second, the relative clause translated *whom I love* occurs here and again in 3:1-5, where the woman searches for her absent lover. Even though in 1:7 the young woman appears to address her lover directly (lit. *tell me, whom I love, where you shepherd, where you cause to rest at midday*), the use of the phrase *whom I love* suggests that he is absent in this poem, just as he is in 3:1-5. The woman speaks to her lover as if he could hear her, but he cannot.

Instead of NIV's *you whom I love* in verse 7 some translations have *you whom my soul loves* (RSV, NRSV, NASB). The Hebrew *nepeš*, which appears in verse 7, is often translated by the English word "soul." It is a difficult word to translate into English because it has many different meanings in the Hebrew Bible. It can refer to the inner person, but in some contexts, when used with the possessive pronoun "my," it becomes a poetic synonym for the pronoun "I." The NIV translators assume that this is the case here and translate this phrase simply, *Tell me, you whom I love*. The noun *nepeš* refers frequently to the "throat" and often occurs in contexts related to thirst, longing, and desire, which makes it especially appropriate in this context. We might translate the Hebrew as *Tell me, you whom I fervently love* in order to emphasize the desire for the beloved that underlies the choice to use *nepeš* in this expression. To end the poetic unit, the friends reply, perhaps somewhat mockingly, that if the young woman has lost her lover, she should simply let the sheep lead her to him.

THE TEXT IN BIBLICAL CONTEXT

Kisses and Kissing

In the Bible, a kiss may outwardly express an inward desire for some level of intimacy between two people. In biblical times, kissing usually involved touching one's lips to another person's face or hands. Kissing another person's feet could indicate devotion, subservience, or humility. Kissing often occurred between family members (Gen

27:27; Exod 4:27; 2 Sam 14:33). In-laws also kiss: Moses kisses his father-in-law (Exod 18:7), and Naomi kisses her daughters-in-law Ruth and Orpah (Ruth 1:9). Close friends who are not family members kiss: David kisses Jonathan (1 Sam 20:41). In the fellowships that formed among Jesus' followers in the first century, kissing expressed spiritual kinship. In four letters, Paul instructs church members to greet each other with a holy kiss (Rom 16:16; 1 Cor 16:20; 2 Cor 13:12; 1 Thess 5:26; cf. the "kiss of love" in 1 Pet 5:14.) Willard Swartley (187) states that "the kiss of peace as practiced in the NT churches" was "a rite of peacemaking." We find kissing connected figuratively with peacemaking in a striking metaphor in Psalm 85:10:

> Love and faithfulness meet together;
> Righteousness and peace kiss each other.

On some occasions, a kiss symbolizes reconciliation, as with Jacob and Esau (Gen 33:4) and Joseph and his brothers (Gen 45:15). Kisses were associated with blessing (Gen 27:26-27) and with the anointing of a king (1 Sam 10:1). Because a kiss usually indicates love and intimacy, Judas's kiss of betrayal strikes us as especially shocking (Mark 14:45 and parallels).

Outside Song of Songs (1:2; 8:1), kissing is rarely mentioned in the Bible as an expression of sexual desire. Jacob and Rachel kiss before they are married, but since they are related, this may be considered the kissing of family members (Gen 29:11). In Proverbs, kissing is related to sexual seduction (7:13). Since the Bible is relatively reticent about physical intimacy between men and women, it is perhaps not surprising that kisses and kissing occur most often within the context of family relationships, rather than in settings related to sexual intimacy [*Figures of Speech, p. 267*].

Wine and Anointing Oils

In the Bible, both wine and anointing oils are associated with joyful celebration.

> You love righteousness and hate wickedness;
>   therefore God, your God, has set you above your companions
>   by anointing you with the oil of joy.
> All your robes are fragrant with myrrh and aloes and cassia;
>   from palaces adorned with ivory
>   the music of the strings makes you glad. (Ps 45:7-8)

The psalmist praises God for having created "wine that gladdens human hearts, oil to make their faces shine, and bread that sustains their hearts" (Ps 104:15). In the ancient world, people sometimes wore cones of ointment on their heads on special occasions. As it melted, the ointment produced a pleasant scent. This practice is likely reflected in Psalm 133, which compares family harmony to precious oil:

> How good and pleasant it is
>   when God's people live together in unity!
> It is like precious oil poured on the head,
>   running down on the beard,
> running down on Aaron's beard,
>   down on the collar of his robe.
> It is as if the dew of Hermon
>   were falling on Mount Zion.
> For there the LORD bestows his blessing,
>   even life forevermore.

Vines and Vineyards

Ancient Israel was a land of vineyards, and the fruit of the vine was one of the most important agricultural products. Consequently, it is not surprising that we read a lot about vineyards in the Bible. Perhaps because vineyards were so central to the life of ancient Israelites, vines and vineyards could symbolize the land and people of ancient Israel. Psalm 80 develops this symbolic imagery in a poetic description of the biblical exodus from Egypt. In a hymn of praise to God, the psalmist addresses God directly:

> You transplanted a vine from Egypt;
>   you drove out the nations and planted it.
> You cleared the ground for it,
>   and it took root and filled the land. (Ps 80:8-9)

The prophet Isaiah also develops the vineyard imagery in the well-known Song of the Vineyard in Isaiah 5:1-7. The prophet begins with a short narrative about a vineyard owner.

> I will sing for the one I love
>   a song about his vineyard;
> My loved one had a vineyard
>   on a fertile hillside.
> He dug it up and cleared it of stones
>   and planted it with the choicest vines.
> He built a watchtower in it

and cut out a winepress as well.
Then he looked for a crop of good grapes,
but it yielded only bad fruit. (Isa 5:1-2)

The poem abruptly shifts to the direct speech of the vineyard owner, in which he announces destruction upon the vineyard that failed to produce good grapes. Finally the prophet explains the symbolism for anyone who may have missed it. The vineyard owner is God. The vineyard is the people of God. The fruit of the vine symbolizes the people's deeds.

The vineyard of the LORD Almighty
is the nation of Israel,
and the people of Judah
are the vines he delighted in.
And he looked for justice, but saw bloodshed;
for righteousness, but heard cries of distress. (Isa 5:7)

Elsewhere in the Bible, the destruction of a vineyard can symbolize divine judgment in response to the disobedience of the people of God (see, e.g., Jer 5:10, 17; Hos 2:12; Amos 4:9). Jesus draws upon this imagery in the parable of the workers in the vineyard (Matt 20:1-16) and the parable of the tenants and the vineyard (Matt 21:33-43). The book of Revelation also develops vineyard imagery in its visions of judgment (14:14-20).

Vineyards also symbolize God's blessing and the restoration of the people of God. The prophet Amos announces that after exile, God's people will be restored to their land. "They will plant vineyards and drink their wine; they will make gardens and eat their fruit" (9:14b). A vineyard is the setting in several of Jesus' parables (Matt 20:1-11; Mark 12:1-12; Luke 13:6-9). In the Fourth Gospel, Jesus uses vine and vineyard imagery in a similar fashion to describe God's expectation that Jesus' disciples will "bear much fruit" (John 15:1-8).

In the Song of Songs, the vineyard appears as the location for the lovers' meetings (7:12). Using grape imagery, the man speaks metaphorically of his beloved (7:8). In two other places, the woman's body, and by extension her sexuality, are described metaphorically as a "vineyard" (1:6; 8:11-12). Although in the Song of Songs, vineyard imagery appears to be used differently, when we read Song of Songs within the context of the Scriptures, we are reminded that the people of God are frequently portrayed as "God's vineyard." The resonance of this imagery serves to support a theological reading of the Song, in which the lover represents God and his beloved, the people of God [*Figures of Speech, p. 267*].

TEXT IN THE LIFE OF THE CHURCH

Embodiment

The term "embodiment" expresses an understanding that human experience is embodied experience. Though it has a distinctive emphasis on human sexuality, the Song of Songs shares a view of human nature that is consistent with the rest of the Bible, both Old and New Testaments. Accordingly, it is essential that we understand that God created humans as physical beings, with desires, needs, and emotions. The Bible offers a complex view of human nature that can be described as "holistic," comprising mind, spirit, self, soul, and body all in one person *[Embodiment, p. 264]*.

Why is this important? Embodiment means that we *are* our bodies. We don't "have" bodies, and we certainly are not imprisoned in sinful bodies. This significant change in the way we think about ourselves can affect self-esteem. It may also influence how we treat our bodies. For example, we may treat our physical selves with more respect. We also may become more aware and more appreciative of the joy that physical experiences can bring. A Christian athlete in the film *Chariots of Fire* says, "When I run, I feel God's pleasure." What do *we do* physically that allows us to feel God's pleasure?

In the area of theology, embodiment reminds us that we humans are one part of a vast web of God's creation. Recognizing our embodied natures, we understand more clearly our vulnerabilities—that we can, and will, experience disease and death as part of what it means to be human. This, in turn, underscores our dependence upon God.

In ethics, embodiment means that what we do with our bodies has moral significance. It reminds us that, on the one hand, we should not despise, ignore, or mistreat bodies. On the other hand, we should not idolize bodies. Acceptance of our bodies as gifts of God can help us to avoid both extreme asceticism and extreme self-indulgence. Further, we become aware of ways in which cultural biases operate to denigrate our physical appearance. Through the voices of the young man and woman, the Song of Songs tells us that we are loved for who we are and not for how the surrounding culture views us.

In spirituality, embodiment reminds us of the role our bodily senses play in the practice of our faith. In baptism, we experience the touch of water upon our bodies, especially in those Christian communions that practice full bodily immersion in water. In congregational life, we hear ourselves and others sing praises to God. Singing, for many Christians, can be a spiritual discipline that helps to form them as disciples. Some Anabaptist traditions regularly observe a love feast, at which both the smell and the taste of the meal contribute to the experience of communion with other believers and with God. Nearly all Christians observe some form of bread-and-cup communion in which they taste the bread or wafer and the juice or wine. In the area of spiritual disciplines, we may think of private prayer as an embodied spiritual discipline, if we concentrate on prayer as a conversation with God in which we both speak and listen. Finally, our vision participates in all these spiritual experiences; additionally for some Christians, meditating upon a drawing or painting can become a concrete means to experience the presence of God.

God's Kiss

For much of Christian history, Song of Songs was mined for its spiritual meanings. The kiss of Song 1:2 is not simply a human expression of physical intimacy; it also points to intimacy with God. Far from negating the literal meaning of Song of Songs (although some readers have rejected a literal reading), a spiritual reading can deepen our appreciation of the Song. Taking embodiment seriously, a spiritual reading begins with an understanding of the goodness of creation and of the human body and proceeds with the realization that we can use human experiences to express our experience of the divine.

For Bernard of Clairvaux (1090–1153), the kiss in 1:2 symbolizes the incarnation, and the woman's yearning for a kiss represents humanity's longing to enter into an intimate relationship with God.

> Normally the touch of lip on lip is the sign of the loving embrace of hearts, but this conjoining of natures brings together the human and divine, shows God reconciling "to himself all things, whether on earth or in heaven." (*Sermons* 2.3)

This is the kiss we all long for, the kiss that brings us into an intimate relationship with God. This kiss is the one that brings peace to the earth, a peace that reconciles us with each other and with God.

In a wonderful piling up of Scripture texts, Jerome (347–420) connects this verse with Psalm 85 and Ephesians 2:14, as well as relating it to the apostle Paul's instruction for Christian brothers and sisters to greet each other with a holy kiss (Rom 16:16; 1 Cor 16:20; 2 Cor 13:12; 1 Thess 5:26):

Justice and peace have kissed. All this becomes one in the mystery of the Lord Savior, the Son of man and of God who is our truth, kindness, peace, justice, in whom the justice of the first people and the mystery of the second people are joined together into one peace. The apostle says, in fact, "He himself is our peace, he it is who has made both one." This is the mystery for which the church longs and cries out in the Canticle of Canticles: "Let him kiss me with kisses of his mouth." This is the kiss of which Paul the Apostle says, "Greet one another with a holy kiss." (Jerome 54: "Homily 64")

If we tried to diagram these connections, it might look like this:

Justice + Peace
=
Jesus
=
Breaking down walls that divide
+
Expressing love for one another in community.

In the sixteenth century, several Anabaptists explored the meaning of the kiss in Song 1:2. For Melchior Hoffman (1495–1543?), the kiss is the gospel message. For Pilgram Marpeck (ca. 1495–1556?) and Dirk Philips (1504–68), the kiss is the Word of God, perhaps understood as God's revelation through both Scripture and the Son. In *True Christian Faith*, Menno Simons (1496–1561) writes: "He would bring us into the chamber of his covenant, kiss us with the lips of His peace, wash us from all our uncleanness, and espouse us as his bride" (*CWMS* 374).

Dirk Philips explains that the bride and groom of the Song of Songs have been spiritually restored in Christ and the church. For Dirk, the kiss represents the restoration of the people of God, described in figurative language as a wedding between Christ as Bridegroom and the church as bride.

> Here in Christ and his congregation, the Song of Solomon about the king and his bride is spiritually repeated. Here the Bridegroom, Christ, kissed his bride with the holy kiss of peace and is joyful because of her beauty and because of the costly fragrance of her ointments; that is, because of her inward gifts, virtues, and the anointment of the Holy Spirit with which she is adorned and anointed. (*WDP* 340)

Isaac Watts (1674–1748), the well-known English hymnist, composed a series of hymn texts based on Song of Songs. In the following stanzas of one of these hymns, Watts (no. 558) relates the kiss of Song 1:2 to the love of Christ, expressed figuratively as an embrace:

Let him embrace my soul, and prove
Mine interest in his heavenly love:
The voice that tells me, *Thou art mine,*
Exceeds the blessings of the vine.

On thee th' anointing Spirit came,
And spreads the savour of thy name;
That oil of gladness and of grace
Draws virgin-souls to meet thy face.

Jesus, allure me by thy charms;
My soul shall fly into thine arms:
Our wandering feet thy favours bring
To the fair chambers of the King.

God's kiss—incarnation, good news, peace, and spiritual renewal. With these in mind, may we meditate upon these words and fervently pray, *Let Him kiss me with the kisses of His mouth!* (AT).

Following Jesus

The NIV translates 1:4 in a way that emphasizes the romance of the young couple in love: *Take me away with you—let us hurry!* The RSV and NRSV have *Draw me after you, let us make haste,* a translation that I think works better with a theological or spiritual reading of the Song, which identifies the man as the Christ, and the woman as the Believer. In this TLC, I am working with the *Draw me after you* translation to connect the verse with a Christian understanding of discipleship as "following Jesus."

This connection struck me in a visual way when I saw a fifteenth-century German woodcut that portrays a female figure being physically drawn after Jesus by means of a rope. The female figure may represent a nun, but she may also be understood to represent any disciple of Christ. Both the woman and Jesus bear a wooden cross on their shoulders, and they are connected by means of a rope tied around their waists. Jesus turns to look back at the woman, with whom he is in conversation. Below the visual image is the text of their conversation, a dialogue in which she wishes to postpone her responsibility to imitate Christ's suffering. Jesus encourages her to persevere, and she agrees to take up the cross and follow Jesus.

Although not exclusive to Anabaptist and Pietist traditions, following Jesus is central to their understanding of what it means to be a Christian. Following Jesus, an act of discipleship, demands both belief and action. It means following Jesus in our everyday lives, expressing our discipleship in acts of love.

Gregory the Great (540–604) explains that because we are weak, we are incapable of following Jesus. That is, we need Christ's help in order to become good disciples. Following Jesus is not an easy thing to do. Consequently, like the woman in 1:4, we must ask Jesus, *Draw me after you.*

In a poem contained within a letter, Clare of Assisi (1194–1253) expresses more the joy of companionship with Jesus, "the heavenly Spouse." Born into a noble family, Clare chose to dedicate herself to a life of poverty after hearing Francis of Assisi preach. Using the Franciscan Order as a model, Clare founded a monastic order for women, known today as the Poor Clares. In this portion of the letter, Clare exhorts her spiritual sister Agnes to "be inflamed more strongly with the fervor of charity."

> Draw me after You!
> We will run in the fragrance of Your perfumes,
> O heavenly Spouse!
> I will run and not tire,
> until You bring me into the wine-cellar,
> until Your left hand is under my head
> and Your right hand will embrace me happily
> and You will kiss me with the happiest kiss of Your mouth.
> (Clare of Assisi: 205)

Interestingly, the Anabaptist Pilgram Marpeck associates the request *Draw me after you* with love rather than with suffering. In a letter in which he expresses the power of nonviolent love, Marpeck quotes Song 1:4. He observes that the possession, or experience, of love only increases our desire for love. This is why in Song of Songs, one lover asks the other, *Draw me after you.*

> For in this time we cannot lay claim to the fullness of love with its power to convince. But [we can] follow her path with sincere desire, and mark her footprints and tracks with earnestness, as love pleads with and speaks to love in the Canticle: "Draw me after you and let us make haste" [1:4] and never to lose sight of her until we completely possess her in that day with Christ. For he who possesses her to the fullest degree possible in this time is merely given a greater desire for her, but can never see her form clearly nor embrace her as she has embraced him. She is like a stag or deer, which, when they see someone, quickly dash out of sight [perhaps alluding to Song 2:9, 17; 8:14]. Thus, her return is swift to human eyes to grant man his desire to see her form and to prove with power why it is that she is called love. She is not to be bought. She cannot be coerced, driven, nor urged. Even if one gave his wealth for her [8:7b], he will not gain her, for she is priceless and unconquerable. (*WPM* 533)

The more we love, the more we desire love. Our desire for love brings us the joy of companionship with Jesus, who empowers us to love even more deeply. Reading Song of Songs in connection with Christian discipleship, may we then pray, using the words of Song 1:4, *Draw me after you [Love and Desire, p. 279].*

Song of Songs 1:9–2:7

Poems of Admiration and Desire

PREVIEW

When two people first fall in love, they are often captivated by each other's physical appearance. They may describe their beloved to others, commenting upon her or his eyes, smile, hair, form. As the relationship develops, they may begin to appreciate other aspects. Does he listen intently when she speaks? Does she laugh at his jokes? Insecurities may surface. How do I compare in his eyes to other women? Does she compare me to other men? These appear to be some of the questions underlying the poems in this unit.

OUTLINE

A Poem of the Lovers' Mutual Admiration, 1:9-17
    1:9-11   He Admires His Lover
    1:12-14   She Admires Her Lover
    1:15-17   Expressions of Mutual Admiration
A Poem of Comparisons and of Her Desire for Him, 2:1-7
    2:7   Refrain: Her Charge to the Daughters of Jerusalem

EXPLANATORY NOTES

A Poem of the Lovers' Mutual Admiration 1:9-17

1:9-11 He Admires His Lover

For the first time in the Song, we encounter the man's use of *my darling* as a term of endearment for the woman. The Hebrew term is usually translated either as *my darling* (NIV, NASB) or *my love* (NRSV, GNB). In this passage, the term *my darling (raʿyati)* helps with the transition to a new poem by creating a wordplay with the Hebrew words *graze (reʿi)* and *shepherds (roʿim)* in 1:8, because all three Hebrew words have the same root (*rʿh*). Hebrew wordplay like this is nearly impossible to capture in English translations, which makes it all the more difficult to comprehend the transitions between poems within Song of Songs.

I liken you, my darling, to a mare harnessed to one of the chariots of Pharaoh (AT). Just as earlier the woman declared herself *lovely* (1:5), her lover now affirms her beauty. The man's comparison of his lover to a mare proves challenging to modern readers, who undoubtedly ask, "Is this supposed to be a flattering comparison?" Introduced to ancient Israel from central Asia, horses were not commonly used in farming or for regular transportation. Rather, they were more frequently associated with the royal court and with war. Richard S. Hess (63) suggests that before the Persian period, most horses would have belonged to the king for use in battle. We can first conclude, then, that a reference to horses brings to mind the royal court, thus implying the woman's excellence in the eyes of her lover.

It seems that chariots were pulled by stallions, not by mares (Pope: 336–41; Keel: 56–58). Some interpreters suggest that we should imagine the reaction of a group of male chariot horses when they come in contact with a mare (Pope; Bergant; Longman). Just as a mare can create confusion among otherwise disciplined chariot horses, so the man's lover has the power to unsettle him. Alternately, we might take this comparison in ancient times as a common way for a man to describe something he values highly (Exum: 108).

A second point of comparison is to beautiful jewelry: *Your cheeks are beautiful with earrings, your neck with strings of jewels. We will make you earrings of gold, studded with silver.* Ancient Near Eastern art depicts women wearing jeweled headdresses, long dangling earrings, and rows of necklaces; we might assume that the woman in the Song is similarly adorned. The shift to *we* in this poem could reflect either an interjection by the daughters of Jerusalem or a comment made by the man in which he includes other unidentified individuals. Because he values his lover's beauty and charm, he may assume that everyone will quite naturally want to make jewelry to frame her lovely face.

1:12-14 She Admires Her Lover

In the previous poem of admiration (1:9-11), the man focuses on the physical attractiveness of his lover; now in 1:12-14, she describes her lover's intoxicating fragrance. Again, the world of the royal court permeates this passage as do the sensual activities of eating and lovemaking, which are frequently intertwined in Song of Songs.

The woman again honors her lover by referring to him as *the king* (1:12) *[King Fiction, p. 278]*. What is the setting for this scene? Is it the dining room, as NIV's *table* might suggest? Or does this take place on the king's couch, as NRSV indicates? As Garrett (146) notes, the Hebrew term has to do with something circular and therefore could be taken as either a circular piece of furniture or a circle of people. Even if the precise setting for this poem is unclear, the following verses give a sexual connotation to the whole poem.

For the first time in the book, in 1:13 we encounter her preferred term of endearment for him: *my beloved* (Heb. *dodi*). Three sources of fragrance are identified in these verses: nard, myrrh, and henna blossoms *[Aromatics, p. 260]*. Although in the NIV we read *my perfume spread its fragrance,* the Hebrew term translated *perfume* is the word *nerd,* which refers to a rare, fragrant ointment from India commonly known as *nard,* or *spikenard.* Myrrh is a gum resin, and in biblical times it was imported from India and Arabia. Henna, shrubs with roselike flowers, grew in both Egypt and Israel. All three produce a pleasing fragrance. Thus the woman declares that just as she is the source of her lover's pleasure, so is he the source of her delight.

Although her speech began with reference to a king located presumably indoors and possibly in Jerusalem, the woman ends with a reference to En Gedi, an oasis located in the Judean wilderness along the western shore of the Dead Sea, about twenty-five miles southeast of Jerusalem *[Geography, p. 269]*. In the midst of the dry Judean wilderness and alongside the saltiest sea in the world, this spring-fed oasis and its verdant flora suggest the beauty of the feelings she has for her beloved.

1:15-17 Expressions of Mutual Admiration

Following two poems in which the lovers express their admiration for each other, we read two exclamations in which each lover proclaims the other "beautiful." In the NIV, he proclaims her *beautiful*, and she proclaims him *handsome*; however, in the Hebrew text the same adjective is used of both. She adds that he is *charming* as well as *handsome*. He comments on her eyes. She draws attention to their bed.

As Exum (112) observes, the poet uses the Hebrew particle *hinneh* (KJV: *behold*; NRSV: *Ah*) as an attention-getter. The man wants his lover to see herself through his eyes when he says to her, *How beautiful you are, my darling!* It may be better to use the word "look" to communicate this use of *hinneh*: *Look at you! You are beautiful, my friend!* (AT). The woman responds similarly, *Look at you! You are beautiful, my love* (Exum's translations: 112). Even more, "the poet directs the reader's gaze as well, creating the illusion of immediacy by bringing what the lovers see immediately before our eyes" (Exum: 112).

The man compares his lover's eyes to doves both here and in a later poem (4:1), and she draws a similar comparison about his eyes (5:12). Modern readers might be perplexed by this comparison. In what way do eyes resemble doves? Interpreters offer different explanations, suggesting that the lover's eyes and doves are similar in shape, color, or in their movement. As Keel (69–71) and others have noted, doves symbolized love in the ancient world. Consequently, the comparison to doves fits the context of love poetry. This short unit concludes with references to the fragrances of the natural world: the fresh smells of cedar and fir.

A Poem of Comparisons and of Her Desire for Him 2:1-7

The poems of admiration continue, but with a shift first to the woman's self-description by way of floral imagery (although it is possible to read 2:1 as spoken by the man).

The identification of the two flowers mentioned in 2:1 as *a rose of Sharon* and *a lily of the valleys* (NRSV) is deeply entrenched in much of the English-speaking world, even though commentators today offer other identifications that better fit the ancient Near Eastern context, with its distinctive climate and rainfall. In North America, the common name "rose of Sharon" refers to an eight- to twelve-foot shrub of east Asian origin and thus cannot be the flower (*ḥabaṣṣelet*) mentioned in Song of Songs. If the term *Sharon* refers to a ten-mile-wide coastal region between Joppa and Mount Carmel, the poet may be referring to a single plant, such as the sea daffodil, which produces a large and showy bloom [*Flowers, p. 268*].

English translations commonly identify the second flower (*šôšannah*) as a type of lily. Again, the precise identification of the plant is unknown. Since the flower known in the United States as "lily of the valley" is native to Europe, we should not picture in our mind's eye that small perennial plant with fragrant bell-shaped white flowers when we read this passage. Possible candidates for this flower include various types of lily, such as the white, or Madonna, lily, as well as varieties of the water lily, or lotus. Several scholars have offered compelling arguments for the identification of this flower as the blue lotus, which was associated in ancient Near Eastern art and poetry with love and with those powers that can overcome death (Keel: 78–80). Derek Suderman (49–53) explains how the identity of the flower affects our understanding of the woman's self-description in 2:1. By identifying herself as a blue lotus blossom, the woman claims that she is beautiful and life giving (not plain and modest). In short, she is magnificent!

The man picks up the floral imagery to assert his lover's uniqueness among other young women. He agrees with her. She *is* a beautiful flower, and compared to her, all other women are thorns. The woman's voice returns as she, in turn, compliments her lover. Just as he has proclaimed her superior to all other women, she contrasts him to other men. In the forest, her lover is the one fruit tree that offers both shade and sweet-tasting fruit (2:3).

As with the flowers, a precise identification of the fruit tree is impossible. Although some interpreters think the Hebrew term (*tappuaḥ*) refers to a type of apple tree, others hold that this identification is unlikely, due to the acidic nature of the type of wild apples that would have grown in ancient Israel at this time. Instead, they propose that the poet here speaks of apricots, which would have been sweeter than wild apples.

The precise meaning of 2:4 is unclear. According to NIV, he brings his lover into *the banquet hall*. Literally translated, the location is *the house of wine* (*bet hayyayin*). The NRSV similarly loses the Hebrew text's reference to wine with its *banqueting house*. As we have already seen in 1:2, wine and love are closely associated (as also in 4:10; 7:9.) The *house of wine* may be a private home where wine is served or an outdoor location, but wherever it is, the *house of wine* represents the couple's lovemaking. It is their trysting place.

In the second half of 2:4, the translations diverge. NRSV has *his intention toward me was love*, but in the NIV, we read, *Let his banner over me be love*. Does the Hebrew word *degel* mean "intention" or "banner"? In the ancient Near East, military groups gathered under banners, and the banner itself might portray a symbol of the army's patron deity. Possibly the banner symbolized the deity's protection of the group that marched under the banner. Since we see military connotations elsewhere in the Song (5:10; 6:4, 10), it makes sense to follow the NIV here. The poet portrays the woman as an army marching under the banner of love. Even more, it is her lover's banner that flies over her, both proclaiming their association and symbolizing the nature of that association.

The woman announces that she is *faint with love*. Paradoxically, although faint with love, she craves a food that will heighten her desire for love. In the ancient Near East, raisin cakes were associated with a Canaanite goddess and with love, and apples were considered an aphrodisiac. When we call somebody "lovesick" today, we don't mean they have an illness for which they need a cure. Rather, we recognize that love can be all-consuming. Young lovers forget to eat. They reject sleep. They use all their strength to remain focused on their beloved.

She next describes his embrace. In the NIV, the description is in the present tense: *His left arm is under my head, and his right arm embraces me.* It is also possible to understand this as a wish on the part of the woman, as the NRSV does: *O that his left hand were under my head, and that his right hand embraced me!* Within this context, it may make sense to follow the NIV since she has just announced that she is "faint with love" and thus in need of a supporting embrace. With either translation, however, we can understand the paradoxical nature of lovesickness, in which the lover wants more of the very thing that causes her to feel faint.

2:7 Refrain: Her Charge to the Daughters of Jerusalem

The entire section of poems of admiration concludes with the following refrain:

> *Daughters of Jerusalem, I charge you*
> *by the gazelles and by the does of the field:*
> *Do not arouse or awaken love*
> *until it so desires.* (2:7)

This refrain occurs three times within Song of Songs. It is repeated verbatim in 3:5. In 8:4, it has a slight variation. The precise function and meaning of this refrain, often referred to as an "adjuration," remains somewhat elusive.

She identifies her audience as the *daughters of Jerusalem*, the same group she addressed earlier (1:5) and will continue to address throughout the poems (3:5; 5:8, 16; 8:4) [*Daughters of Jerusalem, p. 262*].

The opening phrase, *I charge you,* can also be translated *I place you under oath* or *I want you to promise.* The GNT puts it this way: *Promise me, women of Jerusalem; swear by the swift deer and the gazelles.*

In biblical oaths, the person taking an oath often makes a pledge in the name of God. Here, however, the woman charges the daughters of Jerusalem to pledge an oath, not in God's name, but by gazelles and does. This substitution introduces a bit of whimsy appropriate to the subject matter. Gazelles and does belong to the lovers' world created in Song of Songs. References to the male gazelle and deer appear in Song 2:9, 17; 8:14. References to female gazelles can be found in 4:5 and 7:3. In the ancient Near East, these animals were often associated with the love goddess, as Keel (89–94) demonstrates through iconography. The independence of these wild animals may also play into the meaning of the adjuration. As long as love remains unprovoked, one is as free as the wild gazelles and deer, but once love takes over, freedom and independence are overcome by the desire for one's lover (Munro: 90–91).

The substitution also indulges in a bit of Hebrew wordplay. The Hebrew word for *gazelles*, ṣebaʾot, has the same spelling as the word for "hosts," ṣebaʾot, in "Lord of hosts"; and the phrase *does of the field,* ʾayelot haśśadeh, resembles the name Elohim Shaddai, ʾelohim šadday. Some interpreters suggest that the reference to animals in the oath may occur due to sensitivity regarding the invocation of God's name in this context (Gordis: 26–28; Hess: 82).

Interpreters are divided over the meaning of the second half of the refrain, *Do not arouse or awaken love until it so desires.* Some take the term *love* as a reference to physical lovemaking. They understand the verse to mean "Don't interrupt this couple's lovemaking until they are finished." Others offer a more compelling argument by taking the term *love* to refer to love in the abstract, rather than to physical lovemaking. Following this line of argument, the refrain means something like "Don't try to force love, because love has a will of its own." This latter interpretation has the advantage of complementing the book's primary statement about love in 8:6-7, that love is a power that cannot be resisted. It also has the advantage of maintaining the Song of Song's reticence when it comes to describing the couple's actual physical lovemaking. With this first occurrence of the adjuration, as readers we may feel puzzled with regard to its meaning, but as Exum (119) suggests, we continue to explore this couple's love in the next few chapters, and the significance of the adjuration becomes more clear.

THE TEXT IN BIBLICAL CONTEXT

Salvation Imagery: The Land Bursts into Bloom

At one level, we can read this set of poems as descriptions of the feelings of admiration that two lovers have for each other. When people fall in love, the beloved stands head and shoulders above everyone else. He is more handsome than other men. She has more character than other women. At a second level, however, this text reflects the relationship between God and the people of God. By reading this passage alongside passages from the prophetic books, we discover corresponding imagery. In the prophets, agricultural imagery abounds. Flowers and gardens and flourishing crops symbolize salvation in prophetic messages. In a vision of a restored Zion, the prophet Isaiah describes the rejuvenation of the land:

> The desert and the parched land will be glad;
>   the wilderness will rejoice and blossom.
> Like the *rose* [*ḥabaṣṣelet*], it will burst into bloom;
>   it will rejoice greatly and shout for joy.
> The glory of Lebanon will be given to it,
>   the splendor of Carmel and Sharon;
> they will see the glory of the LORD,
>   the splendor of our God. (Isa 35:1-2 AT)

Many English translations try to offer a more accurate identification of the flower in this passage by translating the Hebrew term *ḥabaṣṣelet* as *crocus*, but the Hebrew word is the same one commonly translated *rose* in Song of Songs 2:1. Even though the flower is probably not a rose, what is important to observe is that both the Isaiah text and the poem in Song of Songs use this flower to symbolize joy.

Similarly, the prophet Hosea provides an image of salvation that refers to the lily (*šôšannāh*). God speaks through the prophet to announce a future time of salvation.

> "I will heal their waywardness
>   and love them freely,
>   for my anger has turned away from them.
> I will be like the dew to Israel;
>   he will blossom like a lily [*šôšannāh*]." (Hos 14:4-5a)

Just as the woman of the Song delights in her lover's *shade* (Heb. *ṣēl*, 2:3), so the Israelites will flourish beneath God's shade.

> People will dwell again *in his shade*;
>   they will flourish like the grain.

> They will blossom like the vine—
> Israel's fame will be like the wine of Lebanon.
> (Hos 14:7, emph. added)

If we read Song of Songs at this level, we see echoes of the prophetic tradition within Song of Songs. God will renew the land so that it bursts into bloom. God is the dew that enables people to flourish, to blossom like the lily. God is Israel's tree, providing shade (i.e., protection) to God's people. Reading the Song and the Prophets intertextually leads us to read both the Prophets and the Song in a new light.

THE TEXT IN THE LIFE OF THE CHURCH

Flowers and Spirituality

Flowers play an important role in the Song of Songs. They signal love. They symbolize the beloved. They provide the milieu in which lovemaking occurs. This remains true today. We give flowers as tokens of our love. Roses on Valentine's Day. A special bouquet on a birthday. A potted lily or geranium on Mother's Day. We use flowers to express similar feelings about God and to create a special place in which to experience God's presence. Many churches place a floral arrangement on an altar or worship area in the front of the sanctuary, and flowers and plants may be located in other areas of the church building. Think, too, of the way in which we use flowers to express our feelings of love for those we have lost to death.

Flowers, generally, convey meaning. Specific flowers convey specific meanings (Sill: 50–53; Fisher). In the Song of Songs the flowers identified traditionally as rose and lily have played important symbolic roles in the Christian tradition. The imagery of lily and rose pervades Western art, music, and devotional writing through the centuries. Red roses symbolize martyrdom. White roses symbolize purity and are associated with Mary. Lilies symbolize purity, but also innocence and immortality. Christians hymns refer to Jesus as the "Lily of the Valley" and as the "Rose of Sharon" and to Mary as "the rose that bare Jesu" *[Flowers, p. 268].*

Jesus Christ, the Apple Tree

Chapter 2 of the Song provides us with another arresting image, that of the apple tree. An early American song shares imagery with Song of Songs 2:3. Known as "The Tree of Life" or "Jesus Christ, the Apple Tree," the anonymous eighteenth-century text speaks of

Jesus as "tree of life" and as an "apple tree" (Fyock and Wright: 340, no. 509):

> 1. The tree of life my soul hath seen,
> Laden with fruit and always green:
> The trees of nature fruitless be
> Compared with Christ the apple tree.
>
> 2. His beauty doth all things excel:
> By faith I know, but ne'er can tell
> The glory which I now can see
> In Jesus Christ the apple tree.
>
> 3. For happiness I long have sought,
> And pleasure dearly I have bought:
> I missed of all; but now I see
> 'Tis found in Christ the apple tree.
>
> 4. I'm weary with my former toil,
> Here I will sit and rest awhile:
> Under the shadow I will be,
> Of Jesus Christ the apple tree.
>
> 5. This fruit doth make my soul to thrive,
> It keeps my dying faith alive;
> Which makes my soul in haste to be
> With Jesus Christ the apple tree.

If we reflect on the importance of flowers and trees in the lives of our ancestors, we might ask ourselves, "What place do *we* make for flowers, trees, and other flora in our spiritual lives today?" In this technological age, have photos of flowers and gardens posted on social media sites replaced the actual thing? Perhaps for some. But for others, the natural world continues to serve as an essential means of experiencing the holy. We notice the floral arrangements in worship. And for some of us, gardening, camping, and spiritual retreats in the wilderness (or as close as we can get to wilderness in the contemporary world) play an important role in our spiritual development. We feel God's presence as we dig our hands into the soil, appreciate the beauty of roses, lilies, and other flowers, or sit quietly in the shade of a tree. The Song of Songs reminds us that love—human and divine—touches us in a special way through the natural world.

Song of Songs 2:8-17

An Invitation to Love

PREVIEW

When two people are in love, it may feel like an eternal springtime. Flowers bloom. Birds sing. Trees form fruit. Nevertheless, the experience of love can bring out our deepest insecurities. Lovers begin to ask, "How can he love me? Does he *really* love me? Does he really love me—and *only* me?" If unsure, a lover may become cautious. Although the poems in this section can be read in different ways, this chapter explores the possibility that the woman both pulls her lover toward her and pushes him away.

OUTLINE

Her Description of His Sudden Appearance, 2:8-9
His Expression of Desire for Her, 2:10-13
An Invitation and Response, 2:14-17
    2:16   Refrain: Her Expression of Mutual Belonging

EXPLANATORY NOTES

Her Description of His Sudden Appearance 2:8-9

The poem begins by calling our attention to the senses of sight and sound. Suddenly she hears him and then sees him. The Hebrew of the opening verse of this poem quickly brings the lovers into focus with language of immediacy.

> *The voice of my lover! Look, he's here!* (AT)

The poem opens with two words in Hebrew: *qol dodi*, the voice, or sound, of my beloved. The word *qol* means both "voice" and "sound." Some interpreters suggest that she hears him running toward her. Others propose that the verse anticipates her lover's speech in 2:10 (which she quotes). We can perhaps assume that the poet has both in mind: the sound of the lover bounding toward her like a gazelle and the voice that we soon hear through the woman's own voice in verse 10.

The Hebrew word *hinneh* adds to the sense of immediacy in this poem. The word is often translated "behold." What it means is "Look!" It is an interjection expressing surprise and calling attention to the object of "Look!" The NIV correctly captures the sense of immediacy, surprise, and delight:

> *Listen! My beloved!*
> *Look! Here he comes.*

Using the language of simile, she compares him to a gazelle. But why? Gazelles move with grace and speed. As animals of the forest and wilderness, they have freedom and independence. Gazelles appear frequently on stamp and cylinder seals in the ancient Near East (Hess: 89; Keel: 96–97). As Keel observes, the proverbial speech of the gazelle can be seen in an ancient Egyptian love song, in which a woman invites her lover to come to her.

> *If only you would come to (your) sister swiftly,*
> *like a gazelle bounding over the desert.*
> (Keel: 96; for the entire poem, see Fox 1985: 66–67)

Like a wild gazelle or stag, her lover leaps over mountains to get to her. He then stands outside her house, looking in through the window to gaze upon her, before he speaks.

His Expression of Desire for Her 2:10-13

The woman reveals what her lover says to her. Although the NIV does not indicate this, the Hebrew vocabulary used here indicates that the man's speech is in response to the woman: *My lover responded, saying* . . . (AT). In this poem, the change of speakers is explicitly stated, whereas earlier in Song of Songs, we saw that speakers change without any narrative indication. The speeches are simply juxtaposed, and readers determine who is speaking based upon the content.

The man's speech in 2:10-13 is framed by an invitation to the woman he calls *my darling* and *my beautiful one*. This framing device (often called "inclusio") is commonly used in Biblical Hebrew narrative. As an inclusio, the address *Arise, come, my darling, my beautiful one, come with me* encapsulates the reason the woman should come with the man: spring has arrived.

> *Arise, my darling, my beautiful one, come with me.*
> *See! The winter is past;*
> *the rains are over and gone.*
> *Flowers appear on the earth;*
> *the season of singing has come,*
> *the cooing of doves*
> *is heard in our land.*
> *The fig tree forms its early fruit;*
> *the blossoming vines spread their fragrance.*
> *Arise, come, my darling; my beautiful one, come with me.*

As Exum (126) observes, the second occurrence of the invitation at the end of 2:13 also introduces his motivation in 2:14: he wants to see and hear her. Once again, the poem draws our attention to the senses of sight and sound. As lovers, they enjoy gazing upon each other, and they delight in hearing each other's voice. Notice that the punctuation in the NIV suggests that the man's speech is limited to 2:10-13.

Earlier we encountered the first term of endearment, *my darling* (1:9, 15; 2:2). The second term is new, appearing here and again in later poems in the book (4:1, 7; 6:4). Although in previous poems he has not referred to her as *my beautiful one,* the language of beauty has already been used for both the man and the woman (1:8, 15, 16).

He invites her to come away with him, providing a motivation in 2:11-13a. This unit provides a seasonal reference for the invitation: *winter is past, the rains are over and gone.* In Israel, winter occurs in the months from October to April, which corresponds with the rainy season. If the rainy season has ended, it is probably April or May. Five things occur at this time: (1) flowers appear, (2) singing occurs, (3) doves coo, (4) fig trees begin to form fruit, and (5) vines blossom.

The word *zamir,* translated *singing,* can also mean "pruning." Some interpreters explain that pruning would not take place in April and May, so that it must mean "singing" here. Others propose that the word retains its dual meaning in the context: "singing" points ahead to the turtledoves' cooing (v. 12) and "pruning" points back to the ending of winter and beginning of spring (v. 11). The bird identified as a dove in the NIV is the turtledove (*streptopelia turtur*), a migratory bird that appears in Israel in mid-April, at the end of the rainy season. The Hebrew word here is *tor,* whereas in verse 14, the noun for *dove* is *yonah.* "Fig tree and vine" appear together fairly frequently in the Bible to denote security and prosperity. Fig trees ripen in May, and grapevines blossom at that time.

An Invitation and Response 2:14-17

Suddenly the landscape shifts. From a cultivated garden, we turn to the craggy and distant mountains. Following the second invitation to come away with him, the man addresses his lover as *my dove* (v. 14), and he likens her behavior to that of a dove perched *in the clefts of the rock, in the hiding places of the mountainside.* This is the first of the three occurrences of *my dove* as a term of endearment in Song of Songs. As Keel (103) observes, the ancient Near Eastern association of doves with goddesses may underlie the use of dove in the book. An additional characteristic of doves plays a role in verse 14. They have the ability to hide and nest in secluded places. As doves nest in hidden, hard-to-reach mountainous regions, so the man's lover appears similarly inaccessible to him. He invites her to come to him, complimenting her on her sweet voice and lovely face.

Although the NIV gives verse 15 to the man, it seems best to understand this verse as the beginning of the woman's reply to her lover's request that she come away with him. Exum (128–30) offers a compelling explanation and interpretation of this verse. Elsewhere in Song of Songs, the vineyard symbolizes the woman. Exum explains that in verse 15 the vineyards similarly represent young unmarried women and the foxes stand for lusty young men. In ancient Israelite society, young men would have been able to pursue young women, but young women had to be cautious about their responses. In this verse, the young woman speaks for herself and other young women when she uses figurative language to describe the danger that young men pose to unmarried young women: young men are like foxes who ruin vineyards. As a response to the young man's invitation to come away with him, the young woman uses a proverbial style to say, "Young women have to be cautious with young men. They cannot become sexually involved until they have 'caught' a young man for their own."

The verb for "catching" foxes in 2:15 (*ʾḥz*) appears again in 3:4, where NIV translates it as *I held him.* The use of the same verbal root in both 2:15 and 3:4 supports Exum's interpretation (128–30). Here in verse 15, the woman says, *Let us seize for ourselves the foxes* (AT). In 3:4, after searching for her lover and finding him, she says, *I seized him and would not let him go* (AT).

In her reply, the woman shifts from a teasing response to a more serious response in verse 16. Here in its first occurrence in the book, we encounter a refrain expressing the mutuality of the couple's relationship. (See 6:3 and 7:10 for the later occurrences of the refrain in slightly different form.) As Bergant (32) observes, this refrain of mutual belonging makes explicit the feeling implied by the couple's terms of endearment through the poems to this point in the book. He calls her *my darling* (1:9, 15; 2:2, 10, 13). She calls him *my beloved* (1:13, 14, 16; 2:3, 8, 9, 10). Now she makes a more explicit claim that they belong to each other. Within the context of this poem, she may be testing him. He has called her *my darling*, but how serious is he?

The closing verse of the unit (2:17) contains several difficulties, which contribute to the possibility of interpreting this unit in two entirely different ways. On the one hand, some interpreters conclude that the woman turns her lover away because she is not yet ready to consummate their relationship. By contrast, other interpreters claim that she invites him to join her in an intimate embrace. Some readers may be uncomfortable with this passage because it could be interpreted to mean that even though they are not married, they spend the night together. It is probably better for readers to accept the poem's ambiguity and to refrain from any conclusive position with regard to their sexual relationship—not because we want to avoid any suggestion of premarital sexual intercourse, but because the poem itself is intentionally ambiguous.

The precise difficulties with this verse are as follows: (1) Does she invite him to spend the night with her? (2) What does it mean that she compares the man to a *gazelle* and a *young stag*? (3) To what does the final phrase, which NIV translates *rugged hills*, refer? (4) When she says, *Turn, my beloved*, does she instruct him to turn away from her or to turn toward her? (2:17).

Let us take the last question first. Should we understand *Turn, my beloved* as "turn toward me" or "turn away from me"? Interestingly, scholars are divided on this question. On the basis of the Hebrew root, Hess (99) argues that it "cannot mean 'turn toward me' but must mean 'turn away.'" On the basis of the context, Longman (126) holds that "she desires him to turn toward her, to be with her." Garrett (162) rejects both "turn" and "return" because "neither makes sense in this context"; on the basis of its use in 1 Samuel 16:11, he proposes that the Hebrew verb here means "to sit or recline at a meal." Exum (133) answers the question by proposing that the ambiguity here is intentional. In this poem (2:8-17), the woman appears to say both "turn away from me" and "return to me." In the next poem (3:1-5), we read of how the woman searches for her lover and finds him. Exum concludes, "This pattern indicates that the paradoxical sending away and calling for(th) is a prelude to the lovers' union, a union that throughout the Song is simultaneously assured, deferred, and on a figurative level, enjoyed."

If we accept Exum's reading, we need not try to finally determine if the lovers spend the night together. This seems wise, given the elusiveness of the poetry in this book. Other interpreters become stymied by the erotic character of the poem over against the social reality that unmarried women in ancient Israel were not supposed to have sexual relations with men to whom they were neither married nor engaged. Exum (68) refuses to assume that the love poetry of the Song must correspond to the reality of real men's and women's lives in ancient Israel (about which we know relatively little, in any case). She suggests, instead, that love poetry may offer "an escape from social constraints for women and men."

If we turn now to the other questions regarding this verse (2:17), they appear more manageable. Does she invite him to spend the night with her? It appears so, but the invitation may reflect the reality of desire rather than the reality of an unmarried couple's consummation of that desire. Why does she compare her lover to a gazelle and young stag? As we saw earlier in this poem, the gazelle and stag symbolize sensuality (Longman: 126).

To what does the concluding phrase *rugged hills* refer? Here again, scholars are divided. Some argue that the Hebrew phrase *hare beter* refers to a geographical location, the mountains of Beter. Hess identifies Beter as a village not far from Jerusalem. This fits with Hess's conclusion (100) that the woman tells her lover to turn away from her and run off to the "mountains of Beter" because she is not ready for a sexual relationship with him. Other scholars observe that the root meaning of the Hebrew word *beter* means "cut in pieces, divided." Mountains that are "cut" would appear rugged. Hence, the NIV translation. What if these rugged mountains, however, refer poetically to the woman, as some interpreters propose? Other scholars understand the reference to be to the woman's breasts (Garrett: 163). Again, Exum (132) is helpful in proposing that we accept the phrase—which she translates "cleft mountains"—as "a double entendre suggestive of the woman herself and the various pleasures her body has to offer."

THE TEXT IN BIBLICAL CONTEXT

Fig Trees and Vines

Fig trees and grapevines are closely associated in several texts, where together they symbolize peace, prosperity, safety, and security. First Kings describes the safety and security that existed during the reign of King Solomon: "During Solomon's lifetime Judah and Israel, from Dan to Beersheba, lived in safety, everyone under their own vine and under their own fig tree" (4:25).

Among the prophets, the vine and fig tree appear in messages of judgment as a symbol of the broken covenant relationship between God and the people, as we read in the prophet Joel: "The vine is dried up and the fig tree is withered; the pomegranate, the palm and the apple tree—all the trees of the field—are dried up. Surely the people's joy is withered away" (1:12). Through the prophet Hosea, God announces a future judgment upon the people as a consequence of their behavior: "I will ruin her vines and her fig trees, which she said were her pay from her lovers; I will make them a thicket, and wild animals will devour them" (Hos 2:12).

In Psalm 105, the imagery appears in a hymn of praise in which the psalmist praises God for delivering the people from slavery in Egypt. Their rescue, however, entailed judgment upon their Egyptian oppressors:

> He [God] struck down their vines and fig trees
>   and shattered the trees of their country. (105:33)

The prophets also use the imagery of vine and fig tree to describe the future restoration of Israel, when the people will once again be safe:

> Everyone will sit under their own vine
>   and under their own fig tree,
> and no one will make them afraid,
>   for the Lord Almighty has spoken. (Mic 4:4)

"In that day each of you will invite your neighbor to sit under your vine and fig tree," declares the Lord Almighty. (Zech 3:10)

Doves and Turtledoves

The Song of Songs refers to the dove (Heb. *yonah*) six times and to the turtledove (*tor*) once. In the Bible, doves symbolize the renewal of life. The prophets sometimes use the dove as a symbol of Israel, the people of God (e.g., Hos 7:11; 11:11). Psalm 74 refers specifically to the turtledove as a symbol of the poor, who are in need of God's help (v. 19).

In the flood story, the dove symbolizes the renewal of life (Gen 8). After the rain stops, Noah sends a dove out of the ark to determine if the waters have receded enough for everyone to leave the ark. First, the dove returns to the ark, indicating there is no tree or brush visible. The second time, the dove returns with an olive leaf in its beak. This implies that vegetation has appeared, but it is not yet safe to leave the ark. Noah sends the dove out a third time, and this last time, the dove does not return to the ark. After this, Noah, his family, and the animals leave the ark to repopulate the earth.

Psalm 74 is an interesting community lament over the defeat of God's people, usually understood as referring to the Babylonian defeat of Judah and destruction of Jerusalem and the temple in Jerusalem. The psalmist petitions God to remember both the covenant and, most especially, the poor, comparing the lives of the poor to that of a turtledove:

> Do not hand over the life of your turtledove to wild beasts;
> Do not forget the lives of your afflicted people forever. (v. 19 AT)

The dove is also recognized in the Bible for its ability to nest in places that are out of the way and thus secure, as we see reflected in Song 2:14. The prophet Jeremiah instructs the Moabites to seek safety in light of the approaching divine judgment upon them.

> Abandon your towns and dwell among the rocks,
>   you who live in Moab.
> Be like a dove that makes its nest
>   at the mouth of a cave. (Jer 48:28)

Jeremiah also connects the turtledove to the ability to know the right time. In 8:7, the prophet claims that while birds understand and act in accordance with the seasons, God's people do not understand the divine order of things. This passage connects with Song of Songs 2:13-14 in the association of the turtledove with the natural order and seasonal cycles.

> Even the stork in the heavens knows its times;
> and the turtledove, swallow, and crane
>   observe the time of their coming;
> but my people do not know the ordinance of the LORD. (Jer 8:7 NRSV)

In the New Testament, the dove symbolizes God's Spirit, as in the story of Jesus' baptism, when the Holy Spirit descends upon Jesus after his baptism. The Spirit is described as descending "in bodily form like a dove" (Luke 3:22). In the ancient world, birds often symbolized the heavenly realm, and it is possible that the description of the Holy Spirit in the Gospels' account of Jesus' baptism connects this event with the Genesis account of creation, which describes the movement of the divine Spirit at creation in language that evokes the action of a bird: "and the Spirit of God was hovering over the waters" (Gen 1:2).

The Voice of the Beloved

The voice and the sense of hearing play a major role in the Bible. To hear someone's voice is to form a relationship with that person. Song of Songs emphasizes the role that hearing plays in the relationship of the two lovers. Edmée Kingsmill (242) connects the passage in Song of Songs 2 with four passages in the prophet Jeremiah (7:34; 16:9; 25:10; 33:11). In the first three passages, the prophet describes the silencing of "the voices of the bride and bridegroom" in Judah and Jerusalem because of God's judgment. The fourth passage, however, describes a future scene of forgiveness and healing:

> Yet in the towns of Judah and the streets of Jerusalem that are deserted, inhabited by neither people nor animals, there will be heard once more the sounds of joy and gladness, the voices of bride and bridegroom, and the voices of those who bring thank offerings to the house of the Lord, saying,
> "Give thanks to the Lord Almighty,
> for the Lord is good;
> his love endures forever."
> For I will restore the fortunes of the land as they were before, says the Lord. (Jer 33:10b-11)

THE TEXT IN THE LIFE OF THE CHURCH

Incarnation

It fascinates me to discover the many ways in which Christian readers of Song of Songs connect short phrases and individual images with their experience of the Holy. Take the image of the lover peering in through latticework to see his beloved (2:9), an image so fleeting that we can easily gloss over it. Not so for all readers.

Ancient Jewish readers saw in this image a reference to God's presence. According to *Midrash Rabbah* (II:26), this verse describes how God peers through the gaps in the Western Wall of the Jerusalem temple to keep watch over the people of God.

For Bernard of Clairvaux, this verse illuminates the incarnation. Through the incarnation, God comes to understand humankind in a new and different way. God becoming human in Christ is like a lover peering through a lattice to see his beloved. The wall separates God from the Beloved, but the latticework allows God to come close to the Beloved in an intimate fashion.

> He [God] drew near the wall, therefore, when he joined himself to our flesh. Our flesh is the wall, and the Bridegroom's approach is the incarnation of the Word. The windows and lattices through which he is said to gaze can be understood, I think, as the bodily senses and human feelings by which he began to experience all our human needs. For "he has borne our griefs and carried our sorrows." [Isa 53:4]. On being made man, therefore, he has used our bodily feelings and senses as openings or windows, so that he would know by experience the miseries of men and might become merciful. (*Sermons* 56.2.1)

In his middle age, the French painter James Tissot (1836–1902) returned to the church of his childhood and began illustrating religious subjects. Among his 365 illustrations of the life of Christ is one that portrays Christ peering through latticework. Clinging to the wall is a grapevine, and standing in front of the wall are several sunflowers. The grapevine resonates at multiple levels with both Song of Songs imagery and New Testament imagery. In Christian art, grapes symbolize the wine of the Lord's Supper and the blood of Christ. The vine calls to mind Christ's statement in John 15:1, "I am the true vine, and my Father is the gardener." Although not found in the Bible, the sunflower in Christian art symbolizes the believer who turns to face Christ (or God), just as the sunflower turns toward the sun. Tissot's work will elicit different responses. When we see the way in which he has connected Christ to Song 2:9, it may help us reflect on our own experience that even when we feel separated from God, God's love is nearby, and God, in Christ, keeps watch upon God's Beloved.

New Beginnings

Around February in the northeast part of the United States, people start to ask, "When will spring be here?" By March, we are ready to say good-bye to snow and ice and eager to feel the strong, warm rays of the sun. We look for signs of spring's arrival: crocus, snowdrops, daffodils, pussy willow. In ancient Israel, the end of winter meant the end of the heavy rains, rather than the end of snow, ice, and subzero temperatures; yet the Song expresses joy at the end of winter and the arrival of spring, which brought with it flowers and new growth.

This passage appears to have been a favorite among Anabaptist leaders in the sixteenth century, because Menno Simons (1496-1561), Dirk Philips (1504-68), and Pilgram Marpeck (ca. 1495-1556?) each quotes Song 2:10-13. For each of these writers, the passage in the Song describes a new and hopeful chapter in the story of God's people.

In section E of his *Foundation of Christian Doctrine* (1539), the Dutch Anabaptist Menno Simons directly addresses the "Bride, Kingdom, City, Body, and Church of the Lord." The language of the Song of Songs, especially 2:10-13, pervades the entire passage. Menno associates the spring of the Song with the flowering of the true church, and he exhorts his fellow Anabaptists to live lives worthy of Christ, their Bridegroom.

> Arise, make haste, adorn and beautify yourself, extol and praise Him who has created you, and called you to such a high honor through the Word of His grace.
>
> The winter is past, the rain is over and gone, the flowers appear on the earth, and the voice of the turtle[dove] is heard in our land. There is nothing more which can harm or hinder. Hell, sin, the devil, death, the world, flesh, fire, and sword are already vanquished by the children of God. (*CWMS* 222)

For Pilgram Marpeck, a South German Anabaptist, winter refers to "the time of sin and sleeping," which was brought to an end with Christ's birth (*WPM* 524). Christ's advent initiated a first stage of human flourishing. Humanity could blossom; however, it could not bear fruit. According to Marpeck, only with Christ's death and the appearance of the Holy Spirit could humankind truly flourish: "When the turtledove, that is, the Holy Spirit, was heard, then only the first and earliest fruits were borne" (525).

In a writing on spiritual restitution, Dutch Anabaptist Dirk Philips contrasts the springtime of grace with the winter of law and punishment.

> That is, the time of the law has run its course, the wrath of God is stilled, the punishment of the Lord is taken away, the joyful time of grace has come. The comforting gospel has been heard, the sweet fruits of righteousness blossom. The land has become fruitful in faith and the knowledge of God, the plants of the Lord sprout forth. The branches on the vine of Jesus Christ get buds and give [forth] the sweet fragrance of life through the power of Christ that is in them.

This indeed happened in the time of the first apostolic churches and still happens daily at the present time among all believers. (*WDP* 340)

The language and imagery of Song of Songs 2:10-13 continued to influence the thinking of later writers. The colonial American choral composer William Billings (1746–1800) draws upon the imagery and language of the Song of Songs, chapter 2, in his anthem "I Am the Rose of Sharon." In this work, Billings weaves lines together to create a four-part anthem. Because Billings simply quotes the biblical text, it is difficult to know how he interprets the Song of Songs; however, given his historical context in colonial New England, it seems likely that the Bridegroom of the song is Christ. The anthem concludes with the phrase "the Winter is past, the rain is over and gone" (Billings 2: 225).

In the nineteenth century, the song "Hark! Don't You Hear the Turtledove?" (or simply "The Turtledove") was included in the shape-note tune book *The Southern Harmony*, compiled by American Baptist song leader William Walker (1809–75). The song's five stanzas set imagery from Song of Songs within an eschatological framework. In this song, the turtledove symbolizes God's redeeming love through Jesus Christ. The song connects the voice of the turtledove and the change in seasons to the dawning of the end times.

> Hark! don't you hear the turtle dove,
> The token of redeeming love!
> From hill to hill we hear the sound,
> The neighb'ring valleys echo round.
> O Zion, hear the turtle dove,
> The token of your Saviour's love!
> She comes the desert land to cheer,
> And welcome in the jubil-year.

Stanza 2 introduces imagery from Song of Songs 2:11:

> The winter's past, the rain is o'er,
> We feel the chilling winds no more;
> The spring is come; how sweet the view,
> All things appear divinely new.
> On Zion's mount the watchmen cry,
> "The resurrection's drawing nigh:"
> Behold, the nations from abroad,
> Are flocking to the mount of God. (Walker no. 43)

After reflecting upon the different ways that past writers have understood Song 2:10-13, we may ask ourselves, "What does winter represent to me? Has spring arrived in my life? In the life of my church? Through my way of living, do I express the joy of springtime's arrival?

Taking Refuge in Jesus

In Song of Songs 2:14, the man invites his beloved to come out to him from the inaccessible place where she hides like a *dove in the clefts of the rocks*. She has sought refuge, perhaps because she is unsure of his intentions. He wants her to leave the safety of her hiding place and take a chance on him. There are moments in our lives when we look for a safe place, a place of refuge, in which to rest safely and securely. When we are unsure whom we can trust, we want a place of refuge. The Bible often uses figurative language to describe the divine as a place of refuge. Thus we find God imaged as a rock. Moses refers to God as "Rock" (Deut 32:4). The Psalms frequently praise God as our Rock, as in Psalm 18:

> The LORD is my rock, my fortress and my deliverer;
> my God is my rock, in whom I take refuge,
> my shield and the horn of my salvation, my stronghold. (v. 2)

In the New Testament, Paul speaks of Christ as Rock:

> They all ate the same spiritual food and drank the same spiritual drink; for they drank from the spiritual rock that accompanied them, and that rock was Christ. (1 Cor 10:3-4)

In addition to this figurative language about God and Christ, rocks can literally provide protection for individuals, as when Moses shelters in a rock in order to be protected from the brilliance of God's glory.

> Then the LORD said, "There is a place near me where you may stand on a rock. When my glory passes by, I will put you in a cleft in the rock and cover you with my hand until I have passed by. Then I will remove my hand and you will see my back; but my face must not be seen." (Exod 33:21-23)

The biblical use of rock imagery for the Deity emphasizes the nature of God as protection. God as Rock is our refuge. Christian spiritual writers take this imagery even further by associating the clefts, or crevices, of a rock with the side wound of Christ. Just as a rock's crevices offer a place of refuge, so too is Christ's side wound a place of refuge for his followers. Devotional writers and hymnists as diverse as Bernard of Clairvaux, Gertrude of Helfta, Martin Behm, and Augustus Toplady reflect on the Song of Songs' image of the dove resting in the cleft of the rock in light of their understanding of Jesus as a refuge for Christian disciples. Reading the Bible both allegorically and typologically, they draw their understanding from a nexus of texts that includes Song 2:14; John 19:34 (a soldier pierces Jesus' side); and John 20:20-27 (Jesus invites Thomas to put his hand into Jesus' side wound).

Writing of the church as the Bride, Bernard of Clairvaux (1090-1153) finds in the imagery of Song 2:14 a source of strength for Christian martyrs:

> Accordingly she hears [the words]: "My dove in the clefts of the rock," because all her affections are preoccupied with the wounds of Christ; she abides in them by constant meditation. From this comes endurance for martyrdom, for this her immense trust in the Most High. (*Sermons* 61.7)

German Benedictine mystic and theologian Gertrude of Helfta (1256-1302) reflects on the Christian's need to enter into the divine-human union that exists already in Jesus. In her work *The Herald of Divine Love*, Gertrude uses the image of the dove finding refuge in the rock clefts to describe how her meditation on verses from Psalm 102 helped her overcome her sense of unworthiness.

> At the third verse, "Who forgiveth all thy iniquities," like the dove who builds her nest in the cleft of the rocks, I was to find rest for my soul in the wound of your left hand. (*Herald of Divine Love* 2.4)

Viewing Christ's wounds as a place of refuge can be seen in a Lutheran hymn by Martin Behm (1557-1622). The English version of the hymn is known as "Lord Jesus Christ, My Life, My Light." This verse, from a version translated by Catherine Winkworth, does not appear in many English editions of the hymn:

> Oh, let Thy holy wounds for me
> Clefts in the rock forever be,
> Where as a dove my soul can hide
> And safe from Satan's rage abide. (Polack: 116)

In the Moravian Church tradition, the side wound of Jesus became an object of devotion. According to Nikolaus Zinzendorf (1700-1760), the soldier's spear wound was made directly over Jesus' heart. Craig D. Atwood (2004: 107) explains that for Zinzendorf, the wound in Jesus' side gives Christians direct access to Jesus' heart, "a place where Christians are as safe as a child in its cradle, or a dove in the crevice of the rock." In a painting by the eighteenth-century artist Johann Valentin Haidt, Thomas puts his finger in Jesus's side wound, located on Jesus's left side, close to his heart. Moravian devotional cards express this connection between the piercing of Christ's side and the wound as a place of refuge. At least one of these cards makes explicit the connection with Song 2:14 by including the verse, "In the crevice of the side puncture I sit like a little dove." Another card portrays a fish and a dove and the text "There I am a dove and a fish" (translated from German; Atwood 2009: 64, 73).

Contemporary Christians may be unfamiliar with the works of Bernard and Gertrude. Outside the Moravian Church, devotion to the side wound of Christ may be little known. More familiar today, however, are hymns that draw upon the imagery of seeking shelter in the cleft of the rock that is Jesus. The hymn text "In the Rifted Rock I'm Resting," by Mary Dagworthy James (1810–83), describes taking shelter in the cleft, or rifted, rock, which is equated with Jesus' breast.

> 1. In the rifted Rock I'm resting,
> safely sheltered, I abide.
> There no foes nor storms molest me,
> while within the cleft I hide.

Verse 2 concludes with a reference to the wound in Jesus' breast: "Then I found this heavenly shelter, opened in my Savior's breast" (*HWB* no. 526).

Song of Songs 3:1-11
Seeking and Finding the Beloved

PREVIEW
Lovers long to be together. When they are separated, they may feel unable to do anything other than think about their beloved. Where is he? What is he doing? When will we see each other again? The first poem in this chapter develops the twin themes of "seeking" and "finding" as the woman searches for her beloved. When she finds him, she seizes him and refuses to let him go. The second poem describes a royal procession, which culminates with an expression of joy over a wedding.

OUTLINE
Seeking and Finding the Beloved, 3:1-5
    3:5   Refrain: Her Charge to the Daughters of Jerusalem
A Royal Procession, 3:6-11

EXPLANATORY NOTES
Seeking and Finding the Beloved 3:1-5
This unit can be described as a poem of yearning. The woman is the speaker, but it is less clear whom she addresses. In the first two chapters of the book, she primarily speaks *to* her lover. In this poem, she speaks primarily *about* him. Is this, then, a monologue? Or does she address the daughters of Jerusalem throughout the poem?

Either option is possible. Some interpreters prefer the latter since she explicitly addresses the daughters of Jerusalem in verse 5; but this does not require her to address them in the first four verses of the unit.

A second issue of interpretation has to do with how we understand the action within the woman's speech. Is this a dream report? Or does she describe an event that happened in the past? Because verses 1, 3, and 4 of the poem use Hebrew verb forms that can be translated with the past tense in English, some interpreters read this poem as a description of past events (see Garrett: 170). The verbs do not necessarily describe past actions, and there are other indications in the poem that it does not report on an actual event. Rather, we can view the unit as a poetic exploration of the themes of absence and desire.

By the way they open this unit, some translations suggest that this poem reports a single past event. For example, NIV translates *all night long* and NRSV has *at night*, but the Hebrew expression is better understood as a regular, repeated action: "nightly" or "every night" (cf. Pss 92:2; 134:1). As is often true with lovers, the sense of separation and loss that accompanies the absence of one's lover is magnified at night. This does not necessarily indicate that she wants him to join her in bed, but nighttime is often a time of reflection. The reference to *my bed* (3:1) may suggest to some readers a sexual or erotic connotation to her yearning, but we probably should not limit her yearning to sexual desire.

Ellen Davis (2000a: 256) offers a compelling argument that at one level, this poetic unit has to do with the search for God. Citing several Psalms (4:4; 6:6; 119:62; 149:5) and a verse in Job (33:15), Davis claims that the bed "is also a place of prayer, where God is sought, intently and sometimes in great anxiety, and revelations are granted." This gives a different slant on Song of Songs 3:1. At night, in one's bed, one reflects upon the things that concern us.

Running through this poem are two primary catchwords that serve to define the unit's theme: "search," or "seek" (Heb. *bqš*), and "find" (*mṣʾ*). These two catchwords give this unit a sense of unity, and they highlight the poem's theme of seeking and finding the beloved. Here NIV translates *bqš* as *look for* and *search*, and *mṣʾ* as *find*:

> All night long on my bed
>   I looked for the one my heart loves;
>   I looked for him but did not find him. (3:1)

Another expression similarly serves to unify this short poem: the phrase *the one my heart loves* (vv. 1, 2, 3, 4). The Hebrew term translated *my heart* in the NIV is *nepeš*, a word often translated into English as *soul*. In this passage several English versions actually have the phrase *the one whom my soul loves*. The concrete meaning of *nepeš* is "throat," and in certain contexts, the noun can mean by extension "desire" or "appetite." According to Horst Seebass (*TDOT* 9:506), "The OT considers simple sexual craving, which can be satisfied by prostitution, to be blind and therefore repulsive (Jer 2:24), but erotic desire has positive significance as part of the joy of living." In this passage, *nepeš* refers to the erotic, or desiring, self, which the NIV captures with its use of *my heart* to translate the Hebrew term *napši* in verse 3: *Have you seen the one my heart [napši] loves?*

Although some lovers may sit around pining, this woman takes action to find her lover. The Hebrew verbs in verse 2 are forms called *cohortatives*, which can express determination or desire. The cohortative forms here may express the woman's resolve to act: *I will arise, I will go about, I will seek* (AT). Again we might ask if this poem suggests that she actually gets up out of bed to wander through the city, looking for her lover. Without ruling out this possibility, we can also consider these statements to be figurative expressions of her *intention* to take an active role in the relationship. She is not going to wait around for him to act. Rather, she intends to work actively to create a reality in which her desires can be fulfilled.

The precise role of the watchmen in this poem is puzzling (v. 3). They appear out of the blue, and it is not clear why. In this poem, the watchmen do not block the woman from finding her lover, as they do in a later poem (5:7). Here they simply delay the action. The poem interrupts the woman's search with the statement that *the watchmen found me*, and at nearly the same moment, she asks if they have seen her lover. The delay is brief. The watchmen do not have the opportunity to answer the woman's question, which gives the impression that she inquires of them on the run, without stopping for a reply.

Garrett (172) suggests that the watchmen symbolize the woman's virginity and that when she turns from the watchmen to find her lover (v. 4), she crosses a boundary, and in so doing "she has chosen him over her virginity." Although Garrett's interpretation is possible, the poem eludes our desire as readers to establish one specific explanation of the actions described within the poem. What we understand is that her determination has paid off. She has found the one whom she loves. Both NIV and NRSV report the woman saying,

I held him and would not let him go. The Hebrew word translated *I held him* is the same verb we encountered in the enigmatic saying in 2:15, *Catch for us the foxes.* Has she now caught her fox?

Also puzzling in this passage is the reference to *my mother's house*, the place to which she takes her lover after finding him (also see 8:2). Carol Meyers has argued that the reference to the "mother's house" reflects a social practice in ancient Israel of involving mothers in marriage arrangements (cf. Ruth 1:8-9; Gen 24:67). Diane Bergant (36) suggests that the structure of this verse, which sets in parallel *my mother's house* and *the room of the one who conceived me*, serves to emphasize the eroticism of the passage, noting that the reference is to conception, not birth. What takes place inside the mother's house? Some interpreters attempt to place this poem within the context of a plot; however, it is better simply to accept that the poem draws our attention to sexual desire without explaining whether or not it has been satisfied *in the mother's house.*

The poem ends with a refrain (3:5):

> *Daughters of Jerusalem, I charge you*
> *by the gazelles and by the does of the field:*
> *Do not arouse or awaken love*
> *until it so desires.*

This refrain occurs three times within the book (2:7; 3:5; 8:4). In its first appearance in 2:7, it seemed to support the woman's ambivalence about the relationship. Here the refrain can be taken as support for the opposite. Love is ready, and she is ready for love.

A Royal Procession 3:6-11

The poem that concludes this chapter presents several challenges. First, it is unclear who is speaking. Possibly, as the NIV indicates, the woman continues to speak (Longman: 135). Other scholars propose that the speech shifts in verse 6 to a group of observers (Keel: 125) or a chorus (Garrett: 176). Still others suggest that the daughters of Jerusalem speak some portion of this poem (Fox 1985: 119) Another option is to attribute the speech to the man (Hess: 116). Perhaps the best approach is simply to acknowledge that the identity of the speaker in this passage is unclear (Bergant: 37).

Contributing to the discussion of the speaker's identity is a question about how to translate the first verse. The Hebrew interrogative term in verse 6 is usually translated "who?," as the NIV does; however, it is possible that in some contexts it means "what?," and NRSV chooses this alternative. The Hebrew word translated "this" is a feminine form, but does it refer to a woman who, we assume, occupies the approaching carriage, Solomon's bride, being carried in an elaborate procession to the royal wedding? Or does it refer to the carriage itself, since the Hebrew term translated *carriage, miṭṭah,* is feminine in form (v. 7)?

So much in this book is cloaked in mystery. In this poem, too, there is mystery and ambiguity, rather than clarity. Although the carriage, an elaborately upholstered portable bed sometimes called a palanquin, is described as belonging to King Solomon, the poem never explicitly reveals who approaches. Does the king ride in his own carriage? Or has he sent his carriage to fetch his bride and bring her to him? Both are possible, and perhaps the poet here intends to surround the approach of the carriage in mystery.

Throughout this poem, King Solomon holds center stage. For some interpreters, the poem describes a historical event or reflects some historical memory of the famous king. For example, taking this approach, some interpreters have proposed that the poem describes a journey made by King Solomon to see his beloved. It seems more likely, however, that the poem uses the king fiction and its associated regal and courtly imagery to celebrate love (Longman: 133), rather than to describe a particular historical event *[King Fiction, p. 278].*

In the concluding address to the daughters of Jerusalem (3:11), we encounter the only explicit reference to marriage in the entire book. The verse draws attention to a crown, or wedding garland, that Solomon wears. This poem may reflect an ancient Jewish custom whereby a groom wore a wedding garland and the bride was carried on a palanquin, although it is also possible that the Song influenced the development of these later practices (Garrett: 181). The reference to Solomon's mother may support the view that mothers were directly involved in the marriage arrangements of their children *[Nuptial Imagery in the New Testament, p. 282].*

After the lengthy and elaborate description of the carriage and the accompanying procession, the poem ends with two words describing the effect of the wedding upon the groom. The day of his wedding is the day *his heart rejoiced.*

THE TEXT IN BIBLICAL CONTEXT

Quests

In the Song of Songs, we observe the woman searching until she finds her lover, and we notice that the theme of seeking and finding runs throughout the Bible. When someone undertakes a search with a particular goal in mind, we often say that person is "on a quest." Quests can involve physical journeys, but they can also be intellectual and spiritual pursuits.

Links exist between the Song of Songs and wisdom literature. Seeking and finding is an especially important theme in the book of Proverbs. In that book, wisdom is personified as a woman who proclaims, "I love those who love me, and those who *seek* me *find* me" (Prov 8:17). Chapter 18 of Proverbs contains a saying that "the heart of the discerning acquires knowledge, for the ears of the wise *seek* it out" (18:15).

In the book of Ecclesiastes, the speaker who is identified as "the Teacher" (1:1 NIV, NRSV, NLT) conducts a search for meaning and purpose in life. The Teacher's search reveals that human existence is finite, and the ability to achieve success uncertain. Nevertheless, the search also discovers ways to respond to life's uncertainties. Through his search the Teacher determines that material gain and pleasure do not necessarily bring fulfillment, but he also discovers that it is good to enjoy the gifts of work and pleasure, which God provides humankind.

> There is nothing better for a person than to eat and drink and experience goodness in work. This too, I see, is from the hand of God. (2:24 AT)

In several biblical passages we see that God invites humans to seek the Divine. The prophet Amos delivers to the Israelites the following message from God: "Seek me and live" (Amos 5:4). In Jeremiah, we read the following promise, which God makes to the people who are about to be exiled:

> This is what the LORD says: "When seventy years are completed for Babylon, I will come to you and fulfill my good promise to bring you back to this place. For I know the plans I have for you," declares the LORD, "plans to prosper you and not to harm you, plans to give you hope and a future. Then you will call on me and come and pray to me, and I will listen to you. *You will seek me and find me when you seek me with all your heart.*" (29:10-13, emph. added)

In the Prophets we also read that God is troubled when the people do not search for the Divine. In Isaiah 65:1, for example, we read:

> I revealed myself to those who did not ask for me;
>   I was found by those who did not seek me.
> To a nation that did not call on my name,
>   I said, "Here am I, here am I."

From the Scriptures we know that God also seeks humankind. Exodus offers a wonderful image of a Deity who finds and rescues people from bondage. In speaking to Moses, God instructs him to tell the Israelites, "You yourselves have seen what I did to Egypt, and how I carried you on eagles' wings and brought you to myself" (19:4). Among the Gospels, Luke especially emphasizes the theme of God's "seeking and finding" the lost. In Luke 15 we find a cluster of three parables that reflect this theme. In the parable of the lost sheep, a shepherd abandons the rest of the flock in order to search for the one sheep that has been lost. When he finds the sheep, "he lays it on his shoulders and rejoices" (15:5 NRSV). Following this parable, we read about a woman who turns her house upside down in order to find the one coin she has lost (15:8-10). The chapter concludes with the lengthy parable of the lost son (15:11-32). When the older son complains, the father replies, "But we had to celebrate and be glad, because this brother of yours was dead and is alive again; he was lost and is found" (15:32).

Where Is God?

In the Scriptures we also find expressions of anguish resulting from an individual's experience of the absence of God. We see this most notably in the lament Psalms.

> Why, O LORD, do you stand far off?
> Why do you hide yourself in times of trouble? (Ps 10:1)

> My God, my God, why have you forsaken me?
> Why are you so far from saving me,
> so far from my cries of anguish?
> My God, I cry out by day, but you do not answer,
> By night, but I found no rest. (Ps 22:1-2)

Similarly, Job asks why God seems to have abandoned him.

> Why do you hide your face
> and consider me your enemy? (Job 13:24)

Even Jesus expresses the feeling at his crucifixion that God has withdrawn from him.

> And at three in the afternoon Jesus cried out in a loud voice, "*Eloi, Eloi, lema sabachthani?*" (which means "My God, my God, why have you forsaken me?") (Mark 15:34, from Ps 22)

THE TEXT IN THE LIFE OF THE CHURCH

The Absence of God

It is probably fair to say that many, if not all, people experience times in which they feel God has abandoned them. We find this experience powerfully described in the writings of Christian mystics, many of whom were so moved by the poetry of the Song of Songs that they extended its language and imagery into their own reflection on the pain they experienced at times when God felt distant. The thirteenth-century Beguine Mechtild of Magdeburg draws heavily upon the language and imagery of the Song of Songs in her work *The Flowing Light of the Godhead,* in which she describes her experience of the Divine in terms of a marriage between the soul (the Bride) and Christ (the Bridegroom). In a section in which the individual soul complains that God seems to have withdrawn, Mechtild reports the divine response in language that recalls the woman's experience of her lover's absence in Song of Songs 3:1-4.

> You are like a new bride
> Whose one and only lover has slipped away as she slept.
> She had entrusted him with all her love
> And simply cannot endure his parting from her for one hour.
> ....
> Now let me tell you where I shall then be:
> I am in myself in all places and in all things,
> As I always have been eternally,
> And I shall be waiting for you in the orchard of love
> And shall pluck for you the flowers of sweet union
> And shall make a bed for you out of the soft grass of holy knowledge,
> And the bright sun of my eternal Godhead
> Shall make you radiant with the secret wonder of my attractiveness—
> A bit of which you have intimately revealed.
> (*The Flowing Light of the Godhead* 2.25)

In their compositions hymnists and librettists also express the human desire for the presence of Christ. In an aria from Bach's Cantata 32 ("Liebster Jesu, mein Verlangen"), the soul expresses its deep desire for Christ's embrace.

> Dearest Jesus, my desire,
> Tell me, where do I find You?
> Shall I lose You so soon
> And no longer feel You with me?
> Ah! My refuge, gladden me;
> Utterly contented, let me embrace You. (Dürr and Jones: 188)

A hymn text attributed to the Silesian poet Johannes Scheffler (1624–77) also conveys the Christian's desire to find the Jesus who is lover and friend. The seventeenth-century German mystic and poet Angelus Silesius, whose given name was Johannes Scheffler, wrote a series of poems that draw directly from the imagery and language of the Songs of Songs. This series of poems was published in 1657 under the title *Heilige Seelenlust, oder geistliche Hirtenlieder der in ihren Jesum verliebten Psyche* (The soul's holy delight, or Spiritual songs of the Jesus-loving psyche). Some of the poems from this collection appear in early Brethren hymnals but were not included in later Brethren English-language hymnals.

The poems from *The Soul's Holy Delight* that have been translated into English hymn texts exhibit some of the themes of the Song of Songs, such as longing for the beloved (who in the hymns is Jesus); but in general the English translations tone down the more erotic language and imagery of Scheffler's poems. For example, one English translation of Scheffler's poem *"Ich will dich lieben, meine Stärke"* ("Thee Will I Love, My Strength, My Tower") omits the lines "I will love you, God's Lamb, as my bridegroom" (*Ich will dich lieben, Gottes Lamm, als meinen Bräutigam*) and "I will love you, O my life, as my best friend" (*Ich will dich lieben, O mein Leben, als meinen allerbesten Freund*). Similarly, Scheffler's poem *"Jesu, komm doch selbst zu mir,"* which was translated by Mathias Loy as "Jesus, Savior, Come to Me," replaces terms like "soul's friend" (*Seelenfreund*) and "beloved" (*Liebster*) with the more standard terms "Savior," and "Lord." The following English translation preserves the language of "lover" in the opening lines of a hymn text by Scheffler that explores the Christian's desire to live in the embrace of Jesus, the Lover:

> *Wo ist der Schönste, den ich liebe?*
> *Wo ist mein Seelenbräutigam?* (KDP 492)
>
> Where is the most beautiful one, whom I love?
> Where is my soul's Bridegroom? (AT)

Song of Songs 4:1–5:1

A First Description of Her Beauty

PREVIEW

Love can blind us to our beloved's flaws, and in the first poem of this unit, the young man declares to his beloved, *There is no flaw in you* (v. 7). Love, too, can produce wildly divergent emotions, sometimes occurring at the same time. We sense that this may be happening with the man when he suggests that she is driving him crazy. It feels to him as if she is a million miles away, and he asks if they can be together. She agrees, and the unit concludes with an affirmation of their love.

OUTLINE

His Description of Her Beauty (First *Descriptive Inventory*), 4:1-7
An Invitation, 4:8
His Description of Her Effect on Him, 4:9-15
An Invitation and Response, 4:16–5:1a
An Exhortation to the Lovers, 5:1b

EXPLANATORY NOTES

His Description of Her Beauty (First *Descriptive Inventory*) 4:1-7

In this first of four descriptive poems in which one lover inventories the other lover's attributes, the man directly addresses his lover. As readers, we overhear the man speaking privately and intimately to his beloved, which offers us a glimpse of how he feels about her. Yet we are not invited into the moment but stand, as it were, outside, looking in upon the couple.

This poem begins and ends with general statements of the woman's beauty and perfection. The inventory begins with the woman's eyes and ends with her breasts. Using figurative language, the man describes the woman's eyes, hair, teeth, lips, temples (or cheeks), neck, and breasts. In earlier poems in the book, the man and the woman have used figurative language to describe each other (see, e.g., 1:9-11, 13-14). What differs here is that the description has the feel of an inventory, despite the fact that the inventory seems incomplete. This is the first of three such inventories in which he describes her attributes in terms of their effect upon him. She, too, uses the form and style of an inventory to praise his features in 5:10-16 *[Descriptive Inventories, p. 263]*.

Scholars do not agree on how to interpret these poetic inventories. Some have tried to understand the figurative language in terms of the woman's appearance, which results in absurdity. If we try to sketch what the woman looks like based on 4:1-7, we come up with a grotesque figure. We might then ask if this is intentional on the poet's part? Should we read this poem as a comic piece or as a parody, as some scholars have suggested? The larger context of the descriptive inventories does not point in the direction of a comic reading. Rather, as other scholars propose, we should read the figurative language not as a description of the woman's physical appearance, but rather as a recounting of her characteristics and qualities. The descriptions reveal who she is, not what she looks like. Further, the poems draw the reader into the couple's relationship in order to share in each lover's delight in the beloved. By reading the descriptive inventory of 4:1-7, we can come close to experiencing how she affects him.

As this poem opens, the man proclaims the beauty of his beloved. Verse 1 begins by repeating an exclamation that occurred earlier in the book: *How beautiful you are, my darling! Oh, how beautiful!* (1:15; 4:1). As the poem ends, the man repeats this declaration but intensifies the statement: *All beautiful, you are, my darling, there is no flaw in you* (4:7 AT). The word translated "flaw" is used elsewhere in the Bible to refer to blemishes or disfigurements. Here the lover proclaims that his beloved has no imperfection. Such extravagant praise is not unexpected in love poetry.

The opening proclamation begins with a Hebrew word (*hinneh*) that can be translated in several different ways. The dictionary definition of the word is "look, behold," and some translators use the second of these two words: *Behold, you are beautiful, my love, behold, you are beautiful!* (RSV). Other translations abandon the somewhat archaic term *behold* and use other language to communicate the sense of immediacy this term engenders, such as *Look at you, so beautiful, my darling! Look at you, so beautiful* (Hess: 127).

In the core section of the poem, the man comments upon different parts of his beloved's body, beginning with her eyes and continuing with her hair, teeth, lips, temples (or cheeks), neck, and breasts. The figurative language he uses draws primarily upon the fauna and flora of the natural world (doves, goats, sheep, fawns, pomegranates, lilies, and myrrh), but he also uses architectural and military imagery (a tower of David and warriors' shields). The reference to King David recalls the royal court, which in turn alludes to Jerusalem and contributes to the book's use of the king fiction, even though here the reference is to David, rather than Solomon *[King Fiction, p. 278]*.

Othmar Keel (139) helps us understand these descriptive inventories within an ancient Near Eastern context. Keel explains that these comparisons seek to portray the individual's essential character and significance by identifying their physical features with the splendor of the natural and social world in which the poet resided. According to Keel, the comparisons are "only rarely a matter of shape and form; . . . more often the similarity has to do with color, value, or some dynamic quality" (25). In this inventory, the woman's thick, flowing hair suggests her vitality and sexuality (141). The comparison of the woman's teeth to twin sheep suggests both order and fertility (142). Keel discusses possible associations with the color red and concludes that "the bright red lips of the beloved are an invitation to love" (143). A reference to pomegranates, widely regarded in the ancient Near East as aphrodisiacs and used in ancient art to symbolize life itself, heightens the erotic character of the woman's appearance (144–46). We have no evidence of an actual "tower of David" in ancient Israel. Keel argues that rather than describing the appearance of the woman's neck, reference to *the tower of David* attributes to her the pride associated with cities that have never been conquered (147). This may suggest that the man feels she is inaccessible to him or that she is so powerful that she has conquered him. Finally, Keel suggests that the comparison of the woman's breasts to fawns implies that they are "dispensers of life and joy" (151).

An understanding of the symbolic world of ancient Israel can help readers make sense of the imagery used in the Song's descriptive inventories. Cheryl Exum makes a further observation that distinguishes between the ways in which the man and woman express themselves. Exum proposes that the woman expresses her feelings about her lover by telling stories in which they are the main characters (e.g., 2:8-17; 3:1-4; 5:2–6:3). By contrast, the man expresses his feelings for the woman by describing his beloved's appearance and how it affects him (156). She also suggests that the descriptive inventories simultaneously invite us in and exclude us from the couple's intimate relationship (158).

An Invitation 4:8

Verse 8 serves as a hinge connecting two independent sections (4:1-7 and 4:9–5:1). Wordplay connects verse 8 to the preceding section. In 4:6, the man says, *I will go to the mountain of myrrh and the hill of incense*. The Hebrew word translated *incense* is *lebonah* (4:6), which creates a wordplay with the place name "Lebanon" (*lebanon*) in 4:8. The verse is also connected to the following section through repetition of the term "bride" (4:8, 9, 10, 11, 12; 5:1) and the repeated references to Lebanon (4:8, 11, 15) *[Aromatics, p. 260]*.

The man's invitation to his lover in 4:8 emphasizes the twin themes of separation and desire. The man invites his beloved to come to him from her far-distant mountainous location. In the Hebrew, the verse emphasizes the man's desire to be with his beloved by placing "with me" first in the sentence. Although some translations suggest that he invites her to descend with him from the mountains, the context implies that he is located somewhere else and asks her to descend from the mountains in order to be with him: *Come from Lebanon, bride, to be with me* (AT). Two verbs are used in addressing the woman: *come* and *descend*. As Bergant observes, in English these verbs appear to be commands, but in Hebrew they are imperfect in form and thus may express more of a wish or a hope than a command—as in "I hope you will come from Lebanon to be with me" (Bergant: 50).

Four place names identify the woman's location: Lebanon, Amana, Senir, and Hermon. These place names refer to mountain peaks in the Lebanon and Anti-Lebanon mountain ranges west and northwest of Damascus. Although Lebanon and Hermon are familiar places in the Bible, Amana and Senir are not. Senir may be an alternate name for Hermon (Deut 3:9), although this passage and one other (1 Chron 5:23) suggest they are two different locations. According to Ezekiel 27:5, Senir was a source of fir trees in ancient times. The only other reference to Amana in the Bible is to a river that flows through the city of Damascus (2 Kings 5:12), possibly originating on Mount Amana.

Mount Hermon, the southernmost peak of the Anti-Lebanon Mountains, reaches around 9,200 feet and is usually covered with snow throughout the year. In the Bible, the name Lebanon refers both to a mountain range and to the surrounding region. At the highest point, the Lebanon Mountains reach over 11,000 feet. The name *Lebanon*, which means "white" in Hebrew, may refer to the range's snowy peaks.

In other words, in this verse the man expresses his hope that his beloved will come down from the distant mountain peak where she currently resides in order to be with him. Although some interpreters explain why the woman would be living in the mountains among wild animals, we should likely take this location figuratively. From the man's point of view, his beloved is so distant and inaccessible that it feels as if she is living among the wild animals on a distant mountain peak. The references to lions and leopards, both fierce and dangerous carnivores, may also suggest the sense of awe he feels when he thinks about his beloved. There may be an additional layer to this symbolism, in that, as Keel observes, lions and leopards were often associated with female deities in the ancient world. The Babylonian goddess Ishtar was associated with both lions and the mountains of Lebanon (Keel: 155–58). By drawing upon this broader cultural association, the poet does not deify the woman. Rather, these references describe the powerful attraction this man feels toward his beloved. Today people say, "He's divine," or "She's an angel," without meaning to attribute divinity or heavenly status to the person. Even if the Song here draws upon goddess imagery, it neither attributes divine status to the woman nor imputes polytheism to the poet.

Verse 8 introduces the first occurrence of the word "bride" (*kallah*) in the Song of Songs. The noun is concentrated in this section, occurring six times within the context of 4:8–5:1 (4:8, 9, 10, 11, 12; 5:1) and nowhere else in the book. The precise usage of the term within this book is debated. Some scholars assume that it defines the relationship between the man and the woman in legal terms as a marriage, as either engaged or recently married; thus Garrett (102–4) argues that the couple enjoys a monogamous relationship. Other scholars suggest that "bride" appears here as a term of endearment that expresses the man's feelings toward the woman, but is not to be taken literally as a description of their legal status (R. Murphy: 156; Bergant: 52; Longman: 50). Hess (35) argues that the Song is neither "a manifesto for free love" nor "a description of a married relationship," but rather "a fantasy that explores the commitment of an erotic love affair." Given that this poem emphasizes the couple's separation, it seems unlikely that "bride" refers to the couple's actual status as bride and bridegroom. The evidence of this poem and of the other poems in this book seems to weigh against the view that the couple is either married or engaged to be married. Additionally, in all six occurrences of *kallah* in Song of Songs, the Hebrew word is simply "bride," not "my bride." Although NIV and most English versions do have "my bride," the possessive pronoun is absent from the Hebrew text. The absence of the possessive pronoun in the Hebrew text, along with the other reasons listed above, suggest that she is not "*his* bride."

With the term "bride," the man expresses the desire that his beloved be reserved for him alone, an idea that is continued in verse 12 with the figurative imagery of an enclosed garden. He wants her to be for him, and only him—which is not an unusual desire for a lover to have.

In four of the six occurrences, the term "bride" is paired with "my sister," resulting in the term of endearment, "my sister-bride." The use of the term "sister" in this passage may indicate Egyptian influence, since Egyptian love poetry used "sister" as a term of endearment, as we see in the following lines from an Egyptian text (Papyrus Harris 500), although this way of addressing one's lover can be seen in Canaanite and Sumerian literature as well (Munro: 74).

> I am your sister, your best one;
> I belong to you like this plot of ground
> That I planted with flowers
> And sweet-smelling herbs." (*AEL* 2:192)

As Garrett observes, the use of the term "sister" suggests an emotional bond similar to the bond that exists between family members (194). Together "my sister" and "bride" reflect the man's desire for the familiarity known by family members ("my sister") and the exclusive intimacy experienced within marriage ("bride").

His Description of Her Effect on Him 4:9-15

The man continues to address the woman directly, but now shifts to expressing admiration for her in the sensory language of sight, taste, and smell (4:9-11). The section connects to the larger unit by means of wordplay and repetition, but it also recalls the opening section of the book, where she comments upon his fragrance and compares his love to wine (1:2-3).

Verse 9 contains an interesting verb that is based on the Hebrew noun for heart (*leb*). The verb form is unusual and can be taken in two different ways. It may be understood to have a causative meaning, in which case action is intensified, or it may be understood to have a privative meaning, in which case the action is removed or diminished. Keeping in mind that, in the Bible, the heart is the seat of the will, a privative sense of the verb suggests that she has taken away his will, leaving him weak and unable to resist. Verbs such as "stolen" (NIV), "captured" (*The Message*), and "ravished" (KJV, RSV, NRSV) communicate a privative sense of the verb. This form of the verb can also have an intensifying meaning. Accordingly, it may indicate that she has increased his will, motivating him to act or arousing him sexually: *You have made my heart beat faster* (NASB). This may well be an example of Hebrew wordplay in which *both* meanings are operative: the lover is weakened so that he cannot resist his beloved, and at the same time he becomes sexually aroused by her. Othmar Keel (162) suggests that it means something like "you drive me crazy." The man further emphasizes the power and immediacy of her effect upon him when he explains that this has happened as a result of *just one glance of your eyes, just one jewel of your necklace* (AT).

With his appeal to the senses of taste and smell in this poem of admiration in 4:10, we hear echoes of chapter 1, where she expresses her admiration for him. In 1:2, she proclaims his love to be *better than wine*. In nearly identical language, he makes the same proclamation about her expressions of love: *How much more pleasing is your love than wine.* (In Hebrew, both expressions use a comparative form of the word meaning "good," *ṭob*.) Similarly, she comments on the fragrance of his perfume (1:3a), and he states that the fragrance of her perfume is more pleasing than any spice.

He continues to describe her taste and smell in 4:11. First he describes her lips and tongue, possibly referring to both her kisses and her speech, using imagery that appeals to the sense of taste. The first metaphor has been translated in at least two different ways: *Your lips drop sweetness as the honeycomb* (NIV) and *Your lips distill nectar* (NRSV). *The Message* offers a more straightforward interpretation that equates her lips to kissing: *The kisses of your lips are honey.* Egyptian love poems also admire the lover's speech, so it is possible that the reference to the lips has to do with the woman's speech instead of, or in addition to, her kissing. Although *The Message*'s translation is more concrete, it is better to follow the NIV, which allows the lips to represent both kissing and speech *[Figures of Speech, p. 267]*.

Although before this point in the book we have encountered floral imagery from the natural world, here for the first time the woman is described figuratively in terms of a garden. The term "garden" is used of the woman six times in the Song of Songs, with four of those occurrences found in this unit (the other two occurrences are 6:2 and 8:13). Although readers today might think of a backyard vegetable or flower garden, the poet here draws upon the long tradition of royal gardens in the ancient Near East. Thus we shift here from the mountainous terrain inhabited by wild animals (4:8) to the courtly splendor of a royal garden (4:12–5:1).

In 4:12, the poet uses three related images to describe the woman: she is *a garden locked up, . . . a spring enclosed, a sealed fountain.* Some interpreters take the adjectives *locked up, enclosed,* and *sealed* as figurative references to the woman's virginity; others take them as references to her inaccessibility. Still others suggest that they refer to the anticipated exclusivity of the man's relationship with her. Possibly the language suggests all three. Combined with the epithet "wife," the descriptive terms point to the man's desire for an exclusive relationship with the woman he loves. He invites her to leave her isolation (4:8), because she has stolen his heart (4:9).

Gardens need water in order to flourish. The poet introduces water imagery in 4:12 alongside the garden imagery. In 4:15 the man declares his beloved to be a *fountain of gardens* (AT). The NIV translates the Hebrew phrase in 4:15 as *a garden fountain,* but the Hebrew actually reads *a fountain of gardens,* that is, a fountain that waters many gardens. The imagery of abundance continues in the poetic parallel that describes her as *a well of flowing water streaming down from Lebanon*—which brings us full circle with the opening invitation for her to descend from Mount Lebanon (4:8).

In 4:13-14, the man lists the many plants that grow in this garden of delights that is his beloved. They include choice fruits, and more specifically, pomegranates, including a wide variety of exotic spices *[Aromatics, p. 260].* The term *orchard* (v. 13) translates the Hebrew word *pardes,* a Persian loanword that occurs in the Old Testament only here and two other places (Eccl 2:5 and Neh 2:8, both Persian-period texts), where it designates the parks or forests created for the enjoyment of the king.

An Invitation and Response 4:16–5:1a

It is unclear who is speaking in the first half of 4:16. It could be either the man or the woman. The reference to *my garden* tips the decision in favor of the woman as speaker, since she has not yet become "*his* garden." After the rather lengthy description of the effect he hopes she will have upon him (4:10-15), she responds quickly with her own invitation, which maintains the figurative language of garden and fruits: *Let my beloved come into his garden and taste its choice fruits* (4:16).

He replies, indicating that he has, indeed, accepted her invitation and enjoyed her garden (5:1a). The Hebrew verbs suggest that the action described is complete, and the first-person forms emphasize the man's active role in the relationship: *I have come . . . ; I have gathered . . . ; I have eaten . . . ; I have drunk. . . .* The repetition of the possessive pronoun "my" reinforces his claim to have obtained an exclusive relationship with the woman. *Myrrh*, *spice*, *honey*, *wine*, and *milk* suggest the sensuality and pleasure that characterize their relationship. He has feasted upon love.

An Exhortation to the Lovers 5:1b

The unit concludes with an affirmation of their love (5:1b):

> *Eat, friends, and drink;*
> *drink your fill of love.*

The identity of both the speaker and the audience being addressed in this portion of the verse is unclear. The verbs in Hebrew are plural forms, so it is possible that both the man and the woman are being addressed. But who is speaking? The only other frequent speakers in the book are the "women of Jerusalem," so it could be that they address the couple, which NIV supports by identifying the speakers as the "friends." (The brothers speak only once, in 8:8-9.) Exum (183) suggests that having the women address the couple may be the poet's way of inviting readers to enter the scene described here, in which the couple achieve a sense of intimacy. As a conclusion to this entire unit, the instruction offered by witnesses to the couple's intimacy affirms their relationship.

THE TEXT IN BIBLICAL CONTEXT

Gardens

The imagery of the garden functions within the larger biblical context as a symbol of beauty, harmony, and abundance.

The narrative of Genesis 2–3 provides us with a foundational story set within the context of a garden. Whereas the first couple is exiled from the garden as a consequence of their eating fruit from the tree of the knowledge of good and evil, the couple in Song of Songs seeks to return to a garden in which they may enjoy each other's companionship. In a chapter in her book *God and the Rhetoric of Sexuality*, biblical scholar Phyllis Trible (145) takes the garden of Eden story in Genesis 2–3 as the key to unlock the meaning of the Song of Songs. In Trible's reading of the two stories, she proposes that the Song of Songs redeems the love story of Genesis 2–3, which went awry with the couple's act of disobedience.

In the prophetic writings, gardens symbolize the satisfaction of human need, and especially the fulfillment of desire for a future restoration. The prophet Jeremiah tells the exiles to settle down in Babylon, because their exile there will not be short:

> Build houses and settle down;
>   plant gardens and eat what they produce. (29:5)

> They will come and shout for joy on the heights of Zion;
>   they will rejoice in the bounty of the LORD—
> the grain, the new wine and the oil,
>   the young of the flocks and herds.
> They will be like a well-watered garden,
>   and they will sorrow no more. (31:12)

The prophet Joel sounds an alarm in Zion, announcing the approach of the day of the LORD. One of the images he offers of this coming day of judgment is the contrast of before and after.

> Before them fire devours,
>   behind them a flame blazes.
> Before them the land is like the garden of Eden,
>   behind them, a desert waste—
>   nothing escapes them. (2:3)

Following the destruction that occurred in Judah and Jerusalem with the invasion of the Babylonians, prophets offer hope to the exiled people for a future restoration. To the exiles in Babylon, the prophet Ezekiel announces a future restoration that will resemble Eden.

They will say, "This land that was laid waste has become like the garden of Eden; the cities that were lying in ruins, desolate and destroyed, are now fortified and inhabited." (36:35)

We read a later prophecy to the exiles that offers a similar vision of restoration, using the imagery of the garden of God:

> The Lord will surely comfort Zion
>   and will look with compassion on all her ruins;
> he will make her deserts like Eden,
>   her wastelands like the garden of the Lord.
> Joy and gladness will be found in her,
>   thanksgiving and the sound of singing. (Isa 51:3)

> The Lord will guide you always;
>   he will satisfy your needs in a sun-scorched land
>   and will strengthen your frame.
> You will be like a well-watered garden,
>   like a spring whose waters never fail. (Isa 58:11)

Garden imagery continues in the New Testament, especially in the book of Revelation. We might say that garden imagery bookends the entire Bible, since we begin early in Genesis with the garden of Eden and end in Revelation with the imagery of a city that has at its center a garden and a river. The river is the water of life flowing from God's throne, and on its banks grow trees that produce fruit and leaves intended for healing.

> Then the angel showed me the river of the water of life, as clear as crystal, flowing from the throne of God and of the Lamb down the middle of the great street of the city. On each side of the river stood the tree of life, bearing twelve crops of fruit, yielding its fruit every month. And the leaves of the tree are for the healing of the nations. (Rev 22:1-2)

THE TEXT IN THE LIFE OF THE CHURCH

The Garden of God's Love

Late medieval visual art frequently locates Mary and the infant Jesus within an enclosed garden. Mary may be seated on a throne, grass bench, or on the ground. She holds the infant Jesus on her lap. Around them flowers and other types of vegetation can be seen, and the scene depicts them seated within a walled garden enclosure. Art historians commonly refer to this motif by the phrase found in the Latin version of Song 4:12, *hortus conclusus*, and they suggest that the setting symbolizes Mary's virginity and her immunity to temptation (Schiller: 53; Bucher 2007).

Christian spirituality draws upon the imagery of the garden as a place of beauty, abundance, and harmony. When drawing explicitly upon Song of Songs 4:12, Christian spiritual writers also incorporate the idea of safety and protection offered by an enclosed garden. For mystical writers, the garden may symbolize the individual's experience of union with God.

The sixteenth-century Spanish mystic St. John of the Cross describes in his work *The Spiritual Canticle* the three stages of the mystical experience: the purgative, the illuminative, and the unitive. In stanza 22 of this work, which interprets the biblical Song of Songs as the quest of the individual soul for a unitive experience of the divine, John draws upon the Song's garden imagery. In the following selection, John identifies the speaker in Song 5:1 as the Bridegroom (Christ), who invites his Bride (the soul) into the garden. In *The Spiritual Canticle,* the garden represents the soul's experience of union with God.

> The bride has entered
> Into the pleasant garden of her desire
> And at her pleasure rests,
> Her neck reclining
> On the gentle arms of the Beloved.
> ....
> We learn this truth very clearly from the Bridegroom himself in the Song of Songs, where he invites the soul, now his bride, to enter this state, saying: "Come into my garden, O my sister, my bride: I have gathered my myrrh with my aromatic spices" (Song 5:1). He calls the soul his sister, his bride, for she was such in the love and surrender that she made of herself to him before he had called her to the state of spiritual marriage, where, as he says, he gathered his myrrh with his aromatic spices, that is, the fruits of flowers now ripe and made ready for the soul. These are the delights and grandeurs communicated to her by himself in this state, that is, he communicates them to her in himself, because he is to her the pleasant and desirable garden. (stanza 22; translation from McGinn: 461–62)

In other writers, the garden may symbolize either God's love or the church, perhaps as an expression or gift of God's love, rather than mystical union with God. The colonial composer William Billings (4: 113-19) uses texts from the Song of Songs in his four-part song "I Am Come into My Garden." Conrad Beissel, the Pietist founder of a celibate community at Ephrata, Pennsylvania, also draws upon the imagery of the garden in the four-part song "I Stand Here Implanted in the Garden of His Love."

> I stand here implanted in the garden of His love.
> Many sweet thoughts sustain me, sent from God above.
> The assurance arises, from this heavenly garden,
> that now my corruptible life He will pardon. (Beissel and Getz: 18-19)

The English hymnist Isaac Watts (no. 566) borrows imagery from Song of Songs 4:12-15 and 5:1 in a hymn that describes the church as "a garden walled around" and praises the bounty and the blessings that we receive from God the Father and experience at the Lord's table.

> We are a garden wall'd around,
> Chosen and made peculiar ground;
> A little spot enclos'd by grace
> Out of the world's wide wilderness.

Like the poetry of Song of Songs, Watts appeals to the senses in this hymn celebrating the goodness of God's blessings. The garden is fragrant, and in the following verse, we can almost feel the breeze of the divine spirit:

> Awake, O heavenly wind! and come,
> Blow on this garden of perfume;
> Spirit divine! descend and breathe
> A gracious gale on plants beneath.

Taste joins smell in Watts's description of the "feast divine" and incorporates the imagery of the tree of life from Genesis and Revelation:

> Our Lord into his garden comes,
> Well pleas'd to smell our pure perfumes,
> And calls us to a feast divine,
> Sweeter than honey, milk, or wine.
>
> "Eat of the tree of life, my friends,
> The blessings that thy Father sends;
> Your taste shall all my dainties prove,
> And drink abundance of my love."

In the hymn's concluding verse, the church responds with praise and thanksgiving for the abundant blessings received from the Lord of life and love:

Jesus, we will frequent thy board,
And sing the bounties of our Lord;
But the rich food on which we live,
Demands more praise than tongues can give.

Song of Songs 5:2–6:3

Seeking the Beloved (Again)

PREVIEW

"The course of true love never did run smooth" (Shakespeare, *A Midsummer Night's Dream* 1.1.132). In the first poem of this unit, the woman's lover comes to the door, but she locks him out. When she decides to open the door to her lover, he is gone. She then runs into the streets to look for him, but she encounters opposition. The second poem is an inventory of the lover's attributes, spoken this time by the woman regarding the man. Following the descriptive inventory, the lovers are united once more. A chorus affirms their decision to enjoy the pleasures of each other's company, and the unit concludes with the refrain of mutual belonging: *I am my beloved's and my beloved is mine.*

OUTLINE

A Description of Her Experience Seeking Her Lover, 5:2-9
Her Description of His Beauty (Second *Descriptive Inventory*), 5:10-16
Dialogue between the Woman and the Daughters of Jerusalem, 6:1-3
    6:3   Refrain: Her Second Expression of Their Mutual Belonging

EXPLANATORY NOTES

This unit parallels 2:8–3:5 in complex ways. In the earlier unit, the lover invites her to come outside with him, because it is springtime and he wants to be with her. Now here, he asks to join her inside, because it is night and he is wet with dew. In both units what follows this invitation is the woman's search for her lover, although in 5:2–6:3, the search is delayed by her failure to respond quickly to his invitation. In the earlier unit, her search clearly results in success. She announces, *I found the one my heart loves. I found him and would not let him go* (3:4). But here, she appears not to find him, because she says, *I looked for him but did not find him. I called him but he did not answer* (5:6b), and she instructs the daughters of Jerusalem, *If you find my beloved, what will you tell him?* (v. 8). City watchmen appear in both units, playing slightly different roles. The refrain expressing the mutuality of their relationship appears in both units. In 2:8–3:5, it appears just before the "seeking and finding" episode: *My beloved is mine and I am his; he browses among the lilies* (2:16). In 5:2–6:3, the refrain (reversing the order from the earlier refrain) follows the search: *I am my beloved's and my beloved is mine; he browses among the lilies* (6:3).

A Description of Her Experience Seeking Her Lover 5:2-9

The first poetic unit in this passage presents several challenges. (1) Is the woman reporting a dream she had? Or is she half awake and describing something that happened to her when she woke up? (2) Does this passage describe a sexual encounter between the man and the woman? Or does it deliberately avoid an explicit description of the couple's encounter, and if so, why? (3) Why does the text suggest that she searches for her absent lover, who is, in fact, with her the entire time? Or does she conjure up her absent lover through an inventory of his physical attributes?

The unit opens with her statement: *I slept but my heart was awake.* Both NIV and NRSV use verbs in the past tense to translate the Hebrew; however, the Hebrew text could be translated *I sleep but my heart is awake* (AT). Perhaps this should clue us immediately to the fact that what follows may not be a report of either a dream or a series of events that occur, but rather a poetic description of the experience of being in love. Ellen Davis (2000a: 276) suggests that the Song here reveals "particular moments in the life of love, viewed from inside the relationship."

Sound first indicates the approach of the lover. The NIV correctly grabs our attention: *Listen! My beloved is knocking* (5:2; cf. 2:8, *Listen! My beloved!*). Referring to the scene as "the excluded-lover topos," Exum (193) observes that the scene in which a male lover stands outside a house asking to gain admittance to join his beloved is a common scene in love poetry. Hess (178) points to parallels in ancient Sumerian practice as well as in medieval Europe, concluding that the Song may reflect a similar custom in ancient Israel.

Scholars agree that the poem in 5:2-6 is filled with sexual innuendo. His request that she open the door to him suggests that he wants to gain entry to her body (Longman: 166) or to her "will, body, and being" (Hess: 1168). In the Hebrew Bible, the word "feet" (*raglaim*) can refer euphemistically to both male genitalia (Exod 4:25; Judg 3:24 KJV) and female genitalia (KJV: Deut 28:57; Ezek 16:25). Longman argues that "hole" and "hand" can be understood sexually, given that in Isaiah 57:8-10, the Hebrew word *yad*, translated "hand" (KJV), refers to the penis. Observing that the Hebrew word ḥor nowhere else refers to a hole in a door (NIV, *latch-opening*), Longman (167) concludes that the combination of *hand* and "hole" in 5:4 refers to a "sexual overture" on the part of the man.

Although scholars agree on the eroticism of the language, they disagree on how to understand the poem. Some interpreters read this as an actual report of the male lover's disturbance of his beloved's sleep: he knocks on her door but is denied entry into her house. Others propose that the poem describes a dream the woman experiences. Garrett (204) proposes that this poem refers to a couple's wedding night and argues that this poem expresses symbolically "the woman's loss of virginity" on her wedding night. By contrast, Carey Walsh (113) suggests that this poem unexpectedly describes an act of masturbation on the part of the woman. She states, "This passage, in essence, is a biblical wet dream of a woman."

Longman (161) explains that "this poem, like all the other poems in the Song, are not focused on a real-life occurrence" but rather "are creating moods and sensations." Similarly, Exum (190) explains the use of double entendre in the poem as follows:

> Double entendre, which gives the impression of gratification taking place even as it is longed for, makes it possible to read the woman's account on two different levels. This slippage from one mode to another, the blurring of distinctions between the more literal level of wishing, dreaming, desiring, and the figurative level of consummation is one of the poetic techniques that makes the Song so sensual.

Commentators have proposed a number of different interpretations for verse 7. Some try to explain the watchmen's violent behavior on the basis of historical information. They suggest that when the watchmen see a half-naked young woman in the streets at night, they assume she is a prostitute (Pope: 527; Keel: 195) or that she is a disobedient daughter who should be punished (Hess: 176–77). Garrett (214) assumes that this poem describes a young bride's first night with her husband, and he suggests that the watchmen are a metaphor for the "physical and emotional trauma of losing her virginity." Others assume that the poet uses symbolic language to express something about the experience of love. Both Longman (168–69) and Davis (2000a: 279) suggest that the watchmen symbolize the unfriendly attitude of the public or the city. Exum (199) proposes that the watchmen's treatment of the woman might symbolize the woman's willingness to suffer for her lover, and she provides support from both ancient Egyptian literature and contemporary practice among the Hamar people of southwest Ethiopia *[Figures of Speech, p. 267]*.

Next come verses 8-9, which serve as a transition to the inventory of 5:10-16. She asks the daughters of Jerusalem, *If you find my beloved, what will you tell him?* Immediately she instructs them regarding what to tell him: *Tell him I am faint with love* (v. 8). The daughters of Jerusalem then reply with a question of comparison: *How is your beloved better than others?* This then leads into her inventory of his physical attributes.

Her Description of His Beauty (Second *Descriptive Inventory*) 5:10-16

In this second of four descriptive poems that list the lover's physical features, it is the woman who speaks, praising her lover to a third party, the daughters of Jerusalem, in response to their question, *How is your beloved better than others?* Unlike the descriptive poem in 4:1-7, where a man speaks directly to his beloved, here she describes him to a third party. As in 4:1-7 and the other descriptive poems, this poem offers a partial inventory of the beloved's physical body, using figurative language to describe the beloved's head, hair, eyes, cheeks, lips, arms, torso, legs, and mouth. In her praise of her beloved, the woman begins with the head and then moves down the body to the legs. She then returns to his head, to comment upon his mouth.

As with the other descriptive poems, some interpreters understand this one to be something other than a straightforward poem of descriptive praise. Some scholars take 5:10-16 to be a satiric description of the man, who appears "somewhat awkwardly as a gargantuan, immobile, distant figure" (Whedbee: 274), and others find the description "coldly metallic and disjointed" (Landy: 80).

Rather than a comic, parodic, or satiric description, the context in which this descriptive poem occurs suggests that the woman here praises the man she finds so desirable by comparing him to precious gems and metals.

As this poem opens, she offers a comparative statement about her beloved, pronouncing him *outstanding among ten thousand* (5:10). The poem begins with the woman's favorite term of endearment, *my beloved*. This term and other figurative language in the poem serve to link this unit to the larger context of the book, despite the fact that some of the descriptive terms appear only here within the Song of Songs, such as *radiant and ruddy* (Hess: 181). She concludes with the pronouncement that he is *altogether lovely* (v. 16), thus framing the figurative description of the beloved with more general statements about his value and desirability. In rounding out her descriptive inventory of praise, she repeats her favorite term of endearment, *my beloved,* and adds to it a second term, *my friend*.

In the core section of the poem, she uses figurative language drawn from different realms. Although she draws some of the imagery from the natural realm of fauna and flora, as he does in his descriptive praise of her, this poem emphasizes the imagery of artisanship and architecture in its references to precious metals, ivory, semiprecious stones, and to features of both statuary and buildings. It is also possible that the description intends to recall statements made about God or the gods.

The poem uses both metaphor and simile. Metaphor is used in connection with the woman's description of her beloved's firm body in terms of precious metal (gold), ivory, and valuable stones (chrysolite, sapphires). Simile is used when she compares her beloved's facial features (eyes, cheeks, lips) to flora and fauna (raven, dove, spices, lilies). The imagery appeals to multiple senses. The visual predominates, but the imagery also appeals to the sense of smell—with its references to spices, lilies, and cedars (5:13, 15)—and to taste and touch (5:16) [*Figures of Speech, p. 267*].

First she declares her beloved to be *radiant and ruddy* (5:10). Some scholars think this may be an example of hendiadys, two terms combining to mean "bright red" or "shiny red." The color red (Hebrew ʾ*adom*) suggests male vigor and beauty. The young David is described as "ruddy" in appearance (1 Sam 16:12; 17:42). Similarly Esau, an outdoorsman, is associated with the color red (Gen 25:25). We also know that Egyptian art traditionally used a dark red-brown when coloring the male body. The woman then declares her beloved to be *outstanding among ten thousand*. That is, he is "one in a million."

In the poem, gold is used to describe the man's body three times. As is true today, gold calls to mind wealth and beauty. The poem uses three different terms for "gold." The phrase *purest gold* translates two Hebrew words, *ketem paz* (5:11). The more commonly used word for gold, *zahab*, appears in verse 14, and the word *paz* appears alone in verse 15, translated *pure gold*. As with all the descriptive poems, we get into trouble if we read too literally. Without pressing too hard the question of how a man could have a golden head and a ruddy complexion, we can acknowledge that the gold in this descriptive poem symbolizes the value that the woman sees in her beloved.

Shifting to a different image, she describes his hair as *wavy and black as a raven* (v. 11). Continuing with imagery from the natural world, she next describes her beloved's eyes as being *like doves* (v. 12). We often think of the eyes as mirrors of an individual's true self, and lovers look deeply into each other's eyes. It is not surprising, then, that she emphasizes his eyes in this poem. Earlier in the Song of Songs, he described the powerful effect her eyes have upon him (4:9). He, too, describes her eyes in terms of doves (1:15; 4:1). Again, the comparison of eyes to doves can be taken in different ways. Many interpreters suggest that the pupils are compared to doves in some way and contrasted with the whites of the eyes (*washed in milk*). She completes her description of his face with sensual imagery drawn from the natural world, comparing his cheeks to spice beds and his lips to *lilies dripping with myrrh* (v. 13).

In the next descriptive section, she refers to several different gemstones, which also suggest wealth and beauty. His arms are *rods of gold set with chrysolite* (v. 14a NIV 1984). It is generally accepted that the Hebrew term *taršiš* denotes some type of precious or semi-precious stone; the NIV identifies it as *chrysolite*, a green gemstone. Others translate it as *topaz* (2011 NIV), *beryl* (KJV, NASB) or more generically as *jewels* (NRSV). This is the same word as the place name Tarshish in the book of Jonah, which leads some scholars to speculate that it refers to precious gems that come from Tarshish.

There are several difficulties in verse 14b. The Hebrew word *meʿim*, translated by the NIV as *body*, usually refers to the inner parts of the human body. Here it appears to refer to a part of the body that can be seen, possibly the stomach or the abdomen. Although the NIV translates this as a simile, the Hebrew word meaning "like" is absent. The comparison is to ivory, although it is unclear exactly what the modifier *ʿešet* means, since it occurs only here in the Bible. It may refer to the form the ivory takes, such as "bars" (Hess: 164) or "panels" (Fox 1985: 149), or to work that has been done to the ivory that renders it "polished" or "carved." Still others take the word to refer to the appearance of ivory, which might be described as "bright" or "smooth." Following the last line of thinking, we can translate it as *His belly is polished ivory* (AT). This fits the poem's larger context, which describes the solidity of the beloved's body. The ivory has been decorated in some way. The Hebrew plural noun *sappirim*, which most versions translate by its cognate term *sapphires*, may originally come from a Sanskrit word for lapis lazuli, a precious stone that was imported to western Asia from the region that is now Afghanistan and frequently used in jewelry. The word *marble* (5:15) translates Hebrew *šeš*, which may refer to alabaster, a highly prized stone in the ancient Near East.

In addition to conjuring images of wealth and beauty, the imagery in this poem may suggest that the woman pronounces her beloved "divine" (just as he describes her in terms fitting for a deity in 4:8). In an Egyptian hymn to the sun-god Re, we find similar descriptive language:

His bones are of silver,
his flesh is of gold;
that which was on his head
is of genuine lapis lazuli. (Keel: 202)

To conclude, this inventory of descriptive praise, in which the poem describes the beauty of her beloved, uses figurative language that suggests solidity, beauty, and value.

Dialogue between the Woman and the Daughters of Jerusalem 6:1-3

The descriptive poem is framed by questions addressed to the woman about her lover (5:9; 6:1). The daughters of Jerusalem ask her to explain why her beloved is *better than others* (5:9), to which she responds with the descriptive poem (5:10-16).

Following her pronouncement that her beloved is *altogether lovely,* which she addresses to the daughters of Jerusalem, they ask another set of paralleled questions, inquiring about the location of her beloved (6:1). The woman answers this question more succinctly but ambiguously, using language that has both literal and figurative meanings in this book (6:2; cf. "his garden," 4:16; and "spice" and "lilies" in 5:13).

6:3 Refrain: Her Second Expression of Their Mutual Belonging

The unit concludes with a statement in which the woman describes her relationship with her beloved as one of mutual belonging (6:3a) and with a description of his location (6:3b), which confusingly suggests that they have been together all along. This is the second occurrence of the refrain of mutual belonging.

THE TEXT IN BIBLICAL CONTEXT

Imagery of Well-Being

Two images in this section of Song of Songs connect to images of prosperity and well-being elsewhere in the Bible. One image, "dew," occurs only here within Song of Songs. When the man speaks to his lover, he says, *My head is drenched with dew, my hair with the dampness of the night* (5:2). On the one hand, this may be a simple description of his condition; however, when we recognize the biblical symbolism of "dew," we may discover that this seemingly simple comment has deeper symbolic significance.

Those who live in a region that receives adequate rainfall to support vegetation may be unaware that dew can be a primary source of water in some areas. Israel receives little rainfall in the months between April and October. Today, crops and other vegetation can be watered through the use of irrigation systems. In ancient times, heavy dews served a similar function of maintaining necessary crop growth and even provided water for small animals. Consequently, in the Bible "dew" frequently symbolizes divine favor. When Isaac mistakenly gives his son Jacob the blessing intended for Esau, he says, "May God give you heaven's dew and earth's richness—an abundance of grain and new wine" (Gen 27:28). In the narratives of the wilderness wanderings, dew is associated with the manna from heaven (Exod 16:13-14; Num 11:9). When the prophet Elijah tells King Ahab that God was bringing a drought upon the land, he says, "As the Lord, the God of Israel, lives, whom I serve, there will be neither dew nor rain in the next few years except at my word" (1 Kings 17:1). In a prophetic message of hope, the prophet Zechariah announces that at some time in the future, God will restore the people, and at that time the heavens will provide "their dew" upon the earth again: "The seed will grow well, the vine will yield its fruit, the ground will produce its crops, and the heavens will drop their dew. I will give all these things as an inheritance to the remnant of this people" (Zech 8:12).

The second image, "Lebanon," occurs throughout the poetry of the Song of Songs. Since Lebanon is a geographical location on the northern border of ancient Israel, its symbolic import may be easily overlooked. The term "Lebanon" refers to an area that was defined by two mountain ranges. Located today in modern Lebanon, the Lebanon Mountains border the Mediterranean Sea. Further east lies the Anti-Lebanon range. In between the two mountain ranges lies the fertile Beqaa Valley. Because in biblical times this area received abundant precipitation and the benefits of the snowmelt, "Lebanon" in the Bible symbolizes fertility and abundance.

In a royal psalm asking God to endow the king with justice and righteousness, the psalmist says, "May grain abound throughout the land; on the tops of the hills may it sway. May the crops flourish like Lebanon and thrive like the grass of the field" (72:16). Among the Prophets, Lebanon symbolizes the future restoration of the land, as in this announcement of God's future actions found in Isaiah: "The glory of Lebanon will come to you, the juniper, the fir and the cypress together, to adorn my sanctuary; and I will glorify the place for my feet" (60:13).

In many passages, the cedars of Lebanon are singled out because they were known in ancient Israel as the finest of trees. Notably, they produced wood that was beautiful enough for God's dwelling in Jerusalem, the temple built by King Solomon (1 Kings 5:10; 9:11-19). The psalmist proclaims that God created the cedars of Lebanon (104:16). In one announcement of future restoration, the prophet Hosea joins the imagery of dew and that of the cedars of Lebanon to offer hope to the people. In this prophetic announcement, God is compared to "dew," and Israel will be like "a cedar of Lebanon."

> I will heal their waywardness and love them freely,
>   for my anger has turned away from them.
> I will be like the dew to Israel;
>   he will blossom like a lily.
> Like a cedar of Lebanon he will send down his roots;
>   his young shoots will grow.
> His splendor will be like an olive tree,
>   his fragrance like a cedar of Lebanon.
> People will dwell again in his shade;
>   they will flourish like the grain,
> they will blossom like the vine—
>   Israel's fame will be like the wine of Lebanon. (Hos 14:4-7)

The Beauty of God and of Creation

In the Song of Songs, love is closely associated with beauty. The two lovers admire and comment upon each other's beauty, and the imagery that is used throughout the poetry can itself be described as beautiful. Other passages in the Bible comment upon the beauty of nature, the beauty of individuals, and the beauty of God. Nature's beauty as God's creation is described and praised throughout the Bible. "He has made everything beautiful in its time" (Eccl 3:11a). In the Gospels, Jesus comments upon the beauty of the lilies: "Consider how the wild flowers grow. They do not labor or spin. Yet I tell you, not even Solomon in all his splendor was dressed like one of these" (Luke 12:27). The trees of Eden are declared beautiful (Gen 2:9), and the vision of restoration at the end of Revelation describes, not the destruction of the world, as so many people imagine, but the beauty of "a new heaven and a new earth" (Rev 21:1). New Jerusalem descends to earth. John describes the city by using the imagery of a wedding. He says it is "prepared as a bride beautifully dressed for her husband" (Rev 21:2).

The psalmist expresses the hope of seeing God's beauty in the temple: "One thing I ask from the LORD, this only do I seek: that I may dwell in the house of the LORD all the days of my life, to gaze on the beauty of the LORD and to seek him in his temple" (Ps 27:4). Psalm 50 proclaims that God is "perfect in beauty" (v. 2). The prophet Isaiah describes God as "a beautiful wreath for the remnant of his people" (Isa 28:5). By way of 1 Chronicles 16:29, we are called to "worship the LORD in the beauty of holiness" (KJV). We may sometimes lose sight of the fact that God and God's creation are filled with beauty.

THE TEXT IN THE LIFE OF THE CHURCH

Seeking God

In his work *On the Trinity*, Augustine (354–430), Bishop of Hippo (396–430), discusses the experience of seeking and finding God.

> Directing my purpose by this rule of faith, so far as I have been able (so far as you have made me to be able), I have sought you and have desired to see with my understanding what I believed, and I have argued and labored a great deal. O Lord my God, my one hope, listen to me, lest through weariness I be unwilling to seek you, "but let me always ardently seek your face" (Ps 105:4). Give me strength to seek, you who have made me find you, and given me the hope of finding you more and more. My strength and my infirmity are in your sight: preserve the one, and heal the other. My knowledge and my ignorance are in your sight; where you have opened to me, receive me as I enter; where you have closed, open to me as I knock. May I remember you, understand you, love you. Increase these things in me, until you fully refashion me. (15.28; McGinn: 196)

The hymn "Seek Ye First the Kingdom of God," written by Karen Lafferty (b. 1948), uses the language of the gospel of Matthew to express the understanding that when we ask to be invited into God's kingdom, the door will be opened to us.

> 1. Seek ye first the kingdom of God,
> And His righteousness,
> And all these things shall be added unto you—
> Allelu, alleluia!
>
> 2. Ask and it shall be given unto you,
> Seek and ye shall find,
> Knock and the door shall be opened unto you—
> Allelu, alleluia! (*HWB* no. 324)

Divine Beauty

Christian spiritual writing tends to comment upon the beauty of Jesus rather than the beauty of God. The hymn "Fairest Lord Jesus" describes the beauty of both Jesus and creation. The seventeenth-century hymn text known as *Schönster Herr Jesu* was translated into English in the nineteenth century by Joseph A. Seiss, an American Lutheran pastor with roots in the Moravian tradition. Although the text that follows may be more familiar to twenty-first-century Christians, Seiss's first stanza originally began "Beautiful Savior, King of Creation" and ended with a vow to love and serve Jesus: "Truly I'd love Thee, truly I'd serve Thee, Light of my soul, my joy, my crown."

> 1. Fairest Lord Jesus,
> ruler of all nature,
> O thou of God and Mary's Son,
> thee will I cherish,
> thee will I honor,
> thou, my soul's glory, joy, and crown.
>
> 2. Fair are the meadows,
> fairer still the woodlands,
> robed in the blooming garb of spring.
> Jesus is fairer,
> Jesus is purer,
> who makes the woeful heart to sing.
>
> 3. Fair is the sunshine,
> fairer still the moonlight,
> and all the twinkling, starry host:

Jesus shines brighter,
Jesus shines purer
Than all the angels heav'n can boast. (*HWB* no. 117)

An older hymn, written by Charles W. Fry (1837–82), draws explicitly upon the imagery and language of Song of Songs to describe Jesus as a friend and "the fairest of ten thousand" (see Song 5:10, *outstanding among ten thousand*). The hymn also identifies Jesus as the "Lily of the Valley" (cf. Song 2:1). Fry, a British bricklayer by trade, had ties to the Wesleyan movement in England and to Salvation Army founder William Booth.

1. I have found a friend in Jesus, He's ev'rything to me,
He's the fairest of ten thousand to my soul;
The Lily of the Valley, in Him alone I see
All I need to cleanse and make me fully whole:
In sorrow He's my comfort, in trouble He's my stay;
He tells me ev'ry care on Him to roll;
He's the Lily of the Valley, the Bright and Morning Star,
He's the fairest of ten thousand to my soul. (*Baptist Hymnal* no. 153)

Song of Songs 6:4–7:13

Overwhelmed by Love

PREVIEW

We desire love. We want to love and to be loved. But we also recognize that love can be terrifying. Even the thought of loving someone else can overwhelm us. At times parents can feel overwhelmed by the love for their children and their inability to protect their children from harm. Lovers can experience a loss of independence when they realize the power that love has over them. When we are in relationship with someone, we give up our independence. We acknowledge that our lover has power over us, and we may wonder, "How will my lover use her power over me?" In the poems in this chapter, the man appears overwhelmed by love. He describes his beloved by using both military and celestial imagery. He declares her to be *majestic as troops with banners* and as *majestic as the stars in procession* (vv. 4, 10). Nevertheless, he announces that she is the only one for him (6:9), and she declares that she belongs to him (7:10a).

OUTLINE

His Description of Her Beauty (Third *Descriptive Inventory*), 6:4-10
A Description of an Experience, 6:11-12
An Invitation to the Shulammite to Return, 6:13
His Description of Her Beauty (Fourth *Descriptive Inventory*), 7:1-9a
A Poem Expressing Her Desire for Him, 7:9b-13
    7:10   Refrain: Her Third Expression of Their Mutual Belonging

Song of Songs 6:4–7:13   235

EXPLANATORY NOTES

The identity of the speakers is unclear in some parts of this unit, and the connection of the individual units is not entirely clear. The unit includes the third and fourth poems we have identified as "descriptive inventories of praise." In both of these inventories, the man praises the woman's appearance and attributes.

His Description of Her Beauty (Third *Descriptive Inventory*) 6:4-10

With the third descriptive inventory in 6:4-10, we again encounter the man's praise of his beloved's physical features, using figurative language to describe her attributes. There will be one more descriptive inventory in this book, a final poem in which the man describes and praises his lover's physical features (7:1-9a). This third descriptive inventory is the shortest of the four if we compare just the listing of the lover's body parts. It also has three similes that are identical or nearly identical to the similes in the first descriptive inventory (the comparisons of the woman's hair, teeth, and temples).

Despite the parallels, there are some differences between the two inventories (4:1-7 and 6:4-10). We can also notice the differences in the literary contexts of the two poems. Although the inventory of descriptive praise in this chapter ends in verse 7, the poem continues through verse 10, as the inclusio suggests. Verse 4 and verse 10 both end with the same two Hebrew words ʾayummah kannidgalot (although this repetition is not evident in all major English translations). We might translate the two Hebrew words as follows: *Terrible! Like an army with banners* (AT). NRSV and KJV both demonstrate the inclusio by using the same English phrase to translate the Hebrew: *terrible as an army with banners*. The NIV disguises the parallel by using two different phrases: *as majestic as troops with banners* (v. 4b) and *majestic as the stars in procession* (v. 10b).

This poem, like the first inventory of praise in 4:1-7, opens with a declaration of the woman's beauty. In this poem, however, the observation of her beauty is extended by references to two cities—Tirzah and Jerusalem—and by an intensifying comparison that describes her beauty by using military language. The imagery suggests that this particular poem emphasizes the man's experience of being overcome, overwhelmed by her. Why? Because she is one of a kind. And she is awesome. As Exum (218) observes, this poem reflects a common *topos* in love poetry: the person who is loved is both terrifying and wonderful. With their identification of queens, concubines, and young women, verses 8 and 9b enclose verse 9a, the unit's center, with its emphasis on her one-ness. *She is <u>one</u>, my dove, my perfect one. She is <u>one</u> for her mother* (AT).

A Description of an Experience 6:11-12

These two verses are notoriously difficult to understand. Not even the speaker's identity is clear. The most that can be said about the verses is that the figurative language appears to refer to the woman's developing sexuality.

An Invitation to the Shulammite to Return 6:13

Verse 13 presents a number of difficulties. Who is speaking? What is the meaning of the term "Shulammite"? Where or what is "Mahanaim"? How does this verse connect with its context?

Who is speaking? NIV divides the verse between the "friends" (v. 13a) and the young man (v. 13b). There have been numerous other proposals. Some interpreters suggest that the chorus of women utters the entire verse (Hess: 208-10). Other interpreters propose that the chorus of women issues the invitation (v. 13a), and either the man or the woman responds (Huwiler: 281; Longman: 189). Another possibility is that the man issues the invitation to the woman, and she replies (Exum: 211).

What is the meaning of the term "Shulammite"? There are four main proposals for understanding the meaning of this term: (1) The name resembles *Šulmanitu*, an epithet for Ishtar, the Mesopotamian goddess of love and war. (2) The name is connected to the city of Shunem and consequently to two biblical women associated with the city: Abishag (1 Kings 1:4, 15) and the unnamed Shunammite woman (2 Kings 4:8-37). (3) The name is a feminine form of Solomon. (4) The term reflects the underlying root meaning of "peace" and "completeness." Each of these proposals has some merit, and it is possible that they are not mutually exclusive options. Given the interpretation in this commentary that the poetry has multiple layers of meaning, it makes sense that the term "Shulammite" can be read as an epithet meaning "the perfect one," while at the same time alluding to Solomon and to the goddess Ishtar. The one explanation that seems least likely is the proposal that connects it to one of the Shunammite women (although that possibility cannot be eliminated).

Where or what is "Mahanaim"? The Hebrew word *maḥanaim* means "the two camps" and likely refers to army encampments, although it could also mean a town that lay east of the Jordan River (Josh 21:38). Women frequently danced at victory celebrations after battles. Miriam and other Hebrew women danced and sang after the defeat of the Egyptians, which allowed the Hebrew slaves to escape their bondage in Egypt (Exod 15:19-21). After Jephthah's defeat of the Ammonites, he returned home and was met by his daughter, who was "dancing to the sound of tambourines" (Judg 11:34). These are victory dances, not erotic dances. We have seen other military imagery used in the poetry of Song of Songs, so a reference to a victory dance should not surprise us.

As we consider these pieces of the puzzle—a goddess of love and war, a victory dance of women, gazing upon a woman—we arrive at possibilities rather than certainties. It seems impossible to arrive at a definitive interpretation of this verse, but within its context it may suggest the following. The poet here draws attention to the woman—both the man's attention and our attention as readers—and describes her as being as awe-inspiring as a goddess of love and war. As with the figure of Ishtar, who presides over matters of both love and war, this woman through her "perfection," her "completeness," her shalom (šalom), has won over this man. Simply by being who she is, she has peacefully defeated him in the battle of love.

His Description of Her Beauty (Fourth *Descriptive Inventory*) 7:1-9a

The final poem of descriptive praise that inventories the beloved's physical attributes occurs in 7:1-9. Perhaps because the previous unit ends with a reference to dancing, this poem begins, not at the woman's head, but at her feet, and then moves up her body to conclude in 7:5 with a description of her head and hair. Some interpreters extend the inventory through 7:7. Again, this poem draws upon the "king fiction" in which the lovers compliment each other by using the language and imagery of the royal court *[King Fiction, p. 278]*. Here we see this royal fiction in the reference to the woman as a *prince's daughter* (7:1) and in the description of her hair, in which *the king is held captive*.

> *Your head crowns you like Mount Carmel.*
> *Your hair is like royal tapestry;*
> *the king is held captive by its tresses.* (7:5)

A Poem Expressing Her Desire for Him 7:9b-13

The woman breaks into the man's speech rather suddenly in the middle of 7:9. He has asked for intimacy. She agrees and proposes that they visit the vineyards. She repeats a variation of a refrain that we have encountered earlier in the book: *I belong to my beloved, and his desire is for me* (7:10). In the first of these refrains, she claims, *My beloved is mine and I am his; he browses among the lilies* (2:16). In its second occurrence, she reverses the first half of the verse to say, *I am my beloved's and my beloved is mine* (6:3a). In this poem, rather than describing the mutuality of their relationship, she speaks of his desire for her. The word translated here as *desire* is a Hebrew word that occurs only three times in the Bible (also in Gen 3:16; 4:7). Because the word "desire" alters the structure of the refrain, we need to ask why it is introduced here. As several scholars suggest, we need to read this occurrence of the word "desire" in light of its uses in Genesis. In Genesis 3:16, the woman's "desire" seems undesirable because there appears to be a connection between her desire for her husband and his rule over her. Davis (2000a: 294) pronounces the woman's statement in Song of Songs "radical" in correcting the distortion of the male-female relationship that Genesis associates with the first couple's act of disobedience; she also sets Song of Songs 7:10 in conversation with the story of Cain and Abel, the other biblical occurrence of the word "desire." In that story, God warns Cain of the power that sin holds over people: "But if you do not do what is right, sin is crouching at your door; it desires to have you, but you must rule over it" (Gen 4:7b).

The Genesis texts demonstrate the powerful nature of "desire." In the mouth of the lover, however, "desire" directs itself in a positive way to create a relationship that binds one person to another: not in a hierarchical relationship, in which one person rules over the other, but in a relationship of equals, in which the power of desire serves to benefit both members of the relationship.

THE TEXT IN BIBLICAL CONTEXT

Tirzah and Jerusalem

Jerusalem is certainly familiar to students of the Bible, but Tirzah, by contrast, is barely remembered. Nevertheless, this poet has brought these two cities together in the declaration that the woman is *as beautiful as Tirzah* and *as lovely as Jerusalem*. Jerusalem, of course, was the long-standing capital of the southern kingdom of Judah. Taken by King David from the Jebusites, it became the locus of power in the southern kingdom. David built his palace there, and his son Solomon built a house for the LORD there. King Josiah later declared the Jerusalem temple to be the only legitimate place of worship for Judeans.

Tirzah was a Canaanite town whose king was killed by the Israelites, under the leadership of Joshua (Josh 12:24). The town played no significant role in biblical history until after the formation of the two kingdoms, Judah and Israel, following the death of King Solomon. Jeroboam, the first king of the newly established northern kingdom of Israel, made Tirzah his capital (1 Kings 14:17), and Tirzah remained the northern capital until Omri moved the capital to Samaria (1 Kings 16:23-24).

We may wonder why the Song of Songs refers to Tirzah since the focus of the book's poetry seems to rest upon Judah and Jerusalem. Davis (2000a: 285) suggests that the comparison of the woman in Song of Songs to both Tirzah and Jerusalem serves to "reunite the two kingdoms" within the woman, thus making her a symbol of peace.

Return

It is difficult to read the fourfold call to the Shulammite to *return* (6:13 NRSV; NIV, *come back*) without thinking of the prophets' call to the people to return to God. The Hebrew verb used in both is *šub*, which carries the sense of turning away *from* as well as returning *to* a condition or a location.

The concept of turning away from one's bad ways and returning to the LORD appears throughout the Prophets. In these prophetic calls for the people's return, we see an emphasis on a concept of God's mercy.

> Come, let us return to the LORD.
> He has torn us to pieces
>   but he will heal us;
> he has injured us
>   but he will bind up our wounds. (Hos 6:1)

> Go, proclaim this message toward the north:
> "Return, faithless Israel," declares the LORD,
> "I will frown on you no longer,
> for I am faithful," declares the LORD,
> "I will not be angry forever." (Jer 3:12)

> Say to them, "As surely as I live, declares the Sovereign LORD, I take no pleasure in the death of the wicked, but rather the return of the

wicked from their ways so that they may live. Return! Return from your bad ways! Why would you die, O house of Israel?" (Ezek 33:11 AT)

In the prophet Malachi, we hear the promise that if the people return to God, God will return to them:

> "Ever since the time of your ancestors you have turned away from my decrees and have not kept them. Return to me, and I will return to you," says the LORD Almighty. "But you ask, 'How are we to return?'" (Mal 3:7)

Perhaps one of the best narrative examples of a return that incorporates both a turning away from bad choices and a return to the one who offers love is Jesus' story of the prodigal son in Luke 15. After realizing the error of his ways, the son says, "I will set out and go back to my father and say to him: Father, I have sinned against heaven and against you" (Luke 15:18). The father responds to the son's return by holding a feast to celebrate the return.

THE TEXT IN THE LIFE OF THE CHURCH

Sexual Desire and Sexual Ethics

I belong to my beloved, and his desire is for me (7:10). Longing and belonging. Desire. Intimacy. The term "sexuality" can be defined in several different ways. Thinking broadly, we can use the term *sexuality* to refer to feelings, emotions, and activities related to intimate physical contact between individuals. It can include, but is not limited to, sexual intercourse. It can also refer to sexual feelings, that is, to the *affective* side of human sexuality [*Sexuality, p. 283*].

Perhaps surprisingly, the Bible lacks a word that encompasses what we mean when we say "sexuality." Not only does it lack the term, the Bible has relatively little to say regarding this broader definition of human sexuality that includes sexual feelings, desires, and pleasures. The Song of Songs appears to be the exception, because it has much to say about human sexuality in all its dimensions. Although unusual in its emphasis on sexuality, the Song of Songs is not alone within the Bible in expressing approval of sexual feelings and desire.

Despite the centrality of sexuality to human experience, churches have had relatively little to say on the subject. When sexuality is discussed in churches, it is often because people are debating specific sexual behaviors and activities (e.g., sexual intercourse outside of marriage, premarital sexual intercourse, sexual activity between same-sex partners). Developing a sexual ethic is important, but before that can be done, we have to understand sexuality, including its affective side. The Song of Songs nourishes our understanding of human sexuality. Not only does it celebrate this aspect of human experience; it also explores the various aspects of intimacy: appreciation, trust, commitment, mutuality, and affection.

For those of us within the church, what we do with our bodies matters. It is one of the ways in which we demonstrate faithfulness to God. Erin Dufault-Hunter (727) explains how a communally developed ethic of sexuality fosters the spiritual life:

> Scripture reminds us that sexuality is at its worst when merely utilitarian—solely for our own pleasure, for the conception of heirs, for dominating others. Sexual passion is at its best when it is harnessed so that we are freed to love others faithfully and pursue other important goods. Erotic passion burns without consuming us within intimate commitments marked by the deep satisfaction of mutually self-forgetting, self-offering love. Expressed or restrained, disciplined Christian sexuality sustains and nourishes us for the work of faith, hope, and love.

The Lure of God's Love

As discussed in the TBC, the language of "return" suggests turning away from the attraction of sin and turning to God. What motivates us to turn from sin and to turn, or return, to God? Modern psychology suggests that we are most successful in achieving a goal when we feel motivated internally. Motivation from a source outside ourselves may result in immediate success, but it often fails over the long term. The prophet Jeremiah suggests something like this in the "new covenant" oracle when he transmits God's saying, "I will put my law in their minds and write it on their hearts" (31:33).

Some theologians have moved in this direction with language like "the lure of God" and "the divine Eros." Catherine Keller (104) describes the human response to God in terms of desire and attraction. She argues that we turn from sin and return to God when we respond to the lure of God.

> The lure suggests then the experience of a divine desire that, sweetly or dangerously, in flesh and in spirit, *attracts* us. The touch of truth is not heavy-handed until humans try to force it. So this divine passion influences us not by a power of coercion, from the outside, but by a power of attraction flowing into us. It invites *from within*.

Song of Songs 8:1-14

Love Is Strong as Death

PREVIEW

In the last chapter of the book, we once again encounter short speeches from different speakers, with abrupt transitions between speeches. The poems in this chapter express different understandings about love. In this set of poems, we learn of love's determination, its playfulness, and its value. We reach the climax of the book (8:6-7), which explores love's power and profundity. Finally, we end the Song of Songs as we began it, with an understanding that love is an ongoing process that eludes human attempts to control it. At the end of the book, are the two lovers any closer to achieving what they desire? Yes. And no. Or, maybe.

OUTLINE

A Poem of Desire, 8:1-4
    8:4   Refrain: Her Charge to the Daughters of Jerusalem
A Poem in Praise of Love, 8:5-7
A Poem on Love's Elusive Nature, 8:8-14

EXPLORATORY NOTES

A Poem of Desire 8:1-4

The first poem of this unit (8:1-4) rather closely parallels the poem found in 3:1-5. In both short units, the woman expresses her desire to find her beloved and bring him to her mother's house. Both units conclude with an injunction to the women of Jerusalem, and both units are followed by a similar question, *Who is this coming up from the wilderness* (3:6a; 8:5a).

The unit opens with a wish. She exclaims, *If only you were to me like a brother*. If he were her brother, they could be seen in public, and she could touch him and express affection. We do not know enough about the social context of men and women in ancient Israel to understand this precisely. The literary context of the wish implies that she is unable to relate to him as she would like to do in public without eliciting condemnation.

Interestingly, five verbs in the Hebrew imperfect form appear serially in these two verses: *if I found* (lit. *I would find*); *I would kiss you*; *I would lead you*; *I would bring you*; and *I would give you to drink*. As Hess (229) observes, this form (the imperfect in the first person) occurs only fifteen times in the whole book. Thus, to have five of those fifteen occurrences concentrated in two verses seems significant. Hebrew imperfect verbs often have a future indicative meaning (i.e., they state that something *will* happen), but they can also express a subjunctive mood, in which the speaker expresses the desire or intention that something *might* happen. The NIV translation understands the imperfect verb forms as an expression of the woman's firm intention to act—if she were to locate her beloved.

> Then, <u>*if I found*</u> you outside,
>   I <u>*would kiss*</u> you,
>   and no one would despise me.
> I <u>*would lead*</u> you
>   <u>*and bring*</u> you to my mother's house—
>   she who has taught me.
> I <u>*would give*</u> you spiced wine to drink,
>   the nectar of my pomegranates. (8:1b-2, emph. added)

The phrase translated *if I found you outside* (NIV; NRSV is similar) is perhaps better translated *if I found you in public*. The precise meaning of the verb is unclear. It could mean either that she searched for and then found her lover or that she happened to encounter her lover. The term translated *outside* is better understood as "in public" because in its context the concern is with how her behavior would be viewed in a public context. In other sections of this book, the term "outside" refers to the couple's *private* world in the countryside or the mountains, but here the reference is to the public world in which the couple is unable to appear together without criticism.

Two minor textual problems occur in this section. First, the expression in verse 2 translated *she who has taught me* is sometimes emended to read *she who bore me*. Those who make this emendation

(NRSV) choose to follow the Septuagint and Syriac texts. Some commentators also emend the text in this way, explaining that "she who bore me" offers a better poetic parallel to "my mother's house" (Exum: 247). Such an emendation seems unnecessary since "she who taught me" *does* offer a parallel to "my mother's house." This is further supported by references to the role mothers played in the instruction of children (Prov 1:8; 31:1). Second, NRSV and NIV both read the plural *pomegranates* in verse 2, following the Greek, Latin, and several Hebrew witnesses. The MT reads the singular noun "pomegranate," and it seems unnecessary to emend the text to read the plural.

In the first two verses of this unit, the woman expresses her desire for her beloved. If only she could relate to her lover in public as if he were a family member, then she would embrace him and take him inside the house with her.

Verses 3-4 repeat 2:6-7, with a few minor variations. This repetition suggests to the reader that the poems in the book describe the experiences of a single couple, and consequently we are tempted to overlay the poems with a plot. As in 2:6, the verse can be translated as the description of an embrace the woman experiences at the time of her utterance or as an expression of her desire for his future embrace:

His left arm is under my head
  and his right arm embraces me. (NIV)
OR
O that his left hand were under my head,
  and that his right hand embraced me! (NRSV)

Given that the preceding verses (8:1-2) express the woman's desire for intimacy with her lover, the NRSV translation better fits the context of 8:1-4 as an expression of the woman's desire for intimacy with her lover, rather than a description of her actual experience of intimacy.

In 8:4 the woman directly addresses her companions with a refrain that has appeared twice before in the Song of Songs (2:7; 3:5): *Daughters of Jerusalem, I charge you: Do not arouse or awaken love until it so desires.* In 3:5, it follows the woman's statement that she wants to bring her lover to her *mother's house* (see discussion at 3:4). In both 3:5 and 8:4, the refrain is followed by the question *Who is this coming up from the wilderness?*

A Poem in Praise of Love 8:5-7

For a third time in the book, the question *Who is this?* is asked (3:6; 6:10; 8:5). In each case, the identity of the questioner is unclear, and in two of the three instances, the question remains unanswered (6:10; 8:5). NIV understands the "friends" to be asking the question in 6:10 and 8:5. (In 3:6, NIV has the question asked by the woman.) What does the question mean within its literary context? In 3:6, the question *Who is this?* sets the stage for the entrance of Solomon's palanquin, but here no scene is developed to follow the question. Instead, the question in 8:5 (*Who is this coming up from the wilderness leaning on her beloved?*) seems to be suspended between two units. Both here and in 3:6, the question follows the woman's exhortation to the daughters of Jerusalem (Keel: 265). One possibility in 8:5 is to read the question as a "stylized formula of dramatization," a poetic way of "glorifying the woman" (A. Bloch and C. Bloch: 159). Like the morning star, the woman rises in the east (the wilderness lies to the east).

The speaker(s) is (are) usually understood to be the woman's companions, the *daughters of Jerusalem* (v. 4), which makes sense if the question refers to the two lovers. As in 3:6, we find a reference to a *wilderness*, an area that receives little rainfall and is, therefore, mostly uninhabited, an open area where sheep and goats pasture. The verb translated *leaning on* occurs only here in the entire Bible. The context suggests it means something like "leaning upon" or "reclining against." It could be they are walking together or riding in a conveyance like the carriage of 3:6-11.

In the response to the question, the woman again associates her lover with an apple tree. In 2:3 she proclaims her lover superior to the other young men, using the figurative language of an apple tree. Here she announces that she *roused* her beloved under an apple tree, the same tree under which he was conceived and given birth. As Exum (249) observes, this reference to the moment of their love's arousal precedes the woman's request for a sign of her lover's commitment to a permanent relationship.

In 8:6-7 the woman speaks in a carefully and beautifully constructed poem about love, in which the poet uses parallelism, alliteration, metaphorical language, and repetition to good effect. The unit begins with what Exum (4-5) calls the "erotic imperative," the use of grammatical imperative forms that create a sense of urgency and the illusion of immediacy to the poems *[Erotic Imperative, p. 266]*. In this poem, the woman instructs her lover to keep her close to him and protect her as he would a precious seal or signet:

> *Place me like a seal over your heart,*
> *like a seal on your arm.*

Today we carry a driver's license or credit card, or perhaps a passport, to verify our identity. In ancient Israel and throughout the ancient Near East, a seal served a similar purpose as personal identification for the person who carried or wore the seal. Seals could be made from stone, wood, or metal. They were usually inscribed with an image so that when the image was pressed into wet clay, it stamped the clay with the image. Here the word "seal" refers to the seal itself, not the image made by a seal. A person wore the seal around the neck on a cord or on a hand as a ring. Just as we are careful not to misplace or lose our credit cards and photo IDs, the ancients treated their personal seals as valuables. By asking her beloved to place her as a seal over his heart and on his arm, the woman expresses her desire to be close to him, but also implies that she wants him to treat her with the care and respect he uses to protect his seal. The imperative *place me* lends a sense of urgency to the poem and creates the reader's illusion that the interaction between the two lovers is occurring in real time.

The woman next makes a claim about love (v. 6):

> *For love is as strong as death,*
> *its jealousy unyielding as the grave.*

In Hebrew, both statements lack a verb. As is common in Biblical Hebrew poetry, two juxtaposed terms can indicate similarity in meaning. Love is likened to death in its power. Death is inevitable. The ancients knew this fact as well as we do today (although we moderns are sometimes accused of trying to ignore or escape death's inevitability). To proclaim that *love is as strong as death* is to affirm love's unyielding power [Figures of Speech, p. 267].

The second line occasions more controversy: *its jealousy unyielding as the grave.* The Hebrew lacks the pronoun "its," and the Hebrew word translated *jealousy, qinʾah,* means also "zeal" or "passion." The word translated *grave* in the NIV is the Hebrew term *šeʾol,* which refers to the underworld, the realm of the dead. Thus the second half of the poetic line could be translated: *passion [is] unyielding like the underworld.*

Some translations and some interpreters avoid the term *jealousy* when translating the Hebrew term *qinʾah,* perhaps disliking the negative connotations of the word *jealousy.* Others insist that the term *qinʾah* describes the reaction to something that threatens a relationship. Love and jealousy are paired terms that together describe the experience of love. The first term, *love*, identifies the strength of the desire of lovers for each other. The second term, *jealousy*, characterizes the resistance lovers put up against anything that would threaten their relationship.

Who is the woman's rival? Who threatens their relationship? Although there have been individuals who have blocked the way between the lovers, these are hardly rivals. If the man has other women, the poems have not mentioned these rivals or potential rivals. Given the references to "death" and "the grave," it seems likely that the woman here challenges death as her rival to proclaim that even death cannot overcome the love she feels for the man. Here the woman faces death and utters a challenge: "You are strong and unyielding, but so am I in my desire for my beloved."

Thus far, we observe the poet using parallelism in ways that intensify the meaning of the passage. The woman (v. 6) demands that her lover place her as a seal upon both his heart and his arm. The term "jealousy" intensifies and clarifies the meaning of "love." Here she speaks of love that fiercely defends itself against anyone or anything that would come between lover and beloved, even death and the grave. The last line of verse 6 continues the use of parallelism to describe this unyielding passionate love by means of the image of fire. The NIV makes this a verbal sentence, *It burns like blazing fire, like a mighty flame,* when the Hebrew sentence actually has no verb and simply juxtaposes four nouns. A more word-for-word translation would look something like this: *Its sparks, sparks of fire, an all-powerful flame.* The pronoun "its" refers to the jealous love in the previous paired lines and describes the effects of this fierce love: its sparks have the power to consume anything in its path. The phrase translated *a mighty flame* (NIV) or *an all-powerful flame* (AT) is one word in the Hebrew text: *šalhebetyah*. This is an unusual word, which can be translated in two different ways. The first part of the word, *šalhebet*, means "flame." (1) The ending *yah* may be taken as a superlative, meaning "the mightiest flame," "the hottest flame," or "the most powerful flame." (2) Since the Hebrew word *yah* can also refer to Israel's Deity, Yahweh, some commentators take it to be a reference to God and translate it *the flame of Yah.* If it is a divine name, this would be the only explicit reference to God in the entire book. Quite possibly the word is meant to have a dual meaning: it indicates the superlative ("mightiest") but also refers to God. Since translators must choose one primary translation, it is probably best to translate it as a superlative, as do many versions: *a mighty flame* (NIV), *a raging flame* (NRSV), *a most vehement flame* (KJV). A few versions choose the second option: *divine flame* (CEB) and the *very flame of the* LORD (NASB). My proposal of *an all-powerful flame* intends to evoke the thought of God, who is considered "all-powerful," without directly referring to the Deity.

The metaphors next shift from fire to water. Both fire and water are powerful elements of the natural world, although the poet seems to maintain the comparison of love to fire. Poetic parallelism continues with *many waters* and *rivers* in parallel construction. The expression *many waters* refers to the amount of water and could be translated "floods." If we try to maintain the fire imagery in this verse, it suggests that even a flood could not extinguish the raging fire of passionate love.

In the second half of verse 7, the metaphors again shift—this time from the natural world to the social world. Earlier in this unit we saw a reference to social opinion, when the woman imagines what it would be like to appear with her lover in public without arousing public criticism (8:1). The Hebrew verb translated *despise* or *scorn* recurs at the end of verse 7 (both NIV and NRSV use two different English words to translate the same Hebrew verb, *despise* in v. 1 and *scorn* in v. 7). The first part of the verse, the conditional statement, is clear: *If one were to give all the wealth of his house for love* ... (AT). What follows has two possible meanings. The Hebrew uses the impersonal *they* and reads *they would absolutely scorn* (AT), followed by a masculine singular pronoun that could be translated either *him* (the one who offers his wealth) or *it* (the wealth itself).

If the pronoun refers to the man, the statement would mean something like this: *Anyone who tries to buy love would be scorned*. If the pronoun refers to the wealth, it instead would mean, *If anyone tried to buy love, his money would be scorned* (i.e., *rejected*). Perhaps both meanings apply, in which case we understand that both the person who tries to buy love and the proffered money are scorned. In other words, *You can't buy love*.

A Poem on Love's Elusive Nature 8:8-14

The closing verses of the book present several challenges. First, the identity of the speakers is unclear in verses 8-9 and 11-12. Second, the units appear to be abruptly juxtaposed, lacking connections. Third, after the profound statement about love in 8:6-7, the book seems to shift to inconsequential chatter. Finally, as numerous readers have observed, the book appears not to have an ending—at least, it does not end as we think it should.

The NIV 1984 gives the speech in verses 8-9 to the "friends." Because "brothers" have appeared earlier in the book (1:6), some commentators suggest that the brothers speak in verses 8-9 about the woman, their little sister. Exum (255) offers an alternate view by proposing that the woman speaks in verses 8-10 about a "fictive" younger sister. This fictive sister allows the woman to make the claim that, unlike this little sister, she herself is mature and ready for a relationship with a man.

Whoever speaks in 8:8 makes the claim that the young sister's breasts are not yet developed. The Hebrew states this more dramatically: *She has no breasts!* (so NRSV). That is, this young sister is immature and not ready for a sexual relationship. Given this condition, the speaker wonders what should be done and answers that question in verse 9, using imagery of *wall* and *door*. Some interpreters take the "wall" and "door" to symbolize protection. The NIV 1984 seems to lean in this direction with its choice of the verb *enclose*: *If she is a wall, we will build towers of silver on her. If she is a door, we will enclose her with panels of cedar.* The mention of *silver* and *cedar*, however, caution us to think more of decoration than enclosure. Rather than seeking to protect the little sister, the speaker intends to decorate her in such a way that she will appear mature on that day in the future when she is to become engaged. If we follow this line of thinking, the verse can be translated as follows:

If she is a wall,
  we will build silver battlements upon her.
If she is a door,
  we will fashion upon her a cedar carving.

Following this line of interpretation, the silver battlements and cedar carving may serve to give more shape to the girl's flat chest. In either case, the point of the verse is to describe the sexual immaturity of this "young sister."

If either the friends or the woman's brothers speak in verses 8-9, then the woman in verse 10 challenges them with a statement about herself and her sexual maturity. If we assume that the woman's speech begins in verse 8, then it appears that she contrasts herself with the young sister.

There is no verb in the Hebrew text of verse 10a, although most translations supply a verb. The Hebrew has a noun sentence: *I, a wall, and* (or, *but*) *my breasts, towers.* So the question is, What tense do we supply in this statement? The NIV 1984 supplies present tense in both statements: *I am a wall, and my breasts are like towers.* Does she describe a change in her condition from past (a wall) to present (towers)? If so, she seems to say, *I was sexually immature, but now I am mature*. This appears to make the most sense, especially when we consider that the next sentence begins with a word that suggests a logical consequence. The NIV 1984 captures this with the word *thus*: *Thus I have become in his eyes like one bringing contentment*. The verb translated *bringing* could also mean "finding." With its translation *bringing*, the NIV 1984 assumes that the verb is a causative form of "to come out." But as we have seen, the verb "find" is thematically significant in this book. When read within the larger context of the book, the verb may well communicate both meanings: both *bringing* (to my lover) and *finding* (for myself) contentment.

The word translated in the NIV 1984 as *contentment* is the Hebrew word *shalom* (*šalom*), which has a broad range of meanings yet is often translated simply *peace* (NIV, NRSV). NIV 1984's *contentment* may suggest sexual fulfillment—the woman has become one who brings her beloved sexual fulfillment. It could also suggest completeness or by extension maturity. If taken with the verb *find*, the woman then suggests that she has become like *one who finds sexual maturity*. The word *shalom* (*šalom*) likely has several meanings operating in this verse: sexual maturity, completeness, contentment, sexual fulfillment. It also poetically links to the next section, which begins with the word "Solomon." Thus she is no longer a young, immature girl, but rather, in the eyes of her lover, she has become physically and sexually mature, like one who has found sexual maturity and fulfillment in her relationship with her lover.

The NIV gives verses 11-12 to the woman. Longman (219) and Hess (246–47) agree. Bergant (102), however, identifies these verses as "a boasting song sung by the man." Both Huwiler (289) and Davis (2000a: 301) explain that the identity of the speaker is unclear. Huwiler leans toward the woman as the speaker, but Davis gives a slight edge to the man. If, as Bergant proposes, this is a boasting song uttered by the man, then he boasts of his exclusive rights to the woman, who is "his vineyard." If the woman is the speaker, then she asserts her right to her own body. In either case, the contrast is between the couple's exclusive relationship and the polygamous behavior of King Solomon, who, according to 1 Kings 11:3, had seven hundred wives and three hundred concubines [*King Fiction, p. 278*].

The book ends on an odd note. There is no narrative ending, no explicit "happily ever after." Instead, the book concludes with the woman's address to her lover (v. 14), again in the form of the "erotic imperative" [*Erotic Imperative, p. 266*]. The NIV translation

Come away, my beloved suggests that she invites her lover to run away *with* her, but the Hebrew verb is an imperative form of a word usually translated "flee," which suggests running *from* someone or something. There is no direction given, however. Should he run away *with* her, flee *from* her, or flee *to* her? Some versions make a decision on this question, suggesting that he flee to her: *Come to me, my lover* (GNB) and *Run to me, dear lover* (The Message). Others omit the directional indicator but suggest that there is some urgency for him to act: *Make haste, my beloved* (KJV, ASV, NRSV). The Hebrew verb (*baraḥ*) may have the sense of running from unpleasant situations, but it can also indicate flight to someone, as in 1 Samuel 22:20, "But Abiathar, a son of Ahimelech son of Ahitub, escaped and fled to join David."

A second verb (*damah*) occurs in the verse. The verb occurs elsewhere in Song of Songs in comparisons with the definition "to be like." Here we might understand the two verbs together to mean "flee *like* a gazelle." This would imply both speed (as in *make haste*), but also the ability to leap and bound over obstacles in the way. Additionally, she says that he is to run *on the spice-laden mountains.* "Mountains" may suggest there are still obstacles to overcome, but the reference to spices alludes to the woman's body and the physical pleasures to be enjoyed by the lovers. Thus she may be inviting her lover to speed over obstacles in order to enjoy her own "spice-laden mountains."

What might it mean that the book ends on an inconclusive note? Perhaps it signifies that love cannot be quantified, packaged, and delivered up neatly. The poems in the book have suggested that the lovers experience both the joy of being together and the misery of separation. Although they experience powerful emotions, they are not always certain what to do about those emotions. The book ends, as it began, in the middle of a relationship that is characterized by desire, admiration, appreciation, and a longing for fulfillment.

THE TEXT IN BIBLICAL CONTEXT

Divine Passion

When we think about love that is as fierce and unyielding as death, we remember several biblical passages that speak of God's love for humankind in this way.

Divine passion bursts forth as a theological motif in the book of Hosea. The Israelites turn from an exclusive relationship with their God to worship other gods. Although the Israelites' unfaithfulness could result in their being abandoned by God, that does not happen because God's love for them surpasses even justice. Hosea pursues this theme relentlessly, exploring the depths of God's pain and anger with regard to the Israelites' disloyalty. At one point, Hosea reports that God has come to hate the Israelites:

> Because of all their wickedness in Gilgal,
> I hated them there.
> Because of their sinful deeds,
> I will drive them out of my house.
> I will no longer love them;
>   all their leaders are rebellious. (9:15)

Divine hatred and wrath do not triumph over divine love for the Israelites, however, for Hosea reports that God has a change of heart:

> How can I give you up, Ephraim?
>   How can I hand you over, Israel?
> How can I treat you like Admah?
>   How can I make you like Zeboyim?
> My heart is changed within me;
>   all my compassion is aroused.
> I will not carry out my fierce anger,
>   nor will I devastate Ephraim again.
> For I am God, and not a man—
>   the Holy One among you.
>   I will not come against their cities. (11:8-9)

In the final chapter of the book, using figurative language drawn from the natural world, Hosea reports a speech of God, in which the Deity speaks directly about the overwhelming power of divine love:

> I will heal their waywardness
>   and love them freely,
>   for my anger has turned away from them.
> I will be like the dew to Israel;
>   he will blossom like a lily.
> Like a cedar of Lebanon
>   he will send down his roots;
>   his young shoots will grow.
> His splendor will be like an olive tree,
>   his fragrance like a cedar of Lebanon.
> People will dwell again in his shade;
>   they will flourish like the grain,
>   they will blossom like the vine—
>   Israel's fame will be like the wine of Lebanon. (14:4-7)

In his letter to the Romans, the apostle Paul addresses the question of human suffering and God's providential love. In the face of suffering, persecution, and death, Paul asserts that God stands with humankind:

> For I am convinced that neither death nor life, neither angels nor demons, neither the present nor the future, nor any powers, neither height nor depth, nor anything else in all creation, will be able to separate us from the love of God that is in Christ Jesus our Lord. (8:38-39)

In his commentary on Romans, John Toews discusses Paul's answer to the question "Who shall separate us from the love of Christ? Shall trouble or hardship or persecution or famine or nakedness or danger or sword?" (Rom 8:35).

Paul summarizes his argument with the confident assertion that God is for us. The election and love of God, two sides of the same coin in Jewish thought, are linked in a ringing affirmation of God's commitment. To be children of God means preservation and victory despite the struggles and suffering of living in history. (Toews: 230)

THE TEXT IN THE LIFE OF THE CHURCH

The Overwhelming Power of God's Love

Although North American Christians may be unaware of religious persecution, Christians in other countries around the world experience intimidation, harassment, and sometimes death. Persecution is part of the Anabaptist heritage. Early Anabaptists, many of whom faced persecution and death, expressed their confidence in the power of divine love. In his 1541 essay *True Christian Faith*, Menno Simons uses analogies from daily life in his discussion of divine love, moving from the experiences of human love for children and marriage partners to the nature of human love directed to God:

> That love is of such an effective power and nature may be seen in natural love. We do not have to admonish reasonable parents to provide their children with necessary food and clothing, for natural love will admonish them to these things. Similarly, a husband and wife who sincerely love each other count it no hardship willingly to serve each other and do things together as is proper, they being one flesh. So is also the nature and property of holy, divine love. For all those who by faith are one with the Father and with His Son Christ Jesus in love and spirit, through the true and genuine knowledge of the aforementioned favor, these do not have to be admonished to serve the Lord, to seek the kingdom of God. (*CWMS* 338)

In the same essay, Menno quotes and elaborates upon Song of Songs 8:6b-7a:

> Love, says Solomon, is as strong as death; jealousy is as cruel as the grave. The coals thereof are coals of fire, which have a most vehement flame; many waters cannot quench love. Yes, so firm and strong and ardent is love that it surpasses everything, conquers and consumes what is opposed to Christ and His Word, be it world or flesh, tyrant or devil, sin or death, or whatever we may think of or name; and this is all through the power and Spirit of Jesus Christ from whom it originates. (*CWMS* 339)

For Menno, love motivates Christians to serve God, and love has the power to defeat everything that opposes God and Christ.

In a 1567 letter, Dirk Philips connects Song 8:6-7 to the teaching about love found in the New Testament:

> And this is now the principal teaching and the highest command of our Lord Jesus Christ, that we shall have love one for another just as he has loved us. And this love is not only in words, but lies in power and truth, and must be shown in deeds, 1 John 3:18. For since God is love, as John says, 1 John 4:[7-8], so it is powerful and, according to Solomon's word, stronger than death and firmer than hell, for love is fiery and a flame of the Lord, that waters also cannot extinguish love, nor streams drown it, Song of Sol. 8:6[-7]. And if someone wanted to give all his goods for love, he cannot buy it with them, for it is a gift of the Lord and a special power of God, 1 Cor. 1. (*WDP* 479-80)

In his seventh letter from prison, Thomas von Imbroich, a sixteenth-century Anabaptist martyr, alludes indirectly to Song 8:6-7, writing to his fellow believers that "Christ is a Lord of love" and God is "love itself."

> These words, my dear fellow believers, indicate that Christ is a Lord of love, actually, that God is love itself, which flows from him like a fountain into the hearts of believers, and makes them ardent in doing all that is pleasing and agreeable to the Most Beloved. It is also Christ's will that the fire should burn, since he came to ignite it. He has also promised that he would have the wind blow to increase the fire—namely, his Holy Spirit, which will guide us into all truth (1 John 2, 3, 4; 1 Tim 1; Song of Sol. 8; Luke 12; John 14; Col 3). (*GASB* 135)

The hope of resurrection and life eternal rests in the human capacity to do two things: to love fully and completely and to imagine God's limitless love for creation. Regarding God's limitless love for creation, the hymn writer Charles Wesley expresses the sense of gratitude that Christians feel in response to the love of God. Wesley (1707-88) was a prolific writer, with over six thousand hymns to his name. In the following two stanzas from his hymn "O Love Divine, How Sweet Thou Art," Wesley proclaims that Christ's love for humankind is "stronger than death or hell":

> O love divine, how sweet thou art!
> When shall I find my willing heart
> All taken up by thee?
> I thirst, I faint, I die to prove
> The greatness of redeeming love,
> The love of Christ to me.
>
> Stronger His love than death or hell;
> Its reaches are unsearchable:
> The first-born sons of light
> Desire in vain its depths to see;
> They cannot reach the mystery,
> The length, the breadth, the height. (*HMEC* no. 540)

Outline of Song of Songs

Title: The Most Beautiful of Songs	1:1
In Celebration of Love	**1:2-8**
Her Expression of Desire for Her Lover's Kiss	1:2-4
Her Self-Description	1:5-6
A Dialogue about Her Lover's Whereabouts	1:7-8
Poems of Admiration and Desire	**1:9–2:7**
A Poem of the Lovers' Mutual Admiration	1:9-17
He Admires His Lover	1:9-11
She Admires Her Lover	1:12-14
Expressions of Mutual Admiration	1:15-17
A Poem of Comparisons and of Her Desire for Him	2:1-7
Refrain: Her Charge to the Daughters of Jerusalem	2:7
An Invitation to Love	**2:8-17**
Her Description of His Sudden Appearance	2:8-9
His Expression of Desire for Her	2:10-13
An Invitation and Response	2:14-17
Refrain: Her Expression of Mutual Belonging	2:16
Seeking and Finding the Beloved	**3:1-11**
Seeking and Finding the Beloved	3:1-5
Refrain: Her Charge to the Daughters of Jerusalem	3:5
A Royal Procession	3:6-11

Outline of Song of Songs

A First Description of Her Beauty	**4:1–5:1**
His Description of Her Beauty (First *Descriptive Inventory*)	4:1-7
An Invitation	4:8
His Description of Her Effect on Him	4:9-15
An Invitation and Response	4:16–5:1a
An Exhortation to the Lovers	5:1b
Seeking the Beloved (Again)	**5:2–6:3**
A Description of Her Experience Seeking Her Lover	5:2-9
Her Description of His Beauty (Second *Descriptive Inventory*)	5:10-16
Dialogue between the Woman and the Daughters of Jerusalem	6:1-3
Refrain: Her Second Expression of Their Mutual Belonging	6:3
Overwhelmed by Love	**6:4–7:13**
His Description of Her Beauty (Third *Descriptive Inventory*)	6:4-10
A Description of an Experience	6:11-12
An Invitation to the Shulammite to Return	6:13
His Description of Her Beauty (Fourth *Descriptive Inventory*)	7:1-9a
A Poem Expressing Her Desire for Him	7:9b-13
Refrain: Her Third Expression of Their Mutual Belonging	7:10
Love Is Strong as Death	**8:1-14**
A Poem of Desire	8:1-4
Refrain: Her Charge to the Daughters of Jerusalem	8:4
A Poem in Praise of Love	8:5-7
A Poem on Love's Elusive Nature	8:8-14

Essays for Song of Songs

ALLEGORICAL AND FIGURAL INTERPRETATION
Allegorical Interpretation Scholars commonly use the term "allegorical interpretation" to refer to interpretations of the Song of Songs that identify the two main speakers as someone other than two human lovers. The unnamed woman has been identified as (1) Israel, God's chosen people; (2) the church; (3) Mary, the mother of Jesus; and (4) the individual human soul, or person, who trusts in God. The unnamed man has been identified as God or Jesus.

In the early church allegorical interpretation sought to identify the deeper meaning of a biblical text. With the rise of historical criticism in the nineteenth and twentieth centuries, allegorical interpretation fell out of favor. Contemporary biblical exegesis often emphasizes the meaning behind the text, that is, the event or experience represented by the biblical text. Some historically oriented exegetes have sought to determine, as nearly as possible, the original author's intent, although extreme forms of this approach have largely been abandoned by biblical scholars in the twenty-first century. By contrast, allegorical interpretation of the Bible does not locate meaning behind the text or even necessarily in the author's supposed intention, although that could be considered. Rather, it searches for a deeper meaning within a text.

Jewish allegorical interpretation views the human couple of the Song of Songs as representing God and Israel, or God and the faithful believer. Christian allegorical interpretation has traditionally viewed the couple in terms of the relationship between Christ and the church, or between Christ and the soul (i.e., the individual, believing Christian). Jewish allegorical interpretation goes back at least to Rabbi Akiba (first century CE). The Christian allegorical approach can be traced back to the third century and the commentary of Origen. In the twentieth century, with the influence of the historical-critical approach to the Bible, scholarship shifted, instead asserting that the book contains poems expressing the mutual love and desire of a man and a woman. Interpreters who prefer the historical-critical approach to the Bible sometimes denigrate allegorical readings of Song of Songs; others, however, others are willing to consider both allegorical and literal readings of Song of Songs as appropriate [History of Interpretation, p. 270].

Figural Interpretation In his recent commentary on the Song of Songs, Paul J. Griffiths helpfully distinguishes between allegorical and figural interpretation. Griffiths explains that, unlike allegorical reading, figural reading does not erase the literal level of a text: "One event or utterance figures another when, *while remaining unalterably what it is*, it announces or communicates something other than itself" (xvii; emph. added). In figural reading, the two lovers of the Song may be understood as figures that point to God and Israel, or Christ and the church, but at the same time they remain two human lovers. By contrast, allegorical readings dissolve the text into that which it allegorizes. An allegorical reading of the Song replaces the two human lovers of the Song with other figures, God and Israel, Christ and the church, Christ and the soul. According to Griffiths (xvii), "Following allegorical method strictly means that an allegorical text's literal sense must be ignored except in so far as it permits understanding of what it allegorizes." In practice, the two types of interpretation may be difficult to untangle, but the significance of the contrast deserves our attention, because, as Griffiths explains, allegorical interpretations sever the connection with the Song's literal level of meaning:

> Four principal candidates have emerged among Jews and Christians as answers to the question of who are the Song's human beloved figures. Sometimes, even often, these answers have been given in a flat-footed allegorical way, as if, once the beloved figured by the Song has been identified, the human beloved of the Song—the woman who figures but is not herself figured, this human woman panting for her lover, opening her door and her body to him, praising the beauties of his body, recalling the delights of his kisses, lamenting his absence, imagining his presence—can be left aside, having performed her figuring function and then having nothing left to do. This way of reading dissolves the figuring into the figured and leads all too easily into a dissolution of the text's surface, and even of its very words, into some deeper or higher meaning. On this allegorical view, the human beloved and the eroticism of the text vanishes, is neutered and absorbed. Better, certainly more Christian, is to read in such a way as to preserve both the text's figures and what they figure. (xxxviii–xxxix)

Griffiths' description of the way in which allegorical readings of the Song of Songs erase the text's erotic elements at the level of human sexuality contains an essential insight. In this commentary, I propose that *figural* readings of the Song of Songs offer new levels of understanding. I do not advocate allegorical readings that erase, dissolve, or ignore the literal meaning of the poems as expressions of human love and desire [*Figures of Speech*, p. 267; *History of Interpretation*, p. 270].

AROMATICS People in the ancient Near East used aromatic plants and plant substances in several different ways. Some aromatics could be added to food as spices. Others might be burned as incense or added to oil to create a perfume. Perfumed oils were used in the anointing of kings and priests (Zohary: 183). They were also used then as we use perfume today, to enhance an individual's attractiveness. Some aromatics could be found locally in ancient Israel, but many had to be imported from the East (India or Arabia), which made them expensive and available only to wealthier individuals.

The term **aloes** (Heb. *ʾahalot*) in Song 4:14 refers to the eaglewood tree (*Aquilaria agallocha*), which was imported from the east. The tree's resin, produced by a fungus, has a pleasant odor, which is even sweeter when burned as incense. In the Bible it is often associated with other imported luxury aromatic plant substances, such as myrrh and cinnamon (see Ps 45:8; Prov 7:17).

NIV translates **balsam** (Heb. *bośem*) with the generic term "spice" (4:10, 14, 16; 5:1, 13; 6:2; 8:14).

Calamus (4:14, Heb. *qaneh*) may refer to *Acorus calamus*, an aromatic grass or reed that was imported from the East. When dried, the plant's rhizome has a sweet odor.

Cinnamon (Heb. *qinnamon*) comes from the bark of *Cinnamomum verum*, a small evergreen tree native to Sri Lanka and the coast of India. In ancient times, it was imported from the east for use in cooking, incense, and perfume. Cinnamon is mentioned four times in the Bible (Exod 30:23; Prov 7:17; Song 4:14; Rev 18:13).

Frankincense (Heb. *lebonah*), an aromatic resin, was a key ingredient in incense. The NIV translates the three occurrences of this term in Song of Songs simply as *incense*, but the term refers to a specific aromatic used as incense, made from the secretions of a shrub of the genus *Boswellia* (Zohary: 197). In Song of Songs, it is frequently paired with myrrh: *perfumed with myrrh and frankincense* (3:6 AT); *the mountain of myrrh* and *the hill of frankincense* (4:6 AT); and *incense tree and myrrh* (4:14 AT).

Henna (Heb. *koper*) occurs in the Bible only in the Song of Songs (1:14; 4:13). In the ancient Near East, henna was used as a perfume and as a dye. When in bloom, henna's white flowers emit a wonderful fragrance, and a sweet-smelling oil can be distilled from the flowers. The flowers grow on a treelike shrub.

Myrrh (Heb. *mor*) is a resin from a shrub or tree, possibly *Commiphora abyssinica* (Zohary: 200) or *Commiphora myrrha* (*NIDB*, s.v. "Myrrh"). In ancient times, myrrh was an important ingredient in ointments, perfumes, medicines, and incense (Song 1:13; 3:6; 4:6, 14; 5:1, 5, 13). Matthew's gospel (2:11) records that the Magi brought gifts of gold, frankincense, and myrrh, which indicates the value of the paired aromatics.

Nard (Heb. *nerd*) occurs three times in the Song of Songs (1:12; 4:13, 14). Also known as spikenard, this small aromatic plant grows in the

Himalayas. In biblical times, it was imported to Israel. Nard (Gk. *nardos*) also occurs twice in the NT, in narratives about the anointing of Jesus' head (Mark 14:3) and feet (John 12:3). Because it was imported, it was a luxury item, as the gospel narratives indicate.

Saffron (Heb. *karkom*) appears only one time in the Bible (Song 4:14), in a context in which it is associated with two other spices imported from the east: nard (spikenard) and cinnamon. It is not clear if the Hebrew *karkom* refers to true saffron, *Crocus sativus*, or to turmeric, *Curcuma longa*, both of which would have been imported to Israel in biblical times (Zohary: 206).

AUTHORSHIP AND DATE Before about the nineteenth century, most Jewish and Christian readers assumed that King Solomon had authored the Song of Songs. A tradition in a Jewish work called *Midrash Rabbah* (I: 10) connects Solomon's authorship of three biblical books to specific periods in his life. Rabbi Jonathan connects King Solomon to the books of Song of Songs, Proverbs, and Ecclesiastes by explaining the following: "When a man is young he composes songs; when he grows older he makes sententious remarks; and when he becomes an old man he speaks of the vanity of things" (Freedman: 17).

Internal evidence to support Solomon's authorship of the book begins with the book's superscription *Solomon's Song of Songs* (1:1). This is, perhaps, the most significant piece of evidence. Additional support derives from the book's frequent references to wealth and luxury, which seem to fit the context of the Solomon's royal court. In 1 Kings 4:32-33 we read that Solomon composed songs: "He spoke three thousand proverbs and his songs numbered a thousand and five. He spoke about plant life, from the cedar of Lebanon to the hyssop that grows out of walls. He also spoke about animals and birds, reptiles and fish." The passage's report of Solomon's interest in and knowledge of flora and fauna also correlates with the book's abundant use of imagery from the natural world. The mention of Tirzah (6:4), a city prominent in the Solomonic era, suggests a tenth-century date. Tirzah became the capital of the northern kingdom under Jeroboam I (1 Kings 14:17), but after Omri moved the capital to Samaria, Tirzah declined in importance. It was destroyed during the Babylonian invasion and lay in ruins during the postexilic period. Finally, some scholars argue that the similarities between the love poems of Song of Songs and ancient Egyptian love poetry point to a date of composition in the early first millennium BCE.

Several times the book refers to Solomon, in addition to the superscription (1:5; 3:7, 9, 11; 8:11, 12), and it also contains references to an unnamed *king* (1:4, 12; 7:5). At first glance, these references combined with the superscription may appear to support the Solomonic authorship of the book. This evidence, however, can work against Solomonic authorship since the majority of references to Solomon are in the third person. As Longman (6) observes, in the passages where Solomon is mentioned, he never speaks as subject, but rather he is the object of discussion.

Although the superscription of the book seems to provide strong evidence for Solomonic authorship, the majority of recent commentators do not accept that Solomon wrote this book. To explain their position, scholars begin by discussing the book's internal evidence. They then explain how the superscription can be understood as indicating something other than authorship.

The Hebrew of the Song of Songs exhibits characteristics of postexilic Hebrew. Linguistic evidence may suggest a date in the sixth or fifth century BCE for certain poems or for the final form of the book, thereby ruling out (tenth-century) Solomonic authorship. Linguistic evidence includes the occurrence of Persian terms (*pardes*, translated *orchard* in 4:13), Greek loanwords (*'appiryon*, translated *carriage* in 3:9), and possible Aramaisms (the influence of Aramaic). Such words and influence would almost certainly not have characterized the time of Solomon (Dobbs-Allsopp 2005b). The superscription *Solomon's Song of Songs* can indicate an association of the book with Solomon, rather than authorship by Solomon. In the Hebrew text, the preposition *le* prefixed to a name *can* indicate authorship, but it has other possible meanings. In 1:1 it can be understood as a dedication to Solomon, as in *The Song of Songs for Solomon*. It can also be taken to mean that the book is "Solomonic," that is, the book is written "in the tradition of Solomon" (Longman: 3). Third, Solomon is never identified in the Hebrew text as one of the speakers and, with one exception, is referred to in the third person. References to a "king" in the poems may reflect the poet's employment of what is sometimes called a "king fiction" [*King Fiction, p. 278*].

Roland Murphy (121–22) and Brevard Childs (573–76) propose that the ascription of the book to Solomon promotes the wisdom character of its contents. Childs, especially, emphasizes that the title of the book, rather than informing the reader of the author's identity, instructs the reader on how to read the book's contents. Because Solomon was associated with the wisdom tradition in ancient Israel, the association of the Song of Songs with Solomon characterizes the book's poetry as sapiential (wisdom oriented) and not simply secular. This does not diminish the appreciation of human love in the book, but rather it demands that the reader recognize the correct context in which to locate this most important human experience.

DAUGHTERS OF JERUSALEM A group of women identified as the *daughters of Jerusalem* are addressed seven times in the Song of Songs. In 3:11, they are addressed by the parallel term "daughters of Zion." In all cases (except perhaps 3:10) it is the woman who addresses this group. By giving the female speaker a group of women to address in private, the poet creates an opportunity for the female lover of the poems to express her innermost feelings. In literary terms, the daughters of Jerusalem as a group serve as a foil (Bergant: 12). Addressing this group of women, the female lover expresses concern about her appearance (1:5). On four occasions (2:7; 3:5; 5:8; 8:4), she addresses the daughters of Jerusalem with a charge, or adjuration, in which she comments upon the power of love and the inability of humans to resist love. In the poem describing a royal procession (3:6-11), the *daughters of Jerusalem* and their poetic parallel, the *daughters of Zion*, are told to come out and observe King Solomon. (The NIV 2011 and the NRSV understand the text this way. Other versions, including KJV and NIV 1984, separate the two phrases into two verses that are not in parallel construction with each other.)

DESCRIPTIVE INVENTORIES (*waṣfs*) The Arabic term *waṣf*, which means "description," has been used as a term of reference for the four poems in the Song of Songs in which one of the lovers describes the physical attributes of the other lover, moving either down the body from the head (4:1-7; 5:10-16; 6:4-10) or up the body from the feet (7:1-9a). In three of the poems (4:1-7; 6:4-10; 7:1-9a), the man describes the woman's appearance. In the fourth (5:10-16), the woman describes the man's appearance.

The term *waṣf* was first used of these four poems in a late nineteenth-century commentary by Franz Delitzsch, who learned of a Syrian wedding practice from J. G. Wetzstein, a German diplomat living in Syria. Wetzstein had written to Delitzsch about a Syrian custom in which songs describing the beauty and perfection of both bride and groom were sung at weddings. Delitzsch (172–74) then applied the term *waṣf* to the four descriptive poems in the Song of Songs.

According to Richard Soulen (190), the purpose of the four *waṣfs* is to invite the reader's secondhand participation in the joyful experience of the lovers. Othmar Keel (139) argues that these poems describe the person's character, not their physical appearance, citing in support "the ancient Near Eastern custom of portraying the essential strength and significance of a deity or person (living or dead) by identifying his or her bodily features with the various powers and splendors of the surrounding world."

DRAMATIC INTERPRETATIONS Dramatic interpretations of the Song of Songs build upon the dialogic character of the poems and try to identify a plot underlying the poems in the book *[King Fiction, p. 278]*. Dramatic interpretations of the Song of Songs find few scholarly supporters today.

As early as the third century, the Greek theologian Origen identified four main dramatic parts: bride, bridegroom, the maidens, and the bridegroom's friends (Commentary 1:1; Torjesen: 55). Marginal notes in fourth- and fifth-century Greek manuscripts of the Bible (Codex Sinaiticus and Codex Alexandrinus) assign parts to different speakers. Dramatic interpretations became popular in the nineteenth and early twentieth centuries. Franz Delitzsch, a German Lutheran theologian and scholar (1813–90), interpreted the book as a "dramatic pastoral" (although not a theatrical drama), with two main characters, King Solomon and a country maid. Delitzsch divided the book into six acts, each having two scenes. According to Delitzsch, the plot follows the relationship of Solomon and the Shulammite (6:13) from their initial mutual attraction to their marriage and covenant of love. For Delitzsch (8), the book holds a moral message: King Solomon grew to love the young woman so much that he abandoned polygamy and came to understand and experience true, monogamous love (3). Other interpreters also identify two main characters, but identify the female voice differently; for example, Goulder identifies the woman as an Arabian princess (11–14, 75–78).

Some interpreters propose that the drama has three characters: Solomon, the young woman, and a young shepherd boy. In the three-character dramas, Solomon attempts (unsuccessfully) to steal the young woman from her boyfriend. Iain Provan (246) suggests that the young woman is a member of Solomon's harem whose true love is a young man outside the royal court. He argues that the book has a dramatic form, although he acknowledges that we have no evidence that the drama was actually performed by actors.

Dramatic interpretations of Song of Songs build upon the character of the poems as speeches uttered by two main speakers, a man and a woman. There is a dramatic character to the poems; however, dramatic interpretations are hindered by the lack of a clear plotline and the ambiguity regarding the identification of the speakers. As a result, dramatic interpretations of Song of Songs differ with regard to the number and identity of the main speakers and the basic plot of the book. (For further discussion and analysis of dramatic interpretations, see Garrett: 76–81.)

EMBODIMENT The term "embodiment" expresses an understanding that human experience is embodied experience. Despite its distinctiveness within the Bible, the Song of Songs shares a view of human nature with the rest of the Bible, both OT and NT, which embraces and celebrates bodily human existence. God created humans as physical beings with desires, needs, and emotions. Humans are created as sexual beings, with the capacity for procreation (Gen 1:28). The description of Eden implies that God provides for human physical needs and sets humans within a world of beauty (Gen 2:9). Because humans have the need for companionship, God creates two beings who can be present for each other (Gen 2:18-24).

In the NT, Jesus addresses bodily needs as well as what we may try to separate out as spiritual needs. Jesus heals people with physical and mental infirmities (e.g., Mark 7:24-37) and feeds the hungry (Mark 6:30-44 and parallels). In fact, it is hard to distinguish between bodily and spiritual needs. Jesus blesses those who hunger now (Luke 6:21) as well as those who hunger and thirst for righteousness (Matt 5:6). He responds to both "evil spirits" and "infirmities" (Luke 8:2). In Luke 4:18-19, when Jesus reads from the Isaiah scroll, it is impossible to separate the physical from the spiritual, so closely are the two intertwined:

> The Spirit of the Lord is on me,
>   because he has anointed me
>   to proclaim good news to the poor.
> He has sent me to proclaim freedom for the prisoners
>   and recovery of sight for the blind,
> to set the oppressed free,
>   to proclaim the year of the Lord's favor.

Biblical writers avoid the language of hierarchical dualism when talking about human existence as persons. That is, they do not describe persons as composed of mortal bodies that are inferior to their immortal souls. It is harder to explain precisely how biblical writers *do* view human existence because they use many different terms when referring to the human as person, without explaining how those terms relate to each other. For example, OT writers can talk about the spirit (*ruaḥ*) as a force that animates humans and empowers them to act. They can also refer to the heart (*leb* or *lebab*) as the locus of both human compassion and human thinking. In some places, the OT writers seem to use "heart" as an equivalent to what we today mean by "mind" or to what NT writers meant by the Greek word *nous*. In the OT, in fact, there is no Hebrew equivalent for "mind." In Song 1:7, the word *nepeš*, although often translated "soul," can refer to a person's "throat" or "desire" and can be used to refer to a person, as in *you whom I love* (lit. "whom my *nepeš* loves"). Its meaning needs to be determined from context; when translated as *soul*, it refers to the vital self, not to an immaterial essence that is the "real you" as opposed to the "body" in a dualistic sense. Similarly, in the NT, writers use language of body (Greek *sōma*), soul (Greek *psychē*), and spirit (Greek *pneuma*) without explaining precisely what they mean by those terms or how those aspects of human identity interrelate.

If this is true, how do biblical writers understand death? What happens to the human body at death? If there is life after death, what form does that afterlife take? The OT has little to say on the subject of life after death, but there are several NT texts that help us understand that life after death is envisioned as a bodily existence. In the Gospels, Jesus' post-resurrection appearances clearly portray him as having a bodily form. After Jesus appears to disciples on the road to Emmaus, he shows himself to a larger group in Jerusalem, where he explains, "Look at my hands and my feet. It is I myself! Touch me and see; a ghost does not have flesh and bones, as you see I have" (Luke 24:39). Jesus then proceeds to eat a piece of broiled fish, as if to demonstrate that he is a resurrected *body*.

The most detailed discussion of what believers can anticipate regarding the resurrection life can be found in 1 Corinthians 15, where Paul distinguishes between two types of bodily existence. In this age, each person is a natural body (*sōma psychikos*), but with the resurrection, the natural body that is sown will be raised as a spiritual body (*sōma pneumatikos*, 1 Cor 15:44). Paul talks about both our present human existence and our future resurrection existence in terms of a body. For Paul, we are not immortal souls imprisoned in mortal bodies. Rather, we are bodies that await transformation by God. As NT scholar James D. G. Dunn (61) explains, "Redemption for Paul was not some kind of escape from bodily existence, but a transformation into a different kind of bodily existence."

What does this mean for our study of Song of Songs? It suggests that we resist the temptation to set aside the book's celebration of the human body and of human sexuality in favor of a less earthy, less physical reading. God created humans as physical beings, with sexual needs and desires, and God saw that it was good.

Despite the Bible's understanding that human beings are embodied persons, Christian tradition has not always clearly supported this idea. In conversation with Hellenistic philosophy, early Christian theologians developed an understanding of the human person that subordinated the body to the soul (often referred to as "hierarchical dualism"). In this form of dualism, the body may even be thought to imprison the soul, so that salvation is understood as a release of the soul from the body, its prison.

Contemporary Christian theology, ethics, and spirituality have largely rejected hierarchical dualism in favor of an understanding that is more compatible with the Bible's view of the human person. Although there is no agreement among Christian theologians and philosophers with regard to human nature, there has been a shift toward appreciating the importance of the body and a recognition that historical Christianity has too quickly dismissed the body. In his description of the biblical understanding of the human, John W. Cooper (70–72) accepts the term dualism but rejects the hierarchy that subordinates body to soul or spirit. Cooper proposes that the biblical understanding is best termed "holistic dualism," a view that the human person is a soul comprising both an embodied spirit and a spirited body. Christian philosopher Nancey Murphy rejects the language of dualism altogether in her attempt to articulate a contemporary theological understanding and replaces it with a view she calls "nonreductive physicalism," which holds that we are our bodies. In Murphy's view, the capacities formerly attributed to a nonmaterial "soul"—capacities for morality, rationality, and spirituality—can rightly be understood as capacities of the human as physical being.

EROTIC IMPERATIVE In her commentary on the Song of Songs, Cheryl Exum (250) uses the phrase "erotic imperative" to refer to the poet's frequent use of grammatical imperatives, jussives, and cohortatives to create both a sense of urgency and the illusion of immediacy. According to Exum (123), the use of the erotic imperative "gives the impression of the lovers' presence at the moment of utterance."

Imperative forms usually communicate commands directed to someone, as in the following: *take me away* (Song 1:4); *tell me* (1:7); *strengthen me* (2:5); *arise* (2:10); *show me* (2:14); *turn* (2:17); *come with me* (4:8); *open to me* (5:2); *place me* (8:6); and *come away* (8:14). Jussive forms express the desire that something will occur with reference to a third-person subject: *let him kiss me* (1:2). Cohortatives express in the first person (singular or plural) the desire or intention that something happen: *let us hurry* (1:4); *I will get up, I will go about,* and *I will seek* (3:2 NRSV); and *let us spend the night* (7:11). Exum (5) describes the way in which the erotic imperative functions in the Song of Songs:

> The erotic imperative—the call to love by means of grammatical imperatives, jussives, and cohortatives—lends urgency to the moment. ... The Song begins with the erotic imperative ("let him kiss me," 1:2) and ends with it ("take flight ... be like a gazelle or a young deer," 8:14). Not least, the climactic affirmation of love in 8:6-7 is grounded

in the erotic imperative: "place me like a seal on your heart, for love is strong as death."

FIGURES OF SPEECH

Metaphor A metaphor is a figure of speech in which a word or phrase that ordinarily designates one thing is used to refer to another, thus making an implicit comparison. This implicit comparison of two seemingly unlike objects seeks to express the unfamiliar in terms of the familiar or to make present a reality, sensation, or experience. In the Song of Songs, when the man says of his beloved, *Your eyes are doves* (1:15; 4:1), he describes her "eyes" as being in some way like "doves." That leads us to ask, In what way are the woman's eyes doves? Thus we need a ground against which to understand the comparison. Is the comparison in respect to appearance? Do the woman's eyes look like doves' eyes? Are they the color of doves? Or are they like doves in some other way?

Simile Like metaphor, simile is a figure of speech that describes an object or event by comparing it to another object or event; simile, however, uses the words "like" or "as" to signal that an explicit comparison is being made. (In Hebrew, we look for the words *ke, kemo,* or the verb *dmh.*) "Your eyes are doves" is an example of a metaphor. "Your eyes are *like* doves" is an example of a simile. Similes and metaphors overlap in many ways. In Song of Songs, we often find similes and metaphors paired together, as in 5:13: *His cheeks are like beds of spices, yielding fragrance. His lips are lilies, distilling liquid myrrh* (NRSV).

When searching for the ground against which to understand metaphors and similes, we must attend to their cultural context. Care must be taken not to assume that our contemporary cultural associations are the same as ancient Near Eastern associations. To someone reading the dove metaphor against the background of the North American culture of the 1960s, the dove might symbolize peace. To someone reading the metaphor against the background of the NT, the dove could symbolize innocence ("Be . . . as innocent as doves," Matt. 10:16). As Othmar Keel explains, when viewed against the background of the ancient Near East, the dove in the Song of Songs likely symbolizes love. Thus the man in effect says to his beloved, "Your eyes speak to me of love." (See the commentary by Othmar Keel, who explores the ancient Near Eastern iconographic background to the imagery of the Song of Songs.)

Allegory The term *allegory* refers to discourse that speaks of one thing but means something different. Whereas we can find many examples of metaphor and simile in the Bible, we find fewer examples of allegory. The book of Ezekiel contains several examples of allegories in which the allegorical narrative rests upon an image that suggests the intended subject. For example, Ezekiel 16 and 23 use the image of an adulterous woman to say something about the way in which the people have been unfaithful to God.

The Bible also contains allegorical interpretation, in which a narrative that has historical meaning at one level is explained as meaning something different. In Galatians 4:21-31, the apostle Paul interprets the Genesis narratives about Sarah and Hagar to mean that those who depend on law (Hagar) rather than faith (Sarah) will lose their inheritance [*Allegorical and Figural Interpretation*, p. 258].

FLOWERS The Song of Songs frequently describes vegetation, but it contains only four clear references to flowers. Two flowers are mentioned by name. Many translations, including NIV, identify them with the names *rose* (2:1) and *lily* (2:1, 2, 16; 4:5; 5:13; 6:2, 3; 7:2). In both cases, these are problematic identifications and will be discussed below. A third term, Hebrew *niṣṣanim*, refers generally to spring flowers (2:12), which might include anenomes, crowfoot, poppies, and tulips. The noun may derive from a root meaning "to come into blossom" (Zohary: 169). The Song also refers to *henna* blossoms (1:14), which were fragrant and formed on a treelike shrub [*Aromatics*, p. 260].

Lotus (not lily) Most English Bibles translate the Hebrew terms *šošannah* and *šošannim* with the terms *lily* and *lilies*, but these flowers are probably a type of lotus rather than a lily. Various flowers have been proposed as the correct identification of the *šošannah*: the sea daffodil (*Pancratium maritimum*), narcissus (*Narcissus tazetta*), mountain tulip (*Tulipa agenensis*), iris or hyacinth (*Hyacinthus orientalis*), anemone (*Anemone coronaria*), gladiolus (*Gladiolus illyricus*), and the ranunculus (*Ranunculus asiaticus*; *NIDB*, s.v. "Lily"; Zohary: 178–79). Zohary (176) asserts that it certainly is the true lily (*Lilium candidum*) that grows in Galilee and on Mount Carmel, and he says it was once more widespread in the region. There is general agreement that the reference to the *lily of the valley* in Song 2:1 cannot refer to the flower known by that name in North America (*Convallaria majalis*), which is native to Europe. Keel (78) and Suderman both argue convincingly that Hebrew *šošannah* refers to the water lily or lotus, either the white (*Nymphaea alba*) or blue (*Nymphaea caerulea*). The Hebrew term is an Egyptian loanword, which suggests that it refers to a plant known in Egypt. In the Bible, we read that the form of this flower was used as an architectural element in the Jerusalem temple pillars (1 Kings 7:19, 22) and in the molten sea (7:26). Archaeology has many examples of a lotus motif used in artistic and architectural creations (for examples, see Keel: 79).

Finally, the symbolism of the lotus helps us better understand the figurative language in Song of Songs than does the identification of the flower as a type of lily. The Hebrew word occurs seventeen times in the OT. Eight of those occurrences are in Song of Songs (2:1, 2, 16; 4:5; 5:13; 6:2, 3; 7:2). In seven of the occurrences in Song of Songs, the flower describes or refers to the woman. She is a *lotus of the valleys* (2:1 AT); a *lotus among thorns* (2:2 AT); her waist is a *mound of wheat encircled by lotuses* (7:2 AT). In four places, she is referred to figuratively with regard to her lover's activity, which is described as *browsing among the lotuses* (2:16; 4:5; 6:3 AT) or *gathering lotuses* (6:2 AT). In only one place is her lover described by using figurative language of lotuses: *his lips—lotuses* (5:13 AT).

As Keel (78) explains, the association of the woman with the lotus means something different than an association with other flowers. He argues that the identification "determines how one envisions the young woman." The association with the lotus means that she is "able and willing to bestow renewed power" (Keel: 80).

Rose of Sharon The flower called *rose of Sharon* (Song 2:1) refers neither to the rose (genus *Rosa*) nor to the flowering shrub known in North America as the Rose of Sharon (genus *Hibiscus*). A precise identification is impossible to make. Various suggestions have been made of flowers that grew in ancient Israel: crocus, meadow saffron, narcissus, or a type of tulip. Keel (78) suggests that it could be a sea daffodil (*Pancratium maritimum*), a flower that could have grown in the marshy land near Sharon. The Hebrew noun ḥabaṣelet occurs only here and in Isaiah 35:1.

GEOGRAPHY The Song of Songs contains references to approximately fifteen different geographical locations in the ancient Levant. Many of the references are in the northern part of the Levant (the countries bordering on the eastern Mediterranean Sea), located today on the Lebanon-Syria border. Kedar, in the northern Arabian peninsula, appears to be the southernmost geographical reference. Its western limit is the Mediterranean Sea and its eastern limit, the Syrian Desert.

Without explicitly specifying a geographical location for the lovers, the poems of Song of Songs suggest a central focus upon Jerusalem. They do this in two ways. First, throughout the book we find short conversations between the woman and the *daughters of Jerusalem*. In all, the book contains seven references to the *daughters of Jerusalem* and one reference to the *daughters of Zion*. Second, in several places the poems refer to Solomon, either by name, or by indirect reference to *the king*. The name Solomon occurs seven times within the book, and there are three references to a *king* apart from Solomon. Even if we consider the references to Solomon as a poetic device, the explicit naming of Solomon throughout the book contributes to the focus on Jerusalem, where Solomon lived and ruled. At the same time, references to far-flung locations—the mountains of Lebanon and the Arabian desert—remind us that the expressions of love found in this book cannot be limited to one place.

Some scholars have attempted to use these geographical references to identify the date of the book or the location of the book's author (see, e.g., Garrett: 22, 228), but it seems more likely that the places mentioned in the book should be interpreted in terms of their figurative value. Most of the geographical references fall into one of three main categories: cities, regions known for their productivity, and mountainous regions.

Two major cities are named in the poems of Song of Songs: Jerusalem and Tirzah. Located in the central highlands, Jerusalem was the capital of the united monarchy under David and Solomon and the capital of Judah after the division of the monarchy. The name "Tirzah" means "pleasure" or "beauty," which may have something to do with the beauty of its location in the hill country north of Jerusalem. Tirzah was the capital of the northern kingdom of Israel from 930 to 880 BCE, from the rule of its first king, Jeroboam, to the rule of Omri, who moved the capital to Samaria. As capital cities, Jerusalem and Tirzah represent the wealth and power that belonged to ancient kings.

In line with the poems' emphasis on the beauty of the natural world, regions known for their verdant growth appear in the poems: Carmel, Gilead, and Sharon. The oasis of En Gedi, with its lush vegetation, can also be included in this group. Carmel (7:5) and Sharon (2:1) are situated close to the Mediterranean seacoast. Carmel refers to a wooded mountain range that overlooks the sea. With its mild temperatures and good rainfall, Carmel produced abundant vegetation, and the name "Carmel" is likely derived from a Hebrew word meaning "orchard." Sharon refers to a plain that runs between the mountains and the coast for about fifty miles south of the Carmel Mountain range. Its rich soil produced vineyards, orchards, and beautiful flowers. The term "Gilead" (4:1; 6:5) refers to a mountainous area just east of the Jordan River, with its eastern edge bordering the Syrian desert. In antiquity, Gilead was heavily forested with scrub oak, carob, and pine. The healing ointment known in the Bible as the balm of Gilead may have come from trees that grew in that region, although some scholars speculate that the balm of Gilead was acquired in Gilead through trade, since a major trade route, the King's Highway, ran through Gilead. En Gedi (1:14), an oasis on the western side of the Dead Sea, was known for its vineyards, date palms, and balsam.

In Song 4:8, the man invites his lover to descend from the top of Lebanon, Amana, Senir, and Hermon—that is, from mountains that are over nine thousand feet high. Rather than describing the woman's precise physical location, it seems more likely that the poem refers to her mountain abode either as a way of describing her emotional remoteness or by using hyperbole to describe how their physical separation affects the man. Two mountain ranges run roughly parallel to each other in southern Lebanon. The western range is known as the Lebanon Mountains. In ancient times, Lebanon was known far and wide for its coniferous forests. The cedars of Lebanon were especially desired as a building material. To the east of this range, separated by the Beqaa Valley, lies the Anti-Lebanon range, to which the peaks of Amana, Hermon, and Senir belong (4:8). Amana likely refers to one of the peaks in this range. Mount Hermon, located in the southern portion of the Anti-Lebanon mountain range, looks northeastward toward Damascus. To the south, it overlooks the Jordan River, the Sea of Galilee, and what today is known as the Golan Heights. The term "Senir" may refer to the entire range that includes Hermon, or it may be another name for Mount Hermon. Beyond these three categories, there are single mentions of a few other locations. Heshbon, a city in the Transjordan, is associated with water (7:4). Nothing is known of Baal Hamon outside of Song 8:11.

HISTORY OF INTERPRETATION

Early and Medieval Period Although we know very little about early Jewish interpretation of the Song, it appears that in the first century CE, Rabbi Akiba (also spelled Aqiva and Akiva; d. 135) read the Song of Songs as a description of the relationship of God and the Israelite people (R. Murphy: 13). The Targum (an Aramaic translation/interpretation, which likely achieved its final form in the seventh or eighth century CE), similarly views the Song as representing the relationship of God and Israel; within the book he finds a pattern of Israel's turning from God and returning to God (Alexander). Although he did not write a commentary on the Song of Songs, the medieval Jewish philosopher Maimonides (d. 1204) seems to have interpreted the book as a portrayal of the human soul's desire to reunite with God (*The Guide of the Perplexed* 3.51–54; R. Murphy: 32–33). Some later rabbis took up the view of Maimonides; others associated the woman's voice with personified Wisdom (Beaton: 762–63).

Christian interpretation of the Song of Songs effectively begins with Origen (b. 185 in Egypt, d. 254 in Palestine), who wrote the first significant Christian commentary on the Song of Songs (Matter: 25). Origen treats the Song of Songs as a single, unified text, a spiritual wedding hymn, dramatized with four speakers: the bride, the bridegroom, the maidens, and the bridegroom's friends. The tradition of referring to the unnamed couple in the book as "Bride" and "Bridegroom" has held sway for centuries. Some modern English versions of the book identify the two main speakers in the poems as "Bride" and "Bridegroom," even though these terms do not appear in the Hebrew text to identify the speakers. The term "bride" occurs six times within the book (4:8-12; 5:1), but as a term of endearment within the speeches of the young man, not as an identification of a speaker. This identification began at least as early as Origen's interpretation of the Song, in which he understood the male in the poems to represent Christ (or God) and the female to represent either the church or the individual Christian soul. In the centuries following Origen's interpretation of the Song, commentators followed his approach and identified the two main voices in the Song as Christ and the church.

Origen begins by presenting the words of the text he interprets. Next, he identifies the speakers and determines the dramatic setting of the speeches. Third, he reinterprets the text, with the woman representing the church. He reinterprets the text once again, with the woman representing the soul, the individual Christian. He concludes by equating the reader and the individual soul of his fourth step (Torjesen: 55). Origen's reading of Song of Songs represents two types of allegorical (or figural) interpretation: the ecclesiological (the female speaker is the church) and the spiritual (the female speaker is the individual soul). A third approach associates the female speaker in the Song with the idealized figure of Mary, the Mother of Jesus *[Allegorical and Figural Interpretation, p. 258]*.

The next major Christian interpreter of Song of Songs was the twelfth-century Cistercian monk Bernard of Clairvaux (d. 1153), who adopted Origen's second line of interpretation of the Song and read the book as a dialogue between Christ and the individual Christian soul. Bernard's eighty-six homilies on the Song of Songs became a guide to the spiritual life for Christian monastics. As Amy Hollywood (75) explains, through his interpretation of the Song, Bernard encouraged his fellow monks to experience God:

Bernard calls on his fellow monks to see the gap between their experience of God's love and their love for God and then to meditate on, chew over, and digest the words of the Song so that they might come more fully to inhabit them.

The third approach, identifying the Bride of the Song with the Virgin Mary, both reflected and influenced the developing medieval liturgical tradition. Protestants often find this to be a difficult approach to understand. Ann Matter (151) explains how this identification of the woman in the Song developed:

> As both *Ecclesia* [church] and *anima* [soul] are feminine nouns in Latin, there was no linguistic difficulty in putting the words of the Bride in the mouth of the church or of the human soul. But a logical consequence of medieval fascination with the Song of Songs was an association of the Bride with a human, a woman, although a highly idealized figure, the Virgin Mary. This form of personification begins early in the Latin liturgical tradition, and gradually becomes a part of Song of Songs commentary.

The Song of Songs appealed to many Christian mystics, individuals who sought a direct and transformative experience of the divine. The medieval mystics Mechtild of Magdeburg (c. 1260–1282/94) and Gertrude of Helfta (1256–1302) employed imagery from the Song of Songs in their mystical writings. Mechtild's work *The Flowing Light of the Godhead* is filled with erotic imagery to describe mystical union with God. Focusing on God's love in *The Herald of Divine Love*, Gertrude weaves language and imagery from the Song of Songs throughout her writing.

Reformation Period Interpretation shifted at the time of the Reformation, although nonliteral interpretations of the Song continued to have influence. Martin Luther, who disliked allegorical interpretation, nevertheless maintained a type of allegorical reading of Song of Songs, with Solomon celebrating the relationship between God and his kingdom. Luther (191) explains that King Solomon thus praises God for the creation of the political order on earth:

> I think it is a song in which Solomon honors God with his praises; he gives Him thanks for his divinely established and confirmed kingdom and government; he prays for the preservation and extension of this his kingdom, and at the same time he encourages the inhabitants and citizens of his realm to be of good cheer in their trials and adversities and to trust in God, who is always ready to defend and rescue those who call upon Him.

Not surprisingly, Luther also used the Song to emphasize aspects of his theology. For example, he explains that the twin sheep in Song 4:2 refer to Law and Gospel (229).

For the most part, early Anabaptists did not write commentaries on the Song of Songs, but they did draw upon figurative language and imagery from the Song in their theological and devotional writings and in their hymnody. In their writings, they intertwine quotations and images from the Song with quotations from other biblical books. Not surprisingly, they draw insights from the Song that relate to their view of themselves as restoring the church to its pure condition, and they offer encouragement to other Anabaptists to stand firm through the persecution they are experiencing. A favorite passage, which appears in the writings of Menno Simons, Dirk Philips, and Pilgram Marpeck, is Song 2:10-13. The imagery of the end of winter and appearance of spring seems to have appealed to these leaders, who sought to restore the church to its intended purity.

Although not the founder of the Anabaptist movement in the Netherlands, Menno Simons (1496–1561) is the best-known leader of the movement. At the age of twenty-eight, he entered the priesthood. But after studying Scripture (which he had not done until after entering the priesthood), Menno came to reject both infant baptism and transubstantiation. After much deliberation, he determined that the church in which he held his priesthood had strayed too far from Scripture, and he left the Catholic Church to join the Anabaptists. Menno draws upon the Song of Songs in various places throughout his 1535 *Foundation of Christian Doctrine*. His fullest and most explicit use of the Song appears in the section titled "To the Bride, Kingdom, City, Body and Church of the Lord, to Whom Be Grace and Peace," in which he encourages his fellow believers to prepare themselves for the Bridegroom's coming:

The Bridegroom, Christ Jesus, through Solomon addresses His bride, the church, saying, Rise up, my love, my fair one, and come away. For, lo, the winter is past, the rain is over and gone; the flowers appear on the earth; the time of the singing of birds is come, and the voice of the turtle[dove] is heard in our land; the fig tree putteth forth her green figs, and the vines with the tender grape give a good smell. Arise, my love, my fair one, and come away.

Elect, faithful children, you who with me are called to a like grace, inheritance, portion, and kingdom, and are named after the Lord's name, oh, hear the voice of Christ, our King; hear the voice of your Bridegroom, O thou bride of God, thou friend of the Lord. Arise and adorn thyself to honor the King and Bridegroom. (*CWMS* 221)

Dirk Philips (1504–68) joined the Anabaptist movement in 1533. A former Franciscan monk, Dirk became a leading theologian among the Dutch and North German Anabaptists of his time. Allusions to the Song of Songs can be found in his *Enchiridion*, his answer to Sebastian Frank, and his epistle to four cities.

In 1530, Melchior Hoffman (1495–1543?), a radical lay preacher and apocalyptic visionary in the northern European Anabaptist movement, published *The Ordinance of God*, which uses nuptial imagery in discussing baptism, the Lord's Supper, and the ban. Drawing upon the Gospels, John's Apocalypse, and the Song of Songs, Hoffman uses the language of Bride and Bridegroom to describe the relationship of both the church and the individual believer to Christ. Hoffman also wrote a commentary on the Song, *Dat Boeck Cantica canticorum, edder, dat hoge leedt Salomonis* (That book, Song of Songs, or the Song of Solomon, explained by Melchior Hoffman). (To my knowledge, this 1529 work has not been translated into English.)

The South German Anabaptist leader Pilgram Marpeck (ca. 1495-1556?) considered love a requisite of Christian faith, and the Song of Songs provides one scriptural key to understanding love. In an undated letter probably addressed to one or more groups of Anabaptists in either Strasbourg or Moravia, Marpeck begins by quoting from the "love chapter," 1 Corinthians 13, and later turns to language of the Song in order to describe God's love for humankind. In fact, Marpeck weaves the language and imagery of the Song through the entire letter.

The 1702 Swiss-Mennonite devotional book *Golden Apples in Silver Bowls* was popular among Mennonites and Brethren. The first two editions (1702 and 1742) were printed in Basel. A third edition was printed at Ephrata (Pennsylvania) in 1745. The book contains letters and other personal writings by several sixteenth-century Anabaptist martyrs, and in these writings references and allusions to the Song of Songs appear. Although the Song is not cited frequently in this collection, several of the sixteenth-century writers draw upon words, phrases, and images from the Song in ways that suggest a familiarity with the book. They interpret the book to refer to the love of Christ for the individual believer or for the church, understood as the communities of Anabaptist believers.

Golden Apples contains prison letters written by the Anabaptist martyr Thomas von Imbroich (1533-58), who was arrested, imprisoned, and tortured before being beheaded at the age of twenty-five. In his sixth letter from prison, Thomas encourages his fellow believers to stand firm in their faith.

> Therefore, beloved fellow believers, take heed that you gather a good treasure for the future, and that none may be found among us who has run or toiled in vain. For our adversary does not hesitate to kill and to destroy, for this is his very nature. We are to resist him with faith (1 Tim 6; 1 Pet 5). And if our heart is not united with God, and the sure confidence of the invisible things is not firmly established in faith, wherewith are we to resist? For the dragon will never cease to spew forth floods of water (Heb 11; Rev 12). It is therefore necessary that we so seal our hearts, and embrace the wings of love, which is stronger than death and passion, surer than hell, so that many floods have not been able to extinguish love, nor streams to drown it (Song 8). (*GASB* 129)

Thomas also uses the Song's images of the dove and the kiss to encourage unity among his fellow believers. After citing numerous OT and NT passages and quoting the apocryphal book of Ecclesiasticus

(Sirach 25:1), Thomas draws attention to the Song's imagery of the dove, which he identifies as the church. In an extended description of doves' behavior, he encourages his fellow believers to act like doves by living in unity with one another.

> This peace and unity is also pictured in the book of the Song of Solomon, where the church of God is called a dove, for where doves live together they stay together, fly out together and come home together; they are simple and without bitterness; they do not rage with biting, tear no one apart with their claws, but enjoy living where there are people, know only one home, and have things in common. By a kiss they recognize the unity of peace and at all times they fulfill the law of unity (Song 2). Such simplicity should be known in God's church. Such love must be practiced that brotherly love will follow the pattern of doves, and that in their gentleness and kindness they may be likened to lambs (1 Cor 13, 16; Matt 10; Luke 10). (*GASB* 138)

Roman Catholic writers continued the tradition of reading the Song as a portrayal of Christ's relationship with the church, and the Marian interpretation persisted as well. Representing a mystical approach to the Song, the Carmelites Teresa of Avila (1515–82) and John of the Cross (1542–91) both read the Song as describing the soul's union with God. Teresa composed a collection of *Meditations on the Song of Songs*. John's work, *The Spiritual Canticle*, employs erotic images from the Song.

Seventeenth and Eighteenth Centuries As a religious movement of the seventeenth and eighteenth centuries, Pietism sought to reinvigorate the spiritual life of the Lutheran Church. Gradually Pietism spread beyond the boundaries of the Lutheran Church to influence other traditions as well. Many of the churches that fall within the category "believers churches" reflect, to greater and lesser degrees, Pietist influence. The two primary influences that led to the formation of the Brethren were Anabaptism and radical Pietism. Pietist views also influenced Mennonites, as well as Methodists and Moravians. Pietist threads run through many Christian denominations today, even though they may not be labeled as such. Christian theologians and writers whose work contributed to the development of Pietism include Johann Arndt, Philip Jakob Spener, Paul Gerhardt, Gottfried Arnold, and the mystic Jakob Boehme (Böhme).

Pietists draw heavily upon the language and imagery of the Song of Songs in their writings. Since Pietism is often described as a "religion of the heart," the affinity that Pietists have for the Song of Songs seems only natural. Perhaps the best place to find their use of the Song is in their hymns and devotional writings. Themes that appear in Pietist writings include the following: the desire of the individual Christian, the Bride, for Christ, the Bridegroom; the urgency of preparation for the return of the Bridegroom; the restoration of the image of God in men and women (which might be portrayed as a return to a restored garden of Eden); renewal in Christ, which could be portrayed as a marriage of the Bride-believer and the Groom-Christ. Pietists favored interpretations that viewed the Bride of the Song as the individual believer, the Christian "soul," in relationship with Christ, the Bridegroom.

In a passage in which he discusses baptism, Johann Arndt (1555–1621) uses the language of Bride and Bridegroom to describe the new birth of the individual who has received baptism:

> Therefore, the Bridegroom takes the soul and marries himself to the soul with an eternal binding and attaches himself with as many firm bonds as a husband can attach himself to his wife with. This promise in the betrothal by which the Bridegroom betroths himself to his bride is stronger than any promise. He has so loved that he has given himself up for the soul in death. (265)

Perhaps the two most important radical Pietist works on the Song of Songs from this period are the Marburg Bible and the Berleburg Bible. In 1712 the radical Pietist Heinrich Horch(e) (1652–1729) published *Mystische und profetische Bibel* (Mystical and prophetic Bible), commonly known as the Marburg Bible, in which he focused on two books: the Song of Songs and the Revelation to John. Interpreting the Song allegorically, Horch divided the book into chronological periods. Accordingly, the Song of Songs reflects the history of the church: from its early years, when it lived a pure life as the bride of Christ suffering persecution (chapters 1:5–3:6); through the years when the church lost the purity of its relation to Christ under the Christian emperors (3:7–5:1); and under the antichrist of the Roman Catholic Church (5:2-16). In the final chapters of the Song, according to Horch, the church prepares itself for its wedding to Christ, "the heavenly Solomon" (Bach: 26–27; Shantz 2002).

Published in Berleburg, Germany, the Berleburg Bible is a revision of Martin Luther's German translation. Edited by the German Pietist Johann Friedrich Haug and others, the Berleburg Bible was a massive project: published between 1726 and 1742, the Bible appeared in eight folio volumes and totaled 6,201 pages. The Berleburg Bible is an annotated edition of the Bible, with the commentary portion taking up four times the space of the biblical text itself. Although the commentators provide exposition of the literal meaning of the biblical texts, their real interest is in the texts' spiritual meaning. The commentary reflects the influence of the German mystic Jacob Böhme, the Quietists Madame Guyon and Antoinette Bourignon, and the Philadelphians Thomas Bromley, Jane Ward Leade, and Johanna Eleanora Merlau Petersen. (The Philadelphian Society was a late seventeenth- and early eighteenth-century religious movement strongly influenced by the mystical thought of Jakob Böhme. The adherents rejected the established churches and believed in the universal restoration of all souls.) Radical Pietist and separatist groups favored this Bible, which expresses the view that true faith has to do with an inward discipleship and should not be confused with churchgoing and the church in its institutional form. In this view, discipleship, "following Christ," is what leads to union with Christ. Consequently, the Song of Songs provides the perfect language of Bride and Bridegroom to describe union with Christ (Ensign: 329; D. F. Durnbaugh: 140).

The literature, music, and folk art left behind by the eighteenth-century radical Pietist community in Ephrata, Pennsylvania, reveals a group steeped in the type of mysticism that treasures the Song of Songs. Images of lilies and roses are prominent in Ephrata's folk art, calling to mind Song 2:1-2: *I am a rose of Sharon, a lily of the valleys. Like a lily among thorns is my darling among the young women.* The titles of two of the Ephrata community's hymnals allude to the Song of Songs. The 1739 hymnal *Zionitischer Weyrauchs-Hügel* (Zionitic hill of incense) alludes to Song 4:6b: *I will go to the mountain of myrrh and the hill of incense.* Alluding to Song 2:12, a second Ephrata hymnal (1747) is titled *Turtel Taube* (The song of the solitary and deserted turtle-dove, namely, the Christian church; or spiritual and experienceful-songs of sorrow and love, as therein both a foretaste of the new world as well as the intervening ways of the cross and sorrow, are presented according to their dignity in spiritual rhymes) (Bach: 160–68).

Pietist hymn texts also reflect the influence of the Song of Songs. In the seventeenth and eighteenth centuries, many German-speaking Pietists favored hymn texts written by Johannes Scheffler (1624–77). Born and raised a Lutheran, Scheffler converted to Catholicism, after which he took the name Angelus Silesius. Despite his Catholic conversion, Pietists included thirty of Scheffler's poems in the widely used Pietist hymnal *Geistreiches Gesangbuch* (Spiritual hymnal, 1704), edited by J. A. Freylinghausen. Scheffler wrote a series of poems that draw directly from the imagery and language of the Songs of Songs. This series of poems was published in 1657 under the title *Heilige Seelenlust, oder Geistliche Hirtenlieder der in ihren Jesum verliebten Psyche* (The soul's holy delight, or Spiritual songs of the Jesus-loving psyche). Some of the poems from this collection appear in early Brethren hymnals but were not included in later Brethren English-language hymnals. The first hymnal published for German Baptist Brethren in the new world was called *Das kleine Davidische Psalterspiel der Kinder Zions* (The little Davidic Psalter of the children of Zion). This hymnal was first published in 1744 by Christopher Sauer and must have been very popular, to judge by the number of later editions that appeared (Stoeffler: 146). This *Little Davidic Psalter* was based on a larger hymnal (containing over one thousand hymns) that was used by the Community of True Inspiration (H. T. Durnbaugh: 48).

Many of the hymns of the *Little Davidic Psalter* reflect the mystical tradition and its use of the language and imagery of the Song of Songs (H. T. Durnbaugh: 30–31; Stoeffler: 127). In the introduction to her work on Brethren hymnody, Hedda Durnbaugh (6) describes the dual influences on Brethren hymnody of mysticism and Pietism.

> A product of mysticism and Pietism was a certain type of Jesus-hymn which reflected both the secular erotic poetry and the Baroque reaching for the infinite. The result was religious poems about Jesus, which had themes of mystical eros and/or mystical union and language which borrowed heavily from the Song of Solomon.

For English-speaking Pietists, the hymns of Isaac Watts (1674–1748) and Charles Wesley (1707–88) emphasize the affective experience of the individual Christian who seeks an intimate relationship with Christ.

This overview has focused upon Anabaptist and Pietist approaches to the Song of Songs and on mystics who are mentioned in the commentary's TLC sections. For a more comprehensive but still concise overview, see the essay by Beaton (762–69). For more thorough discussions, see Pope (89–229) and R. Murphy (11–41) *[Nuptial Imagery in the NT, p. 282]*.

KING FICTION The name Solomon occurs seven times in the Song of Songs (1:1, 5; 3:7, 9, 11; 8:11, 12). In addition to the reference in the title (1:1), the poems refer to objects belonging to King Solomon: tent curtains (1:5), a carriage (3:7, 9), a wedding crown (3:11), and a vineyard (8:11-12). Older approaches, including dramatic interpretations, made Solomon a character in the poems *[Dramatic Interpretations, p. 263]*. Most interpreters now view references to Solomon as a poetic device. Roland Murphy (80) uses the term "king fiction" to describe the literary use of Solomon in these poems. He observes that King Solomon "appears to be peripherally related to the dialogic scenario and exchanges of the two lovers." In addition to mentioning Solomon by name, the poems refer more generally to kings, queens, and princes. The young man calls his lover a "prince's daughter" (7:1), and he describes a king held captive in the woman's hair (7:5).

According to Michael V. Fox (1985: 288), "Love makes lovers noble, even royal, and even greater than royalty!" Fox identifies the "nobility of lovers" as a theme in the Song of Songs and describes the woman's use of "king" as a term of affection for her lover. He further explains that in Egyptian love poetry, girls call their lovers "my prince" as a term of affection. "I say to my heart, . . . 'Give me my prince tonight'" (22). In another poem, a young woman claims that being with her lover makes her a royal: "I am the Mistress of the Two Lands, when I am [with you]" (15).

Roland Murphy (47) explains that love literature frequently blurs the lines between reality and fantasy in order to describe the experience of falling in love.

> What has been called "literary fiction"—usually involving role-playing and the blurring of distinctions between reality and fantasy—may be a characteristic feature of ancient love-literature as well as modern romances. The audience or readership is at least implicitly invited to assume the identities of the lovers portrayed, to escape into them and be transformed with them through the experiences of love that are described. As depicted, the lovers may also imagine themselves and each other in fictional dress.

Ariel Bloch and Chana Bloch (10) agree.

> King Solomon is a central figure in the lovers' fantasies, not a character in the poem, as commentators once assumed. His reign is invoked as a symbol of legendary splendor that enhances and ennobles the two young lovers.

Further, references to precious metals (1:11), expensive spices (4:13-14), and objects such as chariots (6:12), all related to the royal court, participate in the poet's construction of this imaginary world in which lovers imagine themselves to be king and queen.

Nevertheless, the final chapter of the book suggests that true love is even better than royalty or nobility. Jill Munro (42) explains how the king fiction functions at the end of the book to demonstrate that love surpasses the wealth and splendor of kings and queens [*Figures of Speech, p. 267*]:

> By deliberately distancing Solomon from the lovers towards the end of the Song, it becomes apparent that, in the end, the metaphor of kingship is inadequate to describe this great love. Love is not for sale, even to the most rich and powerful.... Therein lies the narrative function of the regal imagery, telling as it does a "story" which nevertheless remains metaphor. Solomon is integrated into this metaphorical system only to denounce it at the last minute and thereby lay bare the limits of language to speak about love.

LOVE AND DESIRE

Love The concept of love has a broad range of meaning in the Bible. Love characterizes interpersonal relationships. Husbands love wives. We are told that Isaac loves Rebekah (Gen 24:67), that Elkanah loves Hannah (1 Sam 1:5), and that the king of Persia loves Esther (Esther 2:17). Men and women fall in love without being married to each other. Because Jacob loves Rachel, he offers to work seven years in order to marry her (Gen 29:18). Shechem loves Dinah and, although he wants to marry her, is prevented from doing so by Dinah's brothers (Gen 34). Michal loves David (1 Sam 18:20), leading her father, King Saul, to offer her in marriage to David. Love can also characterize the feelings parents have toward children. Isaac loves Esau, whereas Rebekah loves Jacob.

Love also defines relationships between individuals and God. The LORD loves Solomon (2 Sam 12:24) and Solomon loves the LORD (1 Kings 3:3). Both testaments affirm that God loves humankind (Deut 7:8; 1 Kings 10:9; 2 Chron 2:11; John 3:16), and both testaments instruct humans to love God (Deut 6:5; Matt 22:37). The Bible also instructs us to love neighbors (Lev 19:18; Matt 19:19), resident aliens (Lev 19:34), and enemies (Matt 5:44). When asked to identify the greatest commandment, Jesus quotes Deuteronomy 6:4 on the centrality of loving God with all one's being. Jesus names "love of neighbor" (quoting Lev 19:18) as the second greatest commandment.

Love is central to the theology of both the apostle Paul and the Johannine tradition (gospel and letters of John). In these texts, love of God and love of humankind predominate. While not explicitly rejected, physical, sexual love is not addressed, although the apostle does reject the Corinthians' view that sexuality is wrong and instructs them that married couples should have sexual relations with each other (1 Cor 7). Paul proclaims that the love of God for humankind is so great that nothing can separate humans from that love (Rom 8:31-39). Love is a gift of the Holy Spirit (Gal 5:22). In Paul's estimation, love is the greatest gift, greater even than faith or hope (1 Cor 13).

The Johannine writings emphasize love within the community of Christ's followers. At the same time, these writings deepen our understanding of the nature of God as love and of the connection between God's love and human love. In John 13:34, we find the "love commandment": Jesus says, "A new command I give you: Love one another. As I have loved you, so you must love one another." The letters of John describe the interconnectedness of God's being as love, our love of one another, and the reality of being loved by God.

> Dear friends, let us love one another, for love comes from God. Everyone who loves has been born of God and knows God. Whoever does not love does not know God, because God is love. (1 John 4:7-8)

Desire "Desire" is a more controversial concept than that of "love." Some biblical interpreters and theologians sharply distinguish between *agapē* love and erotic love and find no room in the church for erotic love. It is true that the Greek word *agapē* appears frequently in the NT, but *erōs* does not. In his book *Agape and Eros*, the Swedish theologian Anders Nygren (1890–1978) drew a sharp distinction between the two Greek terms for love. Nygren characterized *agapē* love as the selfless love that God shows for humankind. By contrast, erotic love is self-centered, the type of love that seeks a return on the investment. Theologian Catherine Keller challenges Nygren's polarization of *agapē* and *erōs*. She associates both terms with God, describing *erōs* as the "creative love of God," "desire," and "divine passion." *Agapē* love for Keller is the "responsive love of God," "compassion." She refuses to denigrate the self: "If agape sacrifices the fullness of our selves, it is a false agape, lacking self-esteem and therefore lacking, precisely, the power of persistence." She also refuses to separate *agapē* from *erōs*: "Agape—when it has not been dissociated from eros—regenerates a common life" (Keller: 116).

Desire is woven throughout the poems of the Song of Songs. At first this book's celebration of desire may strike some readers as not quite appropriate for the Bible. Is there something inherently sinful about desire? Although the Bible condemns envy and lust, desire in itself is not condemned. Some sexual desires may be considered wrong, but sexual desire in itself is not wrong. Ellen Davis (2000b: 8) has argued that in the wisdom literature, desire is viewed as a good, if and when the object of desire is good:

> In using the language of love and desire, the sages alert us to the hidden but essential connection between what we want and what we may come to know. Through holy desire, we may indeed gain what Israel called wisdom: true, realistic knowledge of God, ourselves, and the world. But we may also waste our desire, by turning it to things that are unworthy of us, or harmful to us.... The key insight is this: desire is never spiritually neutral. It either sharpens our perception, so that

we see ourselves and the world in something of the same way God sees, or else it distorts our understanding of our God-given situation in the world.

The word "desire" and its synonyms refer broadly to any strong wish to obtain something or to have something happen. Although the Bible denounces desire that is inappropriately directed, desire in itself is acknowledged to be an aspect of human nature, as in the following proverb: "Hope deferred makes the heart sick, but a longing fulfilled is a tree of life" (Prov 13:12).

The Bible records the human desire for specific objects, such as food (Deut 12:15, 20) or a wife (Deut 21:11). Job expresses his desire to argue his case with God (Job 13:3). Paul writes about his desire to visit the community of Christians in Rome (Rom 15:23).

Throughout the Psalms, it is evident that the satisfaction of desires comes from God:

Take delight in the LORD,
   and he will give you the desires of your heart. (37:4)

[Praise the LORD,] ...
who satisfies your desires with good things
   so that your youth is renewed like the eagle's. (103:5)

You [God] open your hand
   and satisfy the desires of every living thing. (145:16)

Frequently God is identified as the object of human desire or yearning, as in this passage from the prophet Isaiah: "My soul yearns for you in the night; in the morning my spirit longs for you. When your judgments come upon the earth, the people of the world learn righteousness" (26:9). The psalmist also speaks of the individual's desire for God: "As the deer pants for streams of water, so my soul pants for you, my God" (Ps 42:1).

Desire also characterizes God, who is said to have specific objects of desire: steadfast love (Hos 6:6), truth (Ps 51:6), Zion (Ps 132:13), godly offspring (Mal 2:15), and mercy (Matt 9:13). First Timothy advises that God "desires everyone to be saved and to come to the knowledge of the truth" (1 Tim 2:4 NRSV).

Sexual desire plays a relatively small role in the Bible. Although no single book of the Bible celebrates human sexual desire to the degree that occurs in the Song of Songs, there are other examples in the Scriptures where we might detect affirmations of human sexual desire. Yet it is sometimes not easy to determine if a given passage affirms sexual desire or procreation (or sexual desire in the service of procreation). The creation of humankind as male and female and the corresponding commandment to "be fruitful and increase in number" fit this category (Gen 1:27-28). The observation that "a man leaves his father and mother and is united to his wife, and they become one flesh" (Gen 2:24) may also be viewed as an affirmation of human sexuality. Both Jesus and Paul quote this verse as evidence in support of their own positions on divorce (Matt 19:5; Mark 10:7-8) and sexual immorality (1 Cor 6:16). And even though Paul recommends celibacy to those who are single, he admonishes husbands and wives to fulfill their marital duties to each other:

> The husband should fulfill his marital duty to his wife, and likewise the wife to her husband. The wife does not have authority over her own body but yields it to her husband. In the same way, the husband does not have authority over his own body but yields it to his wife. (1 Cor 7:3-4)

NUPTIAL IMAGERY IN THE NEW TESTAMENT Nuptial imagery and bride and bridegroom language are used of Jesus' earthly ministry in several gospel passages. For example, John the Baptist explains that he, himself, is only the friend of the bridegroom:

> The bride belongs to the bridegroom. The friend who attends the bridegroom waits and listens for him, and is full of joy when he hears the bridegroom's voice. That joy is mine, and it is now complete. (John 3:29)

In Mark 2:19-20 (and parallels), Jesus himself uses bride and bridegroom language in answer to a question about why Jesus' disciples do not fast as do other Jews:

> How can the guests of the bridegroom fast while he is with them? They cannot, so long as they have him with them. But the time will come when the bridegroom will be taken from them, and on that day they will fast.

Wedding imagery occurs in the parable of the wise and foolish maidens in Matthew 25:1-13. The parable exhorts Jesus' followers to remain faithful. In the parable, the bridegroom is delayed. The wise maidens are those who are prepared with oil for their lamps and able to welcome the bridegroom when he appears. An explicit exhortation occurs at the end of the parable: "Therefore keep watch, because you do not know the day or the hour" (25:13).

Ephesians 5:21-33 explicitly draws the analogy of husband and wife to Christ and the church. This analogy becomes one of the primary ways in which the Song is read allegorically by later Christians. In later Christian spiritual readings of the Song, the male is understood to be Christ. The identity of the female in the Song can shift. In ecclesiological readings, the female beloved is the church, as in Ephesians. In Christian mystical readings, the female is the "soul," the individual believer in relation to Christ. In the medieval period, Mariological readings come to the fore, in which the female in the Song of Songs is identified with Mary. It helps us understand this allegorical interpretation if we know that Mary, the mother of Jesus, was viewed in the medieval period as the "model Christian" and as a symbol of the church.

In the book of Revelation, nuptial imagery symbolizes the eschatological community of the faithful, who join in marriage to Christ, the Bridegroom. In chapter 18, the destruction of Babylon (i.e., Rome) is announced. This destruction is described as ending the joyful celebration that occurs at a wedding: "The voice of bridegroom and bride will never be heard in you [Babylon] again" (Rev 18:23b). Chapter 19 follows with a vision of Christ's victory, which is described with nuptial imagery:

> Then I heard what sounded like a great multitude, like the roar of rushing waters and like loud peals of thunder, shouting:
> "Hallelujah!
> For our Lord God Almighty reigns.
> Let us rejoice and be glad
> and give him glory!
> For the wedding of the Lamb has come,
> and his bride has made herself ready.
> Fine linen, bright and clean,
> was given her to wear." ...
> Then the angel said to me, "Write this: Blessed are those who are invited to the wedding supper of the Lamb!" And he added, "These are the true words of God." (19:6-9)

In Revelation 21, three originally distinct images are brought together. The first two images occur in 21:2, where the visionary describes what he sees: "I saw the Holy City, the new Jerusalem, coming down out of heaven from God, prepared as a bride beautifully dressed for her husband." In this verse, the restored people of God are portrayed as a city, "the new Jerusalem," and as "a bride beautifully dressed for her husband." Later in the chapter, this bride's husband is called "the Lamb" (Rev 21:9). In this apocalyptic vision of John of Patmos, nuptial imagery joins with other imagery and language to figuratively describe the eschatological restoration of God's people.

SEXUALITY In this day and age, we hear a lot of talk about human sexuality, but do we know what the term *sexuality* means? The *Oxford English Dictionary* offers six different definitions of the term, which for our purposes we can narrow down to two primary meanings. First, the term is used in biology to describe the way in which life-forms reproduce. Single-celled organisms, such as bacteria, reproduce asexually; that is, they reproduce without the formation and fusion of gametes. So do some plants and fungi. Sexual reproduction occurs through the combining of genetic material from two different organisms. Most animals and some plants reproduce sexually.

A second way we use the term *sexuality* is less precise and has a broader scope. It also has more relevance to our discussion of sexuality in the Song of Songs. We can use the term *sexuality* to refer to feelings, emotions, and activities related to intimate, physical contact between individuals. It can include, but is not limited to, sexual intercourse. It can also refer to sexual feelings and desires that remain unfulfilled. Christian ethicist Dennis P. Hollinger (15) states, "All humans are sexual beings whether or not they engage in acts of sex." Similarly, Margaret Farley (159), also a Christian ethicist, comments, "Sex can refer to genital and nongenital sex, sex with or without desire, sex with or without pleasure." In this sense of the term, sexuality has psychological and emotional dimensions as well as physical.

Only since the nineteenth century have we talked about "human sexuality" in this way. Certainly people both felt and expressed sexual feelings before then, but they did not categorize those feelings under the term "sexuality." It should not be surprising, then, to discover that the Bible lacks a word for sexuality. Not only does it lack the term, but the Bible also has relatively little to say regarding this broader definition of human sexuality that includes sexual feelings, desires, and pleasures. This is one reason to pay attention to the Song of Songs: it has more to say about human sexual experience in all its dimensions than the rest of the Bible combined.

Nevertheless, we do want to consider the view of sexuality in Song of Songs within its larger canonical context. In the opening chapters of Genesis, we read about sexuality as reproduction and sexuality as relationship. With regard to sexual reproduction, it says that after creating human beings, "God blessed them and said to them, 'Be fruitful and increase in number'" (Gen 1:28a). The very first commandment found in the Bible is positive regarding human sexuality: "Reproduce." Sexuality in Genesis has to do with more than procreation, however. Genesis 2 describes the affective side of sexuality. When only one person exists, he is lonely, but when God creates a partner for him, the creation of humankind is complete. The man sees the woman and says, "This is now bone of my bones, and flesh of my flesh" (Gen 2:23a). Sexuality is more than procreation. It has to do with the intimacy that breaks the solitary person's isolation. This understanding is furthered in the following verse, which offers a sort of editorial commentary on the creation of man and woman: "That is why a man leaves his father and mother and is united to his wife, and they become one flesh" (2:24). While in Eden, the couple feels no sense of shame regarding their naked bodies (2:25); however, changes in their relationship do occur as a consequence of the couple's act of disobedience in Genesis 3. Much more could be said about Genesis, but this glimpse into the creation story of Genesis 1–3 suggests that at its foundation, the Bible views human sexuality positively. (See Eugene Roop's Genesis commentary in the BCBC series for a more in-depth study of Genesis 1–3.)

If we consider OT laws that have something to do with sexuality, we discover that they deal with matters of ritual purity and with prohibited sexual behaviors and activities. Narratives that involve female sexual activity tend to have as their primary concern issues of procreation and male control of the family line. For example, the book of Ruth describes a woman's sexual advances (3:6-15), but it concludes with a genealogy that lists only the males in the line that extends from Perez to David (4:18-22). Or consider the levirate law as it applies to Tamar (Gen 38). The narrative has everything to do with producing a lineage for Tamar's first husband, who has died, and nothing to do with Tamar's sexual needs or desires—or with love. Tamar makes herself sexually available, presumably to secure her dead husband's lineage (Gen 38:14-18). Tamar's story ends, not with a report of love fulfilled or sexual desire satisfied—not even with a marriage—but with a birth report (38:27-30).

Of course, the absence of much explicit discussion of sexuality does not mean that people in biblical times did not experience sexual feelings and desires. Within the Bible, the Song of Songs is one of the few places in which we find much on this subject, although we catch glimpses elsewhere. For example, in Proverbs we read this advice to husbands:

> May your fountain be blessed,
>   and may you rejoice in the wife of your youth.
> A loving doe, a graceful deer—
>   may her breasts satisfy you always,
>   may you ever be intoxicated with her love. (Prov 5:18-19)

The instruction in Proverbs reminds us of the patriarchal context for the Bible's views on sexuality. With few exceptions, men in the ancient Mediterranean world held positions of authority. Social values and norms tended to favor men. The perspective in the Bible is male oriented. Much of the instruction in the book of Proverbs, for example, is directed to a male audience, as is the passage just quoted. When we recognize the male dominance in much of the Bible, it becomes clear how different the Song of Songs is: in Song of Songs we hear a *woman's* voice and the expression of *female* desire. (Some scholars challenge this assumption and argue that Song of Songs uses a female voice to express a male perspective. See, e.g., Clines.)

What about the NT? Unfortunately, the NT has little more to say about sexuality than the OT. What it does contribute, however, is mostly positive about the role of sexuality in human lives. In recent years, the sexuality and marital status of Jesus has been a topic of discussion. Some popular literature has suggested that Jesus was both heterosexual and married (e.g., Dan Brown's *Da Vinci Code*), but the NT never mentions a wife for Jesus. On the subject of human sexuality, Jesus has little to say. He neither denigrates nor promotes heterosexual marriage. He neither affirms nor condemns same-sex relationships. In one cryptic passage (Matt 19:10-12), Jesus appears to endorse the celibate life, but he does not promote celibacy for everyone (although some readers have interpreted this saying in that way).

Unlike the OT, some NT texts express a sense of urgency about the times that affects views of marriage. In Paul's letters, this sense of urgency leads the apostle to promote celibacy (a position not advocated in the OT). For example, in Paul's influential first letter to the Corinthians, he discourages single people from marrying. It appears that Paul thought it was the wrong *time* to marry. Scholars talk about this as Paul's "imminent eschatology," which led him to focus on preparing for the parousia, the reappearance of Christ on the earth. In 1 Corinthians, Paul claims that "the time is short."

> What I mean, brothers and sisters, is that the time is short. From now on those who have wives should live as if they do not; those who mourn, as if they did not; those who are happy, as if they were not; those who buy something, as if it were not theirs to keep; those who use the things of the world, as if not engrossed in them. For this world in its present form is passing away. (7:29-31)

As with Genesis 1-3, this is a complex chapter to interpret, and scholars do not agree on many of the details. Nevertheless, many NT scholars today agree that Paul's eschatological views influenced his advice related to marriage and sexuality. Richard B. Hays (51) comments, "Presumably, Paul's belief in the imminent eschaton made him relatively indifferent to the raising of families." Graydon Snyder (114-15) explains, "Paul calls for an end-time disengagement from life in this world.... Paul meant for the new Christians to live in this age without conferring ultimate value on its institutions."

Although Paul has on occasion been denounced as a misogynist or as "sex-negative," if we dig deeper into 1 Corinthians 7, we discover that he is neither hostile toward women nor antagonistic toward sexuality. In fact, he instructs married people at Corinth *not* to divorce and *not* to deny themselves or their partners physical, sexual intimacy. What is even more remarkable about the following passage from 1 Corinthians is that Paul treats husbands and wives as having mutual obligations and responsibilities to one another:

> The husband should fulfill his marital duty to his wife, and likewise the wife to her husband. The wife does not have authority over her own body but yields it to her husband. In the same way, the husband does not have authority over his own body but yields it to his wife. Do not deprive each other except perhaps by mutual consent and for a time, so that you may devote yourselves to prayer. Then come together again so that Satan will not tempt you because of your lack of self-control. (7:3-5)

What can we learn from this brief look at sexuality in the Bible? Although unusual in its emphasis on sexuality, the Song of Songs is not alone within the Bible in expressing approval of sexual feelings and desire. Also, the Genesis creation stories affirm the goodness of human sexuality. We unfortunately have only glimpses in the Gospels of Jesus' view of human sexuality. Paul's writing emphasizes that human sexuality belongs within relationships consecrated by marriage and that sexuality should be characterized by mutuality within those relationships.

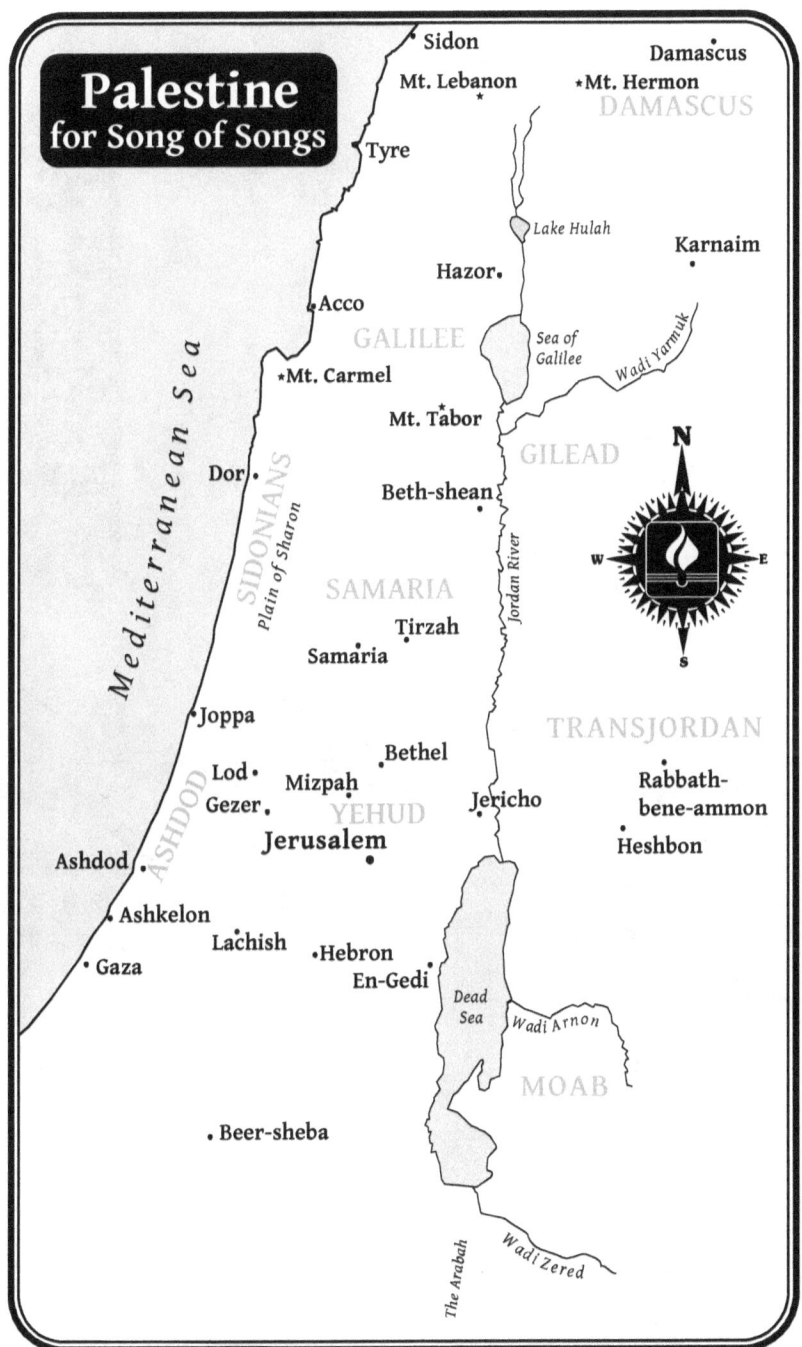

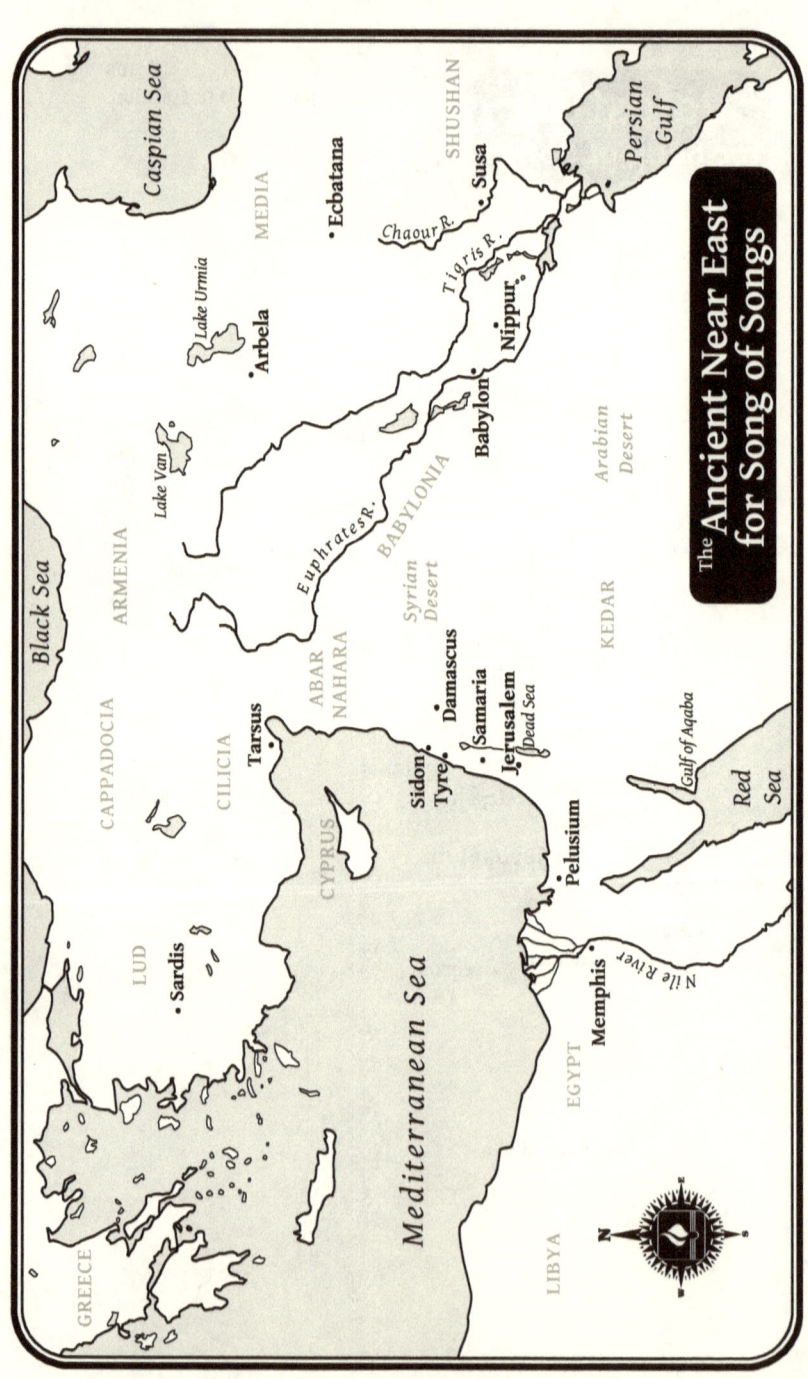

Bibliography for Song of Songs

Alexander, Philip S., ed. and trans.
    2003   *The Targum of Canticles*. Collegeville, MN: Liturgical Press.
Angelus Silesius
    1949   *Sämtliche poetische Werke [des] Angelus Silesius* [pseud.]. Munich: Hanser.
Arndt, Johann
    1979   *True Christianity*. Translated by Peter Erb. Classics of Western Spirituality. New York: Paulist Press.
Arnold, Gottfried
    1963   *Das Geheimnis der göttlichen Sophia*. Stuttgart-Bad Cannstadt: F. Frommann.
Astell, Ann W.
    1990   *The Song of Songs in the Middle Ages*. Ithaca, NY: Cornell University Press.
Atwood, Craig D.
    2004   *Community of the Cross: Moravian Piety in Colonial Bethlehem*. University Park: Pennsylvania State University Press.
    2009   "Little Side Holes: Moravian Devotional Cards of the Mid-Eighteenth Century. *Journal Of Moravian History* 6:61–75.
Bach, Jeff
    2003   *Voices of the Turtledoves: The Sacred World of Ephrata*. University Park: Pennsylvania State University Press.
Baptist Convention, Southern
    2008   *The Baptist Hymnal*. Nashville: LifeWay Worship.
Barton, John
    2005   "The Canonicity of the Song of Songs." In *Perspectives on the Song of Songs*, edited by Anselm Hagedorn, 1–7. Berlin: Walter de Gruyter.

Beaton, Richard
    2008   "Song of Songs 3: History of Interpretation." In *Dictionary of the Old Testament: Wisdom, Poetry and Writings*, edited by Tremper Longman III and Peter Enns, 760-69. Downers Grove, IL: IVP Academic.

Beissel, Conrad, and Russell P. Getz
    1971   *Ephrata Cloister Chorales: A Collection of Hymns and Anthems*. New York: Schirmer.

Bender, Elizabeth, and Leonard Gross, trans.
    1999   *Golden Apples in Silver Bowls: The Rediscovery of Redeeming Love*. Edited by Leonard Gross. Lancaster, PA: Lancaster Mennonite Historical Society.

Bergant, Dianne
    2001   *The Song of Songs*. Berit Olam. Collegeville, MN: Liturgical Press.

Bernard of Clairvaux
    1971   *On the Song of Songs*. Translated by Kilian J. Walsh. 4 vols. Spencer, MA: Cistercian Publications.

Bernat, David A.
    2004   "Biblical *Waṣfs* beyond Song of Songs." *Journal for the Study of the Old Testament* 28:327-49.

Billings, William
    1977   *The Complete Works of William Billings*. 4 vols. Edited by Hans Nathan. Boston: The American Musicological Society & The Colonial Society of Massachusetts.

Bird, Michael S.
    2002   *O Noble Heart/O Edel Herz: Fraktur and Spirituality in Pennsylvania German Folk Art*. Lancaster, PA: The Heritage Center Museum.

Blackburn, Simon
    2004   *Lust: The Seven Deadly Sins*. New York: Oxford University Press.

Bloch, Ariel, and Chana Bloch
    1995   *The Song of Songs: A New Translation with an Introduction and Commentary*. Berkeley: University of California Press.

Brenner, Athalya, ed.
    1993   *A Feminist Companion to the Song of Songs*. Feminist Companion to the Bible. Sheffield, UK: JSOT Press.

Brenner, Athalya, and Carole R. Fontaine, eds.
    2000   *The Song of Songs: A Feminist Companion to the Bible*. A Feminist Companion to the Bible, Second Series. Sheffield, UK: Sheffield Academic.

Brown, Dan
    2003   *The Da Vinci Code: A Novel*. New York: Doubleday.

Bucher, Christina
    2007   "Song of Songs and the Enclosed Garden in Fifteenth-Century Paintings and Engravings of the Virgin Mary and the Christchild." In *Between the Text and the Canvas: The Bible and Art in Dialogue*, edited by J. Cheryl Exum and Ela Nutu, 95-116. Sheffield, UK: Sheffield Phoenix.
    2010   "Love and Desire in the Song of Songs." In *The Witness of the Hebrew Bible for a New Testament Church*, edited by Christina Bucher, David A. Leiter, and Frank Ramirez, 213-35. Elgin, IL: Brethren Press.

Bullough, Vern L., Brenda K. Shelton, and Sarah Slavin
  1988   *The Subordinated Sex: A History of Attitudes toward Women.* Athens: University of Georgia Press.
Burrus, Virginia, and Stephen D. Moore
  2003   "Unsafe Sex: Feminism, Pornography, and the Song of Songs." *Biblical Interpretation* 11:24–52.
Carr, David M.
  2003   *The Erotic Word: Sexuality, Spirituality, and the Bible.* New York: Oxford University Press.
Childs, Brevard S.
  1979   *Introduction to the Old Testament as Scripture.* Philadelphia: Fortress.
Clare of Assisi
  1982   *Francis and Clare: The Complete Works.* Translated by Regis J. Armstrong and Ignatius C. Brady. Classics of Western Spirituality. New York: Paulist Press.
Clines, David J. A.
  1995   "Why Is There a Song of Songs and What Does It Do to You If You Read It?" In *Interested Parties: The Ideology of Writers and Readers of the Hebrew Bible*, 94–121. Sheffield: Sheffield Academic.
Cooper, John W.
  1989   *Body, Soul, and Life Everlasting: Biblical Anthropology and the Monism-Dualism Debate.* Grand Rapids: Eerdmans.
Davis, Ellen F.
  2000a *Proverbs, Ecclesiastes, and the Song of Songs.* Westminster Bible Companion. Louisville, KY: Westminster John Knox.
  2000b "Wisdom, Desire, and Holy Love." *The Living Pulpit* 9, no. 3:8–9.
Delitzsch, Franz
  1872   *Commentary on the Song of Songs and Ecclesiastes.* Translated by M. G. Easton. Edinburgh: T. and T. Clark, 1891.
Dell, Katharine J.
  2005   "Does the Song of Songs Have Any Connections to Wisdom?" In *Perspectives on the Song of Songs*, edited by Anselm C. Hagedorn, 8–26. Berlin: Walter de Gruyter.
Dobbs-Allsopp, Frederick William
  2005a "The Delight of Beauty and Song of Songs 4:1-7." *Interpretation* 59:260–77.
  2005b "Late Linguistic Features in the Song of Songs." In *Perspectives on the Song of Songs*, edited by Anselm C. Hagedorn, 27–77. Berlin: Walter de Gruyter.
Dufault-Hunter, Erin
  2011   "Sexual Ethics." In *Dictionary of Scripture and Ethics*, edited by Joel B. Green et al., 723–28. Grand Rapids: Baker Academic.
Dunn, James D. G.
  1998   *The Theology of Paul the Apostle.* Grand Rapids: Eerdmans.
Durnbaugh, Donald F.
  2005   "Jane Ward Leade (1624–1704) and the Philadelphians." In *The Pietist Theologians*, edited by Carter Lindberg, 128–46. Malden, MA: Blackwell.
Durnbaugh, Hedwig T.
  1986   *The German Hymnody of the Brethren, 1720–1903.* Philadelphia: Brethren Encyclopedia.

Dürr, Alfred, and Richard Douglas Jones
    2006   *The Cantatas of J. S. Bach: With Their Librettos in German-English Parallel Text.* Oxford: Oxford University Press.

Ensign, Chauncey David
    1955   *Radical German Pietism (c. 1675-1760).* Boston: Boston University School of Theology.

Exum, J. Cheryl
    2005   *Song of Songs.* Old Testament Library. Louisville, KY: Westminster John Knox.

Farley, Margaret A.
    2006   *Just Love: A Framework for Christian Sexual Ethics.* New York: Continuum.

Fisher, Celia
    1998   *Pocket Guides: Flowers and Fruit.* London: The National Gallery.

Fox, Michael V.
    1985   *The Song of Songs and the Ancient Egyptian Love Songs.* Madison: University of Wisconsin Press.
    2014   "A Moral Value in the Song of Songs: Reading Shir HaShirim in Its Original Sense." *The Torah.com: A Historical and Contextual Approach.* http://http://thetorah.com/a-moral-value-in-the-song-of-songs/

Freedman, Harry, ed.
    1995   *Canticles Rabbah.* Translated by Maurice Simon. The Soncino Midrash Rabbah. Vol. 9. Chicago: Davka.

Fyock, Joan A., and Lani Wright, eds.
    1996   *Hymnal Companion.* Elgin, IL: Brethren Press.

Garrett, Duane
    2004   "Song of Songs." In *Song of Songs, Lamentations*, by Duane Garrett and Paul R. House, 1–265. Word Biblical Commentary 23B. Nashville: Nelson.

Gertrude of Helfta
    1993   *The Herald of Divine Love.* Translated and edited by Margaret Winkworth. Classics of Western Spirituality. New York: Paulist Press.

Goulder, Michael D.
    1986   *The Song of Fourteen Songs.* Sheffield, UK: JSOT Press.

Green, Arthur
    2002   "Shekhinah, the Virgin Mary, and the Song of Songs: Reflections on a Kabbalistic Symbol in Its Historical Context." *AJS Review* 26:1–52.

Gregory the Great
    2012   *Gregory the Great on the Song of Songs.* Translated by Mark Del Cogliano. Collegeville, MN: Liturgical Press.

Griffiths, Paul J.
    2011   *Song of Songs.* Brazos Theological Commentary on the Bible. Grand Rapids: Brazos.

Hays, Richard B.
    1996   *The Moral Vision of the New Testament.* New York: HarperOne.

Hess, Richard S.
    2005   *Song of Songs.* Baker Commentary on the Old Testament Wisdom and Psalms. Grand Rapids: Baker Academic.

Bibliography for Song of Songs

Hoffman, Melchior
   1529   *Dat Boeck Cantica canticorum, edder, dat hoge leedt Salomonis.* [Kiel]: [Melchior Hoffman].
   1957   "The Ordinance of God." In *Spiritual and Anabaptist Writers: Documents Illustrative of the Radical Reformation*, edited by George H. Williams, 182–203. Philadelphia: Westminster.

Hollinger, Dennis P.
   2009   *The Meaning of Sex: Christian Ethics and the Moral Life.* Grand Rapids: Baker Academic.

Hollywood, Amy
   2012   "Song, Experience, and the Book in Benedictine Monasticism." In *The Cambridge Companion to Christian Mysticism*, edited by A. Hollywood and P. Z. Beckman, 59–79. New York: Cambridge University Press.

Horch, Heinrich
   1712   *Mystische und profetische Bibel.* Marburg: Kürssner.

Huwiler, Elizabeth
   1999   "Song of Songs." In *Proverbs, Ecclesiastes, Song of Songs*, by Roland E. Murphy and Elizabeth Huwiler, 219–90. New International Biblical Commentary. Peabody, MA: Hendrickson.

Jerome
   2001   *The Homilies of Saint Jerome.* Translated by Marie Liguori Ewald. Washington, DC: Catholic University of America Press.

John of the Cross
   1979   *The Collected Works of St. John of the Cross.* Washington, DC: Institute of Carmelite Studies.

Keel, Othmar
   1994   *The Song of Songs: A Continental Commentary.* Translated by Frederick J. Gaiser. Minneapolis: Fortress.

Keller, Catherine
   2008   *On the Mystery: Discerning Divinity in Process.* Minneapolis: Fortress.

Keyte, Hugh, and Andrew Parrott, eds.
   1993   *The Shorter New Oxford Book of Carols.* New York: Oxford University Press.

King, Philip J., and Lawrence E. Stager
   2001   *Life in Biblical Israel.* Louisville, KY: Westminster John Knox.

Kingsmill, Edmée
   2009   *The Song of Songs and the Eros of God: A Study in Biblical Intertextuality.* New York: Oxford University Press.

Das kleine Davidische Psalterspiel der Kinder Zions.
   1829   5th ed. Germany.

Landy, Francis
   1983   *Paradoxes of Paradise: Identity and Difference in the Song of Songs.* Sheffield, UK: Almond.

Lichtheim, Miriam, ed.
   1976   *Ancient Egyptian Literature.* 2 vols. Berkeley: University of California Press.

Linafelt, Tod
   2005   "The Arithmetic of Eros." *Interpretation* 59:244–58.

Lindberg, Carter, ed.
  2005 *The Pietist Theologians: An Introduction to Theology in the Seventeenth and Eighteenth Centuries.* Malden, MA: Blackwell.

Longman, Tremper, III
  2001 *Song of Songs.* The New International Commentary on the Old Testament. Grand Rapids: Eerdmans.

Luther, Martin
  1972 *Notes on Ecclesiastes; Lectures on the Song of Solomon; Treatise on the Last Words of David.* In *Luther's Works*, vol. 15. Saint Louis: Concordia.

Maimonides, Moses
  1963 *The Guide of the Perplexed.* Edited by Shlomo Pines. Chicago: University of Chicago Press.

Marpeck, Pilgram
  1978 *The Writings of Pilgram Marpeck.* Translated and edited by William Klassen and Walter Klaassen. Classics of the Radical Reformation. Kitchener, ON: Herald.

Matter, E. Ann
  1990 *The Voice of My Beloved: The Song of Songs in Western Medieval Christianity.* Philadelphia: University of Pennsylvania Press.

McFague, Sallie
  1987 *Models of God: Theology for an Ecological, Nuclear Age.* Philadelphia: Fortress.

McGinn, Bernard, ed.
  2006 *The Essential Writings of Christian Mysticism.* New York: The Modern Library.

Mechtild of Magdeburg
  1997 *The Flowing Light of the Godhead.* Translated and edited by Frank Tobin and Margot Schmidt. Classics of Western Spirituality. New York: Paulist Press.

Menno Simons
  1956 *The Complete Writings of Menno Simons, c. 1496-1561.* Translated by Leonard Verduin. Edited by John Christian Wenger. Scottdale, PA: Herald Press.

Methodist Episcopal Church
  1882 *Hymnal of the Methodist Episcopal Church with Tunes.* New York: Phillips & Hunt.

Meyers, Carol L.
  1991 "'To Her Mother's House': Considering a Counterpart to the Israelite bêt ʾāb." In *The Bible and the Politics of Exegesis*, edited by David Jobling, 39-51. Cleveland: Pilgrim.

Miller, Keith Graber
  2010 "Guidelines from the Gift-Giver: Sexuality and Scripture." In *Sexuality: God's Gift*, edited by Anne Krabill Hershberger, 35-51. 2nd ed. Scottdale, PA: Herald Press.

Munro, Jill M.
  1995 *Spikenard and Saffron: The Imagery of the Song of Songs.* Journal for the Study of the Old Testament: Supplement Series 203. Sheffield, UK: Sheffield Academic.

Murphy, Nancey
  2006 *Bodies and Souls, or Spirited Bodies?* Cambridge: Cambridge University Press.

Murphy, Roland E.
　1990　*The Song of Songs*. Hermeneia. Minneapolis: Fortress.
Musselman, Lytton John
　2007　*Figs, Dates, Laurel, and Myrrh: Plants of the Bible and the Quran*. Portland, OR: Timber.
Nelson, Tommy
　1998　*The Book of Romance: What Solomon Says about Love, Sex, and Intimacy*. Nashville: Nelson.
Norris, Richard A., Jr., trans. and ed.
　2003　*The Song of Songs: Interpreted by Early Christian and Medieval Commentators*. The Church's Bible. Grand Rapids: Eerdmans.
Origen
　1957　*The Song of Songs: Commentary and Homilies*. Translated and annotated by R. P. Lawson. Westminster, MD: Newman.
Paulsell, Stephanie
　2012　"The Song of Songs." In *Lamentations and the Song of Songs*, by Harvey Cox and Stephanie Paulsell, 169–279. Louisville, KY: Westminster John Knox.
Philips, Dirk
　1992　*The Writings of Dirk Philips, 1504–1568*. Translated and edited by Cornelius J. Dyck, William E. Keeney, and Alvin J. Beachy. Classics of the Radical Reformation. Scottdale, PA: Herald Press.
Polack, William Gustave
　1958　*The Handbook to the Lutheran Hymnal*. St. Louis: Concordia Publishing House.
Pope, Marvin H.
　1977　*Song of Songs*. Anchor Bible. Garden City, NY: Doubleday.
Provan, Iain
　2001　*Ecclesiastes, Song of Songs*. NIV Application Commentary. Grand Rapids: Zondervan.
Roop, Eugene F.
　1987　*Genesis*. Believers Church Bible Commentary. Scottdale, PA: Herald Press.
Sayn-Wittgenstein-Berleburg, Casimr, and Johann Heinrich Haug
　1726–42　*Biblia germanica: Berleburger Bibel; Die Heilige Schrift Altes und Neues Testaments, nach dem Grund-Text [Luthers] aufs neue übersehen und übersetzt*. 8 vols. Berleburg.
Schiller, Gertrud
　1971　*Iconography of Christian Art*. Vol. 1. Greenwich, CT: New York Graphic Society.
Schweitzer, Carol. L. Schnabl
　2005　"Song of Songs: A Metaphorical Vision for Pastoral Care." *Interpretation* 59:278–89.
Shantz, Douglas H.
　2002　"The Millennial Study Bible of Heinrich Horch: A Case Study in Early Modern Reformed Hermeneutics." In *The Practical Calvinist: An Introduction to the Presbyterian and Reformed Heritage*, edited by Peter A. Lillback, 391–414. Fearn, Ross-shire, UK: Christian Focus.
　2013　*An Introduction to German Pietism: Protestant Renewal at the Dawn of Modern Europe*. Baltimore: John Hopkins University Press.

Sill, Gertrude Grace
    1975   *A Handbook of Symbols in Christian Art.* New York: Simon & Schuster.
Snyder, Graydon F.
    1992   *First Corinthians: A Faith Community Commentary.* Macon, GA: Mercer University Press.
Soulen, Richard N.
    1967   "The Waṣfs of the Song of Songs and Hermeneutic." *Journal of Biblical Literature* 86:183–90.
Stoeffler, E. Ernest
    1949   *Mysticism in the German Devotional Literature of Colonial Pennsylvania.* Allentown, PA: Pennsylvania German Folklore Society.
Stoudt, John Joseph
    1937   *Consider the Lilies, How They Grow: An Interpretation of the Symbolism of Pennsylvania German Art.* Allentown, PA: Pennsylvania German Folklore Society.
Suderman, W. Derek
    2005   "Modest or Magnificent? Lotus versus Lily in Canticles." *Catholic Biblical Quarterly* 67:42–58.
Swartley, Willard M.
    2006   *Covenant of Peace: The Missing Peace in New Testament Theology and Ethics.* Grand Rapids: Eerdmans.
Teresa of Avila
    1976   *The Collected Works of St. Teresa of Avila.* Washington: Institute of Carmelite Studies.
Toews, John E.
    2004   *Romans.* Believers Church Bible Commentary. Scottdale, PA: Herald Press.
Torjesen, Karen Jo
    1985   *Hermeneutical Procedure and Theological Structure in Origen's Exegesis.* Berlin: Walter de Gruyter.
Trible, Phyllis
    1978   *God and the Rhetoric of Sexuality.* Philadelphia: Fortress.
Walker, William.
    1835   *The Southern Harmony, and Musical Companion.* New York: Hastings House.
Walsh, Carey Ellen
    2000   *Exquisite Desire: Religion, the Erotic and the Song of Songs.* Minneapolis: Augsburg Fortress.
Watts, Isaac
    1827   *The Psalms and Hymns of Dr. Watts, Arranged by Dr. Rippon.* Philadelphia: David Clark.
Whedbee, J. William
    1998   *The Bible and the Comic Vision.* Cambridge: Cambridge University Press.
Wright, J. Robert, ed.
    2005   *Proverbs, Ecclesiastes, Song of Solomon.* Ancient Christian Commentary on Scripture: Old Testament 9. Downers Grove, IL: InterVarsity.
Zohary, Michael
    1982   *Plants of the Bible.* New York: Cambridge University Press.

Selected Resources for Song of Songs

Commentaries

Davis, Ellen F. *Proverbs, Ecclesiastes, and the Song of Songs.* Westminster Bible Companion. Louisville, KY: Westminster John Knox, 2000. Davis offers an intertextual reading of the Song of Songs with other biblical texts.

Exum, J. Cheryl. *Song of Songs.* Old Testament Library. Louisville, KY: Westminster John Knox, 2005. A thorough analysis of the literary characteristics of the Song of Songs.

Hess, Richard S. *Song of Songs.* Baker Commentary on the Old Testament Wisdom and Psalms. Grand Rapids: Baker Academic, 2005. A solid commentary that is especially good with linguistic matters and cultural background.

Keel, Othmar. *The Song of Songs: A Continental Commentary.* Translated by Frederick J. Gaiser. Minneapolis: Fortress, 1994. The distinctive feature of this commentary is Keel's use of ancient Near Eastern iconography to interpret the imagery of the Song of Songs. Includes 158 illustrations.

Paulsell, Stephanie. "The Song of Songs." In *Lamentations and the Song of Songs,* by Harvey Cox and Stephanie Paulsell, 169–279. Louisville, KY: Westminster John Knox, 2012. Writing for the series Belief: A Theological Commentary on the Bible, Paulsell offers engagement between the Song of Songs and Christian spirituality.

Other Resources

Carr, David M. *The Erotic Word: Sexuality, Spirituality, and the Bible.* New York: Oxford University Press, 2003. A work by a biblical scholar who argues that sexuality and spirituality are intricately intertwined.

Green, Joel B., ed. *Dictionary of Scripture and Ethics.* Grand Rapids: Baker Academic, 2011. This volume contains many helpful essays, including two by Erin Dufault-Hunter on "Sex and Sexuality" and "Sexual Ethics."

Hershberger, Anne Krabill, ed. *Sexuality: God's Gift.* 2nd ed. Scottdale, PA: Herald Press, 2010. This volume contains short essays written by medical professionals, ministers, and theologians.

McGinn, Bernard, ed. *The Essential Writings of Christian Mysticism.* New York: Modern Library, 2006. Anything by McGinn on mysticism is good, and this volume of selected writings is a nice place to start.

Index of Ancient Sources for Song of Songs

OLD TESTAMENT

Genesis
1–3 .... 284, 286
1:2 192
1:27-28 281
1:28 .... 264, 284
2 284
2–3 .... 152, 217
2:9 .... 231, 264
2:18-24 264
2:23-25 284
2:24 282
3 284
3:16 238
4:7 238
8 191
24:67 .... 202, 279
25:25 226
27:26-27 165
27:27 164–65
27:28 229
29:11 165
29:18 279
34 279
38 285
38:14-18 285
38:27-30 285
45:15 165

Exodus
.... 272
4:25 224
4:27 165
15:19-21 237
16:13-14 229
18:7 165
19:4 205
30:23 260
33:21-23 196

Leviticus
19:18 .... 151, 279
19:34 279

Numbers
11:9 229

Deuteronomy
3:9 212
6:4 279
6:5 .... 151, 279
7:8 279
10:17 156
12:15 281
12:20 281
21:11 281
28:57 224
32:4 196

Joshua
12:24 239
21:38 237

Judges
3:24 224
11:34 237

Ruth
1:8-9 202
1:9 165
3:6-15 285
4:18-22 285

1 Samuel
1:5 279
10:1 165
16:11 188
16:12 226
17:42 226
18:20 279
20:41 165
22:20 251

2 Samuel
12:24 279
14:33 165

1 Kings
1:4 236
1:15 236
3:3 279
4:25 190
4:32 156
4:32-33 .... 148, 261
5:10 230
7:19 268
7:22 268
7:26 268
8:6 156
9-10 148
9:11-19 230
10:9 279
11:1-3 148
11:3 250
14:17 .... 239, 261
16:23-24 239
17:1 229

2 Kings
4:8-37 236
5:12 212

1 Chronicles
5:23 212
13:8 147
16:29 231

2 Chronicles
2:11 279

Nehemiah
2:8 216

Esther
2:17 279

Job
13:3 281
13:24 205

Psalms
4:4 200
6:6 200
10:1 205
18:2 196
22:1 205
22:1-2 205
27:4 231
37:4 281
45 156
45:7-8 165
45:8 260
50:2 231
51:6 281
72:16 230
74:19 190-91
80 166
85 169
85:10 165
92 156
92:2 200
103:5 281
104:15 166
104:16 230
105:4 231
105:33 190
119:62 200
132:13 281
133 166
134:1 200
137:3 156
145:16 281
149:5 200

Proverbs
 .... 261, 285
1:8 244
5:18-19 285
7:13 165
7:17 260
8:17 204
13:12 281
18:15 204
31:1 244

Ecclesiastes
 261
1:1 204
2:5 216
2:24 204
3:11a 231

Isaiah
5:1 156
5:1-7 166-67
26:9 281
35:1 269
35:1-2 181
51:3 218
53:4 193
57:8-10 224
58:11 218
60:13 230
65:1 204

Jeremiah
2:24 201
3:12 239
5:10 167
5:17 167
7:34 192
8:7 191
16:9 192
25:10 192
29:5 217
29:10-13 204
31:33 241
33:10b-11 192
48:28 191

Ezekiel
16 267
16:25 224
23 267
27:5 212
33:11 240
36:35 218

Daniel
2:37 156

Hosea
2:12 .... 167, 190
6:1 239
6:6 281
7:11 190
9:15 252
11:8-9 252
11:11 190
14:4-5a 181
14:4-7 230
14:7 181-82

Joel
1:12 190
2:3 217

Amos
4:9 167
5:4 204

Index of Ancient Sources for Song of Songs

6:5-6 156
9:14b 167

Jonah
1:3 227

Micah
4:4 190

Zechariah
3:10 190
8:12 229

Malachi
2:15 281
3:7 240

NEW TESTAMENT

Matthew
.... 272
2:11 260
5:6 264
5:44 .... 151, 279
9:13 281
10 275
10:16 267
19:5 282
19:10-12 285
19:19 279
20:1-11 167
20:1-16 167
21:33-43 167
22:37 .... 151, 279
22:39 151
25:1-13 282

Mark
2:19-20 282
6:30-44 264
7:24-37 264
10:7-8 282
12:1-12 167
12:29-30 151
12:31 151
14:3 261
14:45 165
15:34 205

Luke
3:22 192
4:18-19 264
6:21 264
6:27 151
8:2 264
10 275
10:27 151
12 254
12:27 231
13:6-9 167
15 205
15:11-32 140
15:18-23 240
24:39 265
24:42-43 265

John
3:16 279
3:29 282
12:3 261
13:34 .... 151, 280
14 254
15:1-8 167
19:34 197
20:20-27 197

Romans
8:31-39 .... 151, 280
8:35 253
8:38-39 253
15:23 281
16:16 .... 165, 169

1 Corinthians
1 254
6:16 282
7 .... 279, 286
7:3-4 282
7:3-5 286
7:29-31 286
10:3-4 196
13 .... 151, 274-75, 280
15 265
15:44 265
15:51-54 265
16 275
16:20 .... 165, 169

2 Corinthians
13:12 .... 165, 169

Galatians
4:21-31 268
5:22 280

Ephesians
2:14 169
5:21-33 282

Colossians
3 254

1 Thessalonians
5:26 .... 165, 169

1 Timothy
1 254
2:4 281
6 274

Hebrews
11 274

1 Peter
5 274
5:14 165

1 John
2-4 254
3:18 254
4 151
4:7-8 .... 254, 280

Revelation
12 274
14:14-20 167
18 283
18:13 260
18:23b 283
19:6-9 283
21:1-2 231
21:2 283
21:9 283
22:1-2 218

OTHER JEWISH SOURCES

Akiba, Rabbi
.... 258, 270-71

Midrash Rabbah
.....................192–93, 261

Sirach
25:1........................... 275

OTHER CHRISTIAN SOURCES

Augustine
.....................152–53, 231

Codex Alexandrinus notes........................ 263

Codex Sinaiticus notes........................ 263

Jerome 169–70

Origen 258, 263, 271

OTHER ANCIENT SOURCES

Ancient Egyptian love songs 143, 185, 278

Ancient Near Eastern culture 175, 178–80

Greek plays............ 146

The Author of the Commentary on Song of Songs

Christina Bucher holds the Carl W. Zeigler Chair in Religious Studies at Elizabethtown College, where she offers courses in Bible and biblical languages. She has degrees from Elizabethtown College and Bethany Theological Seminary and completed her PhD in Hebrew Scriptures at Claremont Graduate University. Before finishing her doctorate, Bucher worked as a research assistant at the Institute for Antiquity and Christianity in Claremont, California, and later spent nine months at the *Institut für ökumenische Forschung* in Tübingen, Germany.

Bucher currently represents the Church of the Brethren on the editorial board of the Believers Church Bible Commentary series and is a member of the Bethany Theological Seminary board of trustees. She served the Church of the Brethren as a member of the planning team for the Covenant Bible Study program and wrote two studies for the Covenant Bible Study series. Bucher has contributed articles to *Brethren Life and Thought* and *Messenger*, and in 2010, she coedited a volume published by Brethren Press: *The Witness of the Hebrew Bible for a New Testament Church*. She is a member of the Elizabethtown Church of the Brethren.

Bucher lives in Elizabethtown, Pennsylvania, with her husband, Theodore M. Bushong. They have two adult sons.

Lamentations, Song of Songs

"When you read Lamentations and Song of Songs, you must also read this very fine commentary by Wilma Ann Bailey and Christina Bucher. The authors are alert to the texture and details and layers of meaning in the poetry, as well as to the complicated reverberations of the books in later contexts. I can think of no better guides to a fruitful interpretive engagement with these two brief but unforgettable biblical books." —*Tod Linafelt, professor of biblical literature, Georgetown University*

"Both erudite and earthy, this commentary is the one I'll be drawing on for future sermons and lectures from these multivalent texts. Bursting with a full range of human emotions—lamenting, loving, yearning—the text is a gift for pastors and scholars wanting to apply these ancient, sacred songs to twenty-first-century faithful living. Bailey and Bucher build bridges for us between lament and love and between spirituality and sexuality in ways that are honest, expansive, and grounded." —*Keith Graber Miller, professor of Bible, religion, and philosophy, Goshen College*

"Wilma Ann Bailey and Christina Bucher have written clear, lyrical, and academically solid studies on Lamentations and the Song of Songs. Paired together, the two scholars make the texts live. They plunge readers into questions about human life in its tragic and joyous dimensions. I recommend this work for believers, for those seeking for God, and for those who love biblical literature." —*Kathleen M. O'Connor, professor emerita of the Old Testament, Columbia Theological Seminary*

"Bailey and Bucher wisely amplify the voices of these ancient texts and the communities that have read them as they speak to timeless human experiences of war, communal devastation, sexuality, and love. Preachers, teachers, laypersons, and anyone interested in reflecting on God's presence in the midst of two poles of human experience—violence and love—will be glad they have read this volume."
—*Andrea Saner, assistant professor of Old Testament and Hebrew language, Eastern Mennonite Seminary*

"The pairing of Lamentations and Song of Songs might seem the ultimate scriptural odd couple, but Bucher and Bailey explicate these powerful testimonies to the outer and opposite limits of human experience with striking clarity, revealing strong, authentic biblical testimonies to the voice and experience of women and men in Scripture."
—*Frank Ramirez, senior pastor, Union Center Church of the Brethren*

www.ingramcontent.com/pod-product-compliance
Lightning Source LLC
Chambersburg PA
CBHW030525230426
43665CB00010B/771